YUM DI DEE DAH

Jean Newlove

Copyright © 2013 Jean Newlove
All rights reserved.
ISBN-13: 978-1492315308

Acknowledgements

My thanks are due to Nick de Somergyi for starting me off on this journey and organising my early life memories. To an old friend, Denise Keir, who typed at all hours, to my son Hamish MacColl who has designed the book cover and restored all the old photographs, to Murray Melvin (head of the Archives department at Theatre Royal Stratford E15) for all his help in gathering the photographs, and finally to Alan Officer who runs Kirsty's web site. I am grateful for his ability to steer me through the intricacies of electronic publishing!

Jean Newlove - Yum Di Dee Dah

To all my Laban students with love

Contents

Introduction	1
1. I Am Introduced to Dancing	9
2. The Outbreak of War:	
My Career Plans in Jeopardy	22
3. The Dream Comes True	34
4. Laban's Assistant Hits the Road	47
5. My Country Needs Me	61
6. I Seem to be Surplus to Requirements	80
7. I Exchange Bombs for Doodlebugs	94
8. D-Day: A Night to Remember,	
and Grim New Circumstances	106
9. The Wanderer Returns	118
10. I Survive my Living Quarters in Barnsley	127
11. Back to Civvy Street	136
12. The Best of All Worlds	146
13. 'In the Mirk'	157
14. Taking Flight in the Parrot House	169
15. Given a Great Welcome,	
Despite Recent Horrors	190
16. The War Had Not Touched Sweden	198
Back to Poverty:	
17. From Parrot House to Dilapidated Schloss	211
18. The Knights Save 'Alice' in Barnsley	225
19. A Special 'Production'	235
20. The Edinburgh Festival	246
21. Even the Swings were	
Chained Up on the Sabbath	256
22. Conditions Force a Final Decision	265
23. Stratford East and Bucharest	277
24. London and Warsaw	289
25. The Soho Festival	303
26. Moscow	312
27. London – and Paul Robeson	324
Epilogue	339
Post Script	353
Other Books by Jean Newlove	354
Index of photographs	355

iii

Introduction

It is a fortunately rare circumstance that compels a mother to write the story of her daughter's life, and prosecute the fight for justice over her death. In the terrible months and years following the death of my brilliant daughter, the singer-songwriter Kirsty MacColl, many people offered to tell her story. It took me some years before I realised that I should write it myself, and still further years before I felt able to take on the task. But I am very glad I did, as I lived again through a host of precious moments of our time together – Kirsty, her brother Hamish, and me. 'Sun on the Water' was published some eighteen months ago. It was only then that I began to listen seriously to my many colleagues in the theatre and considered writing my own story up to Kirsty's birth in October 1959.

Over the years I have regularly entertained my friends, colleagues, and family with anecdotes of my early days while working as Rudolf Laban's assistant during the Second World War, and my subsequent career in Theatre Workshop as a choreographer, dancer, movement-teacher, and part-time actress. It was a truly extraordinary time in my life – as it was for so many of us, whether back-stage or front-of-house, audiences and cast alike.

My one concern remained that I was so ancient that my theatrical origins would be lost in the mists of time – though friends reassured me that even these early memories were of 'historical interest' (rather like a fossil's). Even now, more than fifty years on, I am still proud to have played an integral part in one of the most influential and innovative companies ever to have performed on the stage. Despite the passage of years since its last production, Theatre Workshop's reputation continues to rise. Conceived by Joan Littlewood and Ewan MacColl as a 'theatre of action' before the Second World War, the agit-prop of Ewan's Theatre Union developed into the professionally based Theatre Workshop in 1945. By an accident of history, Joan's visionary direction and Ewan's extraordinary gifts as a dramatist and singer required a third element, that of choreography, to realise their genius: and that is when I joined the company, in my early twenties – young in years but having already spent what seemed a lifetime of work and study with another giant of the twentieth-century stage: the movement theorist Rudolf Laban.

In those very early days Rudolf Laban (1879–1958) was virtually unknown in this country; all I knew of him as a schoolgirl was his unusual name, and his striking photograph in a library book. His reputation as a scientist, philosopher, mathematician, and theoretician has since risen dramatically; he was also an architect, an artist, a dancer, and a choreographer; a man of colossal vision, and one of the greatest theatrical innovators of our time. The actors in Theatre Workshop were the first professional company to use his understanding of movement, through their regular classes with me. I am delighted to say that, sixty years on, they have passed their training on to new generations, many of whom are directors.

As the following pages tell, I was greatly fortunate to study with Laban himself during the war, as part of a concerted training programme designed to help women factory workers avoid strain (many having taken over jobs until recently exclusive to men), while also increasing factory production as part of the wider war effort. By the time the war ended, I had served out an apprenticeship with Laban – and it was then that he received a letter from Joan Littlewood asking for help in training the young Theatre Workshop company in movement. She was a great fan of his movement theory, having read about his pre-war work in Germany; she had also been introduced to his movement classes at RADA – though her teacher had frustratingly little English and was unable to give a detailed explanation. And so Laban asked me whether I would like to offer my services, and I went along on a 'temporary' basis. Instead I embarked on a lifelong career under his inspiration. Laban was also to become a 'fan' of the company after seeing some of our productions, expressing the wish that had he been allowed to continue his theatre work in Germany, this was the way he would have worked. In the words of the original Theatre Workshop 'Manifesto':

The great theatres of all times have been popular theatres, theatres which reflected the dreams and struggles of the people of their time. The theatre of Aeschylus and Sophocles, of Shakespeare and Ben Jonson, of the Commedia del Arte and Moliere derived their inspiration, their language, and their art from the common people.

We want a theatre with a living language, a theatre which is not afraid of the sound of its own voice and which will comment as fearlessly on society as Ben Jonson and Aristophanes did.

Theatre Workshop is a team of skilled artists and technicians who have broken with the moribund conventions of the commercial theatre. We believe that by combining all that is best in the great theatres of the past with the most recent scientific and technical developments we can create a theatrical form sufficiently flexible to reflect the rapidly changing twentieth century scene. (Its purpose is to create a flexible theatre art, as swift moving and plastic as the cinema, by applying the recent technical advances in light and sound introducing music and the 'dance theatre' style of production.)

As Howard Goorney admitted in his book 'The Theatre Workshop Story', these were ambitious aims, but in the company's first production of Ewan's 'Johnny Noble' in the 1940s I think we almost achieved it.

A man and a woman, each dressed in oilskins and standing on either side of the proscenium arch, sing in front of a darkened stage that gradually increases in light as they explain in song what the audience will see. Different parts of the stage light up momentarily as the cast silently portray the boredom of an unemployed man, three boys gambling and starting a fight, a young girl dancing alone and finally Johnny Noble, a merchant seaman, sitting on a box on an empty stage playing a harmonica while the effects of the light, sound and carefully rehearsed movement give the audience the full and uncanny effect of a man aboard a ship rising and falling in mid ocean. . . .

Magical.

Introduction

Bathing Belle 1925

Jean Newlove - Yum Di Dee Dah

William G Newlove, Paris 1912/1913

Introduction

Norrie L Newlove, Holidays 1937

The 'Yum Di Dee Dah Lady' was the nickname given to me by Joan Littlewood. In the early days we had no recorded music for classes and I would beat out rhythm with a drum or accompany the movement vocally.

Chapter One

I Am Introduced to Dancing

1923–1942

I looked at the small, unprepossessing brown envelope addressed to me at my home in Lincoln, propped upright on the table where I would be sure to see it. It looked vaguely official, and I didn't give it a second thought, assuming it probably contained news of an evening class I had signed up for with a friend. That day, though, I was far more concerned with my own immediate future. I was eighteen years old, I had just left school, and there were life-changing decisions to be made. After a childhood spent preparing myself for a career in dance, all my plans now seemed to lie in tatters. Dance study was the last thing on anyone's mind: for this was early 1942, in the darkest days of the Second World War, and the evening class I had volunteered to attend was on the recognition of enemy aircraft.

The headmistress at my school had sympathised with my ambitions, and during my final term the previous year had suggested I consider the 'next best thing' and try for a teachers' training college in Yorkshire, where dance at least featured on the curriculum. The competition was stiff, however, since there were only three places and the college principal had already received over three hundred applications. I knew that school teaching was not for me, and that the dance they offered did not meet my standard, but I kept to my part of the bargain and, with a few misgivings, went along for the interview.

Setting off from home at six in the morning – the later train would have meant arriving in Sheffield with very little time to spare – I walked the mile to the station in the complete darkness of the black-out, passing a few shadowy figures on their way to work on an early shift. I bought a ticket and took my seat on a virtually empty train. No sooner had we started to move off than the air-raid sirens blared and we came to a juddering halt. Ten minutes later the All Clear sounded, and I heard a faint cheer from the next carriage and we continued on our way. Half an hour later, the sirens went again and the train stopped in the tunnel which was just ahead. I heard the drone of planes overhead, and waited for the All Clear which came some half an hour later. This time the cheers were more ironic, and having built up steam again, we finally arrived in Sheffield in early daylight, much later than anticipated.

Running all the way to the address printed in my instructions, I arrived at the college breathless but punctual, to discover I was the first interviewee to arrive. The principal greeted me warmly, shaking my hand and asking me if my train had been affected by the air raids and whether I had come on my own. I nodded, volunteering that I had caught the earlier train just in case of problems. This information got the interview off to a good start.

A letter from the college principal arrived a few days later, just as I was setting out for school. Against all the odds, I had been offered one of the three available places. My feelings at this surprising news were mixed – I was pleased at my success, of course, but I felt confirmed in my determination to make a career for myself in the study of dance alone. I sat down immediately, and wrote a letter to thank the principal for her offer, but also to explain frankly my position and why I couldn't accept it. I posted it on the way to school, then went to see the headmistress. She had been charming, though, gracefully acknowledging that I had only attended the interview at her request. But what was I going to do now?

I had made a determined, perhaps foolhardy, decision not to compromise my ideals and to keep my options open. But had I burned my boats? And what options were there, in early 1942, for an eighteen-year-old school-leaver devoted to the study of dance? Preoccupied with such thoughts, my attention returned to the brown envelope left out for me on the table. When I finally opened

I Am Introduced to Dancing

it, it seemed to be some sort of circular; then I read the words 'Dartington Hall', and I immediately realised this wasn't the notice I was expecting from my evening class about German aircraft. As things turned out, this piece of paper that had landed out of the blue, would change my life for ever.

What I told the principal of Bingley Training College was true: I still can't remember a time when I did not want to dance. When I was nearly three, the family – my parents, brother Pip, and I – moved from our village to the county town of Lincoln itself. I developed a stammer in these early days, severe enough to be taken to see a consultant. After checking my reflexes by tapping my knees with a small hammer, he suggested to my mother that I should have dancing lessons, presumably as a means to exercise my sense of physical and verbal rhythm. He could not have known how profoundly his advice was to change my life.

Dance classes were duly arranged, and I attended my first around my third birthday, shortly after our move to Lincoln. The studio was in the middle of the market area of this cathedral city, which came to life every Friday when farmers brought their produce to sell and the whole area was packed with shoppers and stallholders shouting out their wares. My first dance teacher there was Marianne Woodman, and I clearly remember my first sight of her. I was waiting in the empty studio, barefoot, but wearing the silver-threaded bodice and a rose-pink skirt of my party dress (looking rather like a strawberry ice cream sundae), when a door opened at the end of the long room and an angelic creature glided in. Tall and slender, her light brown hair smoothed back into a bun, this apparition of everything I wanted to be can only have been in her early twenties.

She asked me to 'go to the barre': when I looked blank, she pointed languidly to the horizontal bar set into the mirrored wall. Holding the barre with one hand, she demonstrated how I should turn my feet out and bend my knees. Determined to do my best, I could barely reach the barre when standing. Bending my knees, I continued to reach upward, despite having lost contact with the barre, and hoped she wouldn't notice my shortcomings. My first plié!

This was followed by a few more barre exercises. Miss Woodman then asked me to come to the centre of the room and 'dance' for her. Now feeling more relaxed, I was happy to oblige – so much so in fact that I was surprised and disappointed to be told a little later that the lesson was over. But I was determined to come back. Miss Woodman had also survived the ordeal, and was to take me through classes and exams for the next ten years or so. My first pair of ballet shoes was from Porselli's in London, size treble-nought. In later years, my mother would leave me to try on new ballet shoes, as I was very particular and they had to be just right.

I learned to read at an early age, and books soon became a passion. I remember being allowed to choose two or three books from the estate of an elderly relative (recently deceased), and I spent a happy time going through them, finally selecting a huge old folio volume (so old it used f's for s's), which I thought I would study later (though it subsequently disappeared). The other book described the abominable treatment of the Armenians by the Turks during the Great War. Neither of these was particularly suitable, of course, but I do remember the newspaper cutting that fell out of the latter book. It mentioned a 'Captain Newlove' – later identified as a relative – who had taken his ship to Archangel, and on the voyage home encountered a dreadful storm, so bad that he had tied his wife and daughter to the mast to prevent them being swept overboard. I was most impressed.

By this time, at around the age of seven, I had also begun taking piano lessons. I would walk over to my teacher's house, and sit in the entrance hall until invited to sit in and listen to the last part of the previous pupil's lesson. She was an advanced pupil, certainly compared to me, and always finished with a lively technical piece. On one occasion I brought a few friends with me, and when I was asked to go into the music room, I whispered to my friends that I would cough loudly when it was my turn to play. In fact, though, I coughed when the more advanced pianist started her final piece. I'm sure my deception could not have lasted very long, as the girl left and my beginner's lesson started.

I Am Introduced to Dancing

Pip and Jean, 1928/29

Jean Newlove - Yum Di Dee Dah

1934

I Am Introduced to Dancing

One afternoon, my piano teacher asked me if I could sing any nursery rhymes, offering to accompany me on the piano. I explained that I only knew a couple, but I could sing some French songs. She was very impressed by this, and together we got through 'Elle était une bergère' and 'Frère Jacques'. Carried away by my success, I then launched into 'Marlboro' va-t-on son guerre', an obscure song about the Seven Years War. Unsurprisingly enough, my teacher didn't know the music for that one, so I tried one more song, this time a popular cabaret number that went something like 'Mimosette, jolie brunette, petite brune de mimosa'. She didn't know the tune for that one either, which was disappointing. I owed this curious repertoire to my mother, who would occasionally play the piano and sing the songs popular in the years she had spent in France, many of them in Paris, before I was born. My piano teacher called her friend, Miss Harrison, with whom she shared the house, to come and listen. Miss Harrison took a regular Saturday morning class in eurythmics for all young students. As far as I remember, this discipline, which was enormously popular at the time (around the early 1930s), consisted of beating out rhythms with percussion instruments, and reciting 'Ta-tay, ta-tay, taffa, teffi, ta-tay', according to the crotchets and quavers written on the blackboard of the music being played. (I was to meet Miss Harrison again, many years later.)

But neither my reading about Turkish massacres nor my knowledge of French popular song was allowed to interfere with my one and only passion, dance, and by the age of seven I was preparing to take my first ballet exam. It is astonishing to think that the examiner was the famous international dancer Edouard Espinosa, who had now retired as a performer and was Chairman and Chief Examiner for the British Ballet Organization. I remember him as a slight figure, with shoulder-length white hair, white trousers, and red kid shoes, and a kindly and benign manner, who took the time to talk to my seven-year-old self, almost as an equal, after the exam. It turned out that my performance had so impressed him that he wanted me to join the select band of pupils he had chosen to train privately at his studio in London. My mother and I duly travelled down to London to visit one weekend, and while she chatted to Espinosa about the practicalities of this plan, I remember looking on at a group of children of about my age playing a lively game outside. I thought they seemed a jolly group, and happy in their environment. The stumbling block, I learned from my mother, was the matter of my general education. Espinosa had seemed surprised at the question, casually mentioning a school 'around the corner'. One look by my mother at that rather down-at-heel building put paid to my joining the rest of those children.

I was not unduly disappointed. My school had much to offer, my stammer had long since disappeared, and I continued going to ballet class with seniors for exam work, and as I got older helping the teacher with the younger pupils.

When I later moved to big school, Christ's Hospital Girls' School in Lincoln, at the age of eight, I had to change my piano teacher to fit in with the curriculum. This was a shame since her replacement was an extremely neurotic individual. The small practice rooms were soundproofed, and she would indulge in the occasional screaming outburst. I learned from other pupils that it wasn't just me who had to endure this unpleasant and frightening behaviour. Even so, I decided to give up my lessons, politely explaining that I would not be returning for the new term. In retrospect, I think this was an occasion when my mother should have sent a letter. Perhaps she did later – but I needed to muster quite a lot of courage to confront this unpredictable and explosive character.

Although I was still at a very elementary stage, however, I still liked to play the piano for my own pleasure, and so I would go and search through the music section of the local library for pieces I thought I might be able to manage. These were usually Strauss waltzes, but I occasionally found other pieces, often parts of operas and operettas I liked, bringing them back home to learn the words and attempt the music – a difficult, self-imposed task that completely absorbed me.

In time, I also had to change ballet teachers too, when Marianne Woodman left Lincoln, and her place was taken by a friendly blonde called Joan Leaning, who travelled in daily from the nearby town of Gainsborough, where her mother ran a dance school. By this time, my regular studio had moved to an older part of Lincoln, under the shadow of the cathedral itself, which we reached by walking up the aptly named Steep Hill.

During later school holidays – by around the age of fourteen – I also made the journey to Gainsborough to spend Saturdays with the full-time dance students. They were learning tap and Greek dance, as well as ballet, so I joined in too. The Greek dance was taught by Joan's sister Nina – who was built in the svelte mode of the departed Marianne. After a morning's work, we would all go back to the large family home run by Joan and Nina's mother for our lunch. As far as I remember, this generally consisted of a splendid roast beef and Yorkshire pudding main course followed by a fruit crumble, so I can't imagine how we managed to do any dancing afterwards. Perhaps the long walk back to the studio helped. I usually caught the 10 p.m. train home to Lincoln.

It was about this time that my dance teacher asked me to participate in the Skegness Open Dance Festival. This was a popular event and attracted dancers from across Britain. There was a feeling that this would be the last one if war broke out. As a 'senior', I was enrolled in the advanced ballet and national dance competitions. With my hat box containing my costumes, I was given a lift by a junior competitor's mother.

During the lunch break I found myself chatting to a girl about my own age. She had come with her mother and had impressively entered some five or six categories of dance. Her mother was busily engaged in hanging all her costumes and fixing her hair. She also wore some makeup and, to my mind, was obviously a very experienced competitor. I liked her and when she told me her name was Dorothy van Zyl and she was off to the USA very soon, I was impressed. She won all the earlier categories and now we were both competing for Ballet and National Dance. My friends were eager for me to beat her on marks.

The ballet results were read out. There was very little in it but she came first and I, second. Now for the National Dance. I don't remember her dance but mine was a Russian one. Much to my friends' delight, I came first and Dorothy came second. Perhaps my interest in dramatic dance was gradually taking over. I returned home with a gold and silver medal.

Having started to explore the music section of the local library, I then discovered a dance section. Very much smaller than the music section, it was nevertheless very informative. There were many books on the Russian ballet, both pre- and post-Revolution. Indeed, I gained much of my knowledge of that period of European history from reading about Karsavina, the Tsar's favourite ballerina, and Diaghilev's tour of the West with Nijinski. Working my way through the classical ballet section, I learned along the way about the Russian Revolution and its aftermath, supplementing my knowledge by the purchase of Igor Schwezoff's 'Borzoi' (now recognised as a classic) remaindered in a local bookshop for five shillings, which told the prize-winning story of a male dancer who continued to train for the ballet despite those terrible hardships, eventually continuing his career in the Chinese city of Harbin. Intending to go to the Soviet Union at some distant point in the future to study ballet, I started to learn Russian. At least, I learned the Cyrillic alphabet.

I still have the Borzoi book. The only reason I could afford to buy it was that I had by now taken my father to task about my meagre pocket money. I think it had stayed at fourpence a week for most of my childhood, which actually hadn't bothered me that much since I spent so much of my spare time dancing. I was now in my early teens, though, and my father said he would think about it. That night, he came up with the solution. I was to get 35 shillings a month, which was to cover my clothing, bus pass and pocket money. With my new-found wealth I took great pleasure shopping for the best school Panama hat for the summer and the smoothest velour hat for the winter. I also saw a beautiful green coat in a shop window, which was put aside for me until I could pay for it in total after a few weeks.

My self-imposed reading course from the library meanwhile took in square dancing and ballroom dancing. When my science teacher asked if I would teach the young people at her church ballroom dancing, I had no hesitation in accepting her offer.

I Am Introduced to Dancing

'London Bridge'
Dance school, featuring Jean as the 'Muffin Boy'

My family on holiday 1938

In sublime ignorance, I decided to concentrate on the tango. I vividly remember walking through the black-out at sixteen, with my friend and piano-playing accompanist, to a rather dingy church hall lit by a single feeble bulb. The room was long and narrow, with benches on either side, where the young people of All Saints Church were waiting for us. In some curiosity, I noticed that all the girls were sitting on one side, and all the boys on the other. This was a situation I had not anticipated. I had done my homework, and knew that the tango is a passionate dance; I began to realise that perhaps a waltz or foxtrot might under the circumstances have been more appropriate. However, a tango was what I had studied, and a tango I would teach. I started off by suggesting that they should all stand up, move around the room, and choose a partner. This they were reluctant to do, the girls eventually pairing up with their best friends, also girls, while the boys stood around in rather awkward clusters of onlookers. I patiently explained that the tango was a dance for a man and a woman, and said they must each choose a partner of the opposite sex. After what seemed an age, a few brave hearts drifted together, though even these couples kept a wary distance from one another, off-handedly refusing any physical contact at all. Then the music struck up – but by now our time was more or less up. By the end of the following week's class, the boys and girls were dancing together, and while no respectable Brazilian would have recognised their version of the dance as a tango, the 'All Saints' of Lincoln were certainly performing it with gusto.

Ballroom, ballet, Greek, square, tango, tap – it was only a matter of time before I came across a library book on 'modern' dance. It mentioned the Jooss Ballet Company, who danced without using blocked ballet shoes or wearing tutus. Kurt Jooss, I read, was the pupil of Rudolf Laban, a choreographer, architect, innovator, and 'crystallographer'. The book included a photograph of Laban's handsome moustachioed face, studying some abstract models on a table, with Jooss, equally striking but plumper of face and with a shock of dark curly hair. These models apparently represented Laban's 'crystals', and formed part of his theoretical approach to human movement in general. I was immediately fascinated and intrigued, and though understanding very little of

I Am Introduced to Dancing

this new and complicated philosophy of dance, I knew that, one day, I would have to find out more.

While still enjoying ballet, I began to realise that attempting to express human emotions on stage, as an actor would, was limited by classical movement clichés. I found myself asking difficult questions about the classical ballet I had enjoyed for so long – questions that perhaps might find answers, however dimly I could recognise them, in the work of these extraordinary practitioners. The names of Kurt Jooss and Rudolf Laban remained in my memory, along with their photograph, long after I returned the book to the library. It seems amazing to me, even thinking about it now, that within a few short years of reading that chapter as a schoolgirl in the mid-1930s, when war was only a pessimistic forecast, I would actually come to meet both the men in that photograph – Jooss in Cambridge before leaving school, and Laban himself after receiving that brown envelope from Dartington Hall, in early 1942.

My spare time at this age was taken up with dance classes, reading, and art. The Cyrillic alphabet would come in useful for when I visited the Soviet Union to see the Bolshoi and Kirov ballet companies – as I was so sure that I would. Against all the odds, this ambition, too, came true, albeit nearly twenty years later. At the time I was dreaming such dreams, though, the world around me was about to change for ever in the nightmare of war.

Chapter Two

The Outbreak of War: My Career Plans in Jeopardy

1939–1942

The situation in Europe had steadily deteriorated through my childhood, but it was over my brother Pip, seven years older than me, that the full shadow of the gathering war clouds fell. By the time war was declared, on 3 September 1939, he had already joined up, and was in constant training at the nearby barracks for what became the British Expeditionary Force (B.E.F.) to France. In the run-up to the war, many thousands of British children had been offered homes by American friends and relatives for the duration – among them our own relatives in Ohio, who suggested to my parents that I, then in my mid-teens, should make the same journey. After much discussion, they agreed.

My planned emigration went so far as to include a visit with my mother to the American Legation – which was in turmoil. We entered a vast room hastily divided into a series of makeshift cubicles with white sheets for walls, though they did not afford much privacy. Everywhere we looked there were children in various stages of undress, and an army of harassed-looking medical staff in white coats with stethoscopes, carrying clipboards, who dashed about ticking off the names of those with a clean bill of health. We were told to go home and wait for news of a sailing date. The Pathé News bulletins in the local cinema would often show footage of waving children arriving in the States, and for a little while we all thought I would eventually join them. In the event, though, following the outbreak of war, the papers filled with reports that German U-boats had aimed their torpedoes at liners displaying the Red Cross who were ferrying children to their new homes across the Atlantic. I remember reading of one couple who, after long deliberation, had sent their five children, aged between two and ten years old, to a new life in America. All of them perished, along with many others in those terrible days, and the emigration scheme was halted. This was brought home to me when three girls from my own school returned to Lincoln in that winter of 1939, wearing cardigans over their summer cotton dresses, having lost everything else in a shipwreck.

A break from working on the land, 1940

It was the fear of devastating bombing in Britain, though, in the early days of the war that also made an impact on our home. Arriving early at school on the day after the declaration, we were told that a girls' High School from Leeds would from now on be sharing our buildings – our school would use the classrooms on certain timetabled mornings and afternoons, the other school for the remainder – and the evacuee girls themselves would also urgently need our families' hospitality. So it was that a coach pulled up outside our house on South Park, very late one evening, from which a tired-looking girl stepped down, with a large suitcase and school bag, accompanied by her anxious parents. We hadn't been expecting anyone for a few days, so the girl had to share my bed with me for the night before a better arrangement was sorted out. Her parents were anyway reassured and pleased that there was someone near her own age, and after a private and brief goodbye outside, they were back on the bus, which rumbled off to its next drop-off. Appropriately named Peggy Dove, I liked this gentle and pleasant new friend, and she fitted in to the routines of our house very well. By the end of term, however, the expected mayhem of aerial bombing had not materialised – this was the period that later came to be known as the 'Phoney War' – and the Leeds school, with Peggy Dove among them, had returned home.

Both my parents were also contributing to the war effort. My mother had volunteered as a nurse in the local hospital, while my father, previously a manager for an American oil company, was now appointed to a position in charge of supplying fuel to all the local aerodromes, as well as to its farmers – a daunting task when one realises what a big county Lincolnshire is, and how many aerodromes there were in the vicinity. He later nearly lost his life while personally checking the inside of an enormous fuel tank, a job he had decided was too dangerous for his men to undertake: overcome by fumes, it was only when his foreman suddenly realised he was missing that the alarm was raised and he was rescued.

Meanwhile, my brother Pip had himself left for France with the B.E.F. Before embarkation, he and my father had devised a plan to bypass the military censors who they knew would scrutinise his letters – a rudimentary sort of code by which my father would always know exactly Pip's whereabouts whenever he wrote home. There was a large map of France on the wall, I remember, where each move was marked. Then, following the invasion of France in May 1940, and the scramble to evacuate the stranded B.E.F. from the beaches of Dunkirk, we heard nothing from him for a long time. When he did not return with his regiment, we were sick with worry. In fact he had been kept behind as part of the tactical retreat, blowing up bridges to delay the approaching Germans. Before reaching the Normandy beaches, he had contacted Paul

Bouthors (whose family were great friends of my mother), with whom both Pip and I had

stayed before the war at Chateau Valvion in Beauquesne. When I met Paul many years later, he told me that he had travelled to Dunkirk in the hope of finding Pip, to take him back and hide him, but discovered that he was one of the very last soldiers to get away.

I vividly remember my father taking a phone call and asking, 'Are you sure you know my son?' Then I heard a laugh at the other end, and someone say, 'We all know Pip!' Sure enough, he and his men had just safely disembarked in Ramsgate, so exhausted, Pip told us, that when a bugler blew reveille he was nearly lynched. But before long, inevitably, he was off again to serve his country, first in the Middle East and then on to Italy. When my grandfather (my mother's father) was bombed out during the London Blitz of 1940, he came to join us at South Park. Although Peggy Dove had long since returned home to Leeds, two officers in the A.T.S. – the Auxiliary Territorial Service, the women's branch of the Army – had been billeted on us, along with 'Merry', short for Meredith, another grown-up 'evacuee' working all hours at a local aerodrome, whose own home and family were in Leicester. As well as this succession of new faces, my family also always welcomed servicemen, stationed nearby, whether British, Free French, Polish, or (in due course) American. There were even in time a couple of weddings from our house, and years later, when my mother visited the States, she was greeted by a huge crowd of ex-GIs and their families.

Pip in Tobruk

The Outbreak of War: My Career Plans in Jeopardy

Lincoln was surrounded by aerodromes and word had gone around that the Poles now had a local base from where they could renew their battle for a free Poland. Apart from knowing that we had gone to war on their account, we hadn't heard much about Poland. To us Lincolnians, the Poles were rather exotic. To welcome our new allies, the city council put on an Anglo-Polish Ball at the Assembly Rooms, to which I was invited to go by a friend's brother who was my age, sixteen. I remember I wore a shot silk taffeta ball-dress in fine stripes. The skirt was very full but the bodice was a tight fit, with the tiniest shoestring bows down the front. The neckline was low and heartshaped and the sleeves slightly puffed. This was the first time I had worn it, and with my silver shoes, and my hair tied back with a matching ribbon, I was ready to dance – which came as something of a disappointment to my escort, who was not a great fan of dancing.

On entering the ballroom I soon realised that almost everyone I knew was there, including the young women who were the gym teachers at the local schools, whom I knew from the Girls Training Corps. The RAF were there in force, and so were the Poles, all resplendent in their uniforms. Looking back on that night, I think the average age can only have been around twenty-one. Glances were exchanged as the band tuned up, the girls mostly grouped near the double doors from which they had just emerged, the young men nearer the band and the bar beyond. The microphone voice welcomed our friends, the Free Polish Air Force, and said that later that evening the orchestra would play Polish dance tunes in honour of our guests. With that we started with a waltz, and the RAF came over to invite their chosen partners onto the floor. Only a few girls were left over, and a few more men, who seemed either to be shy or biding their time as they checked the standard of the dancing. After the waltz came a 'Paul Jones', and nearly everyone was now on the floor for this 'mixer' dance – except my own date, who had by now retired to the bar.

After about half an hour, during which I thoroughly enjoyed the continual changes of partners and dances, a ten-minute interval was announced, and I went in search of him. I found him nursing a drink and talking about football with a couple of other non-dancers. I explained to him that I had come to dance, and hoped he might like to try, but to no avail. He was happy where he was, so I returned to the dance floor just in time to hear the Master of ceremonies announce the Polish Waltz. The music struck up, and a Polish officer came over to me, clicked his heels and bowed – and we were off. He was an excellent dancer, and the dance flew by. A mazurka followed, and I now had the choice of two or three young men. I discovered that these Poles could really dance, and I was secretly delighted that I knew all these dances – my studies had not been in vain! After polonaises and polkas, we were back to foxtrots, quicksteps and the Lambeth Walk, in a whirl of separate partners, the Poles and RAF now vying for favours.

It was a magical evening, and though my partner joined me for the walk home, even his sulky mood could not spoil my delight in it. At the age of sixteen, the competition of uniformed young men must have been hard for him, I suppose. Anyway, I didn't see him again until he called one day and invited me out to dinner, to apologise for his behaviour that night. Mind you, that was sixty years later. And I sometimes wonder how many of those handsome young airmen even survived the war.

*

In such times, of course, I could scarcely dream of fulfilling my lifetime's ambition for a professional career in dance, but my love of the subject, as well as allowing me to enjoy events like the Anglo-Polish Ball, also kept my mind focused, a distraction and a solace, I suppose, from the dark world around us all.

It was as part of my network of contacts in various local dance organizations that I came to learn that Kurt Jooss – the German choreographer whose name and picture I had come across in a library book a few years before – was now living in Cambridge. I secretly wrote to him, asking for an audition – on a Saturday, I explained, since I was still at school. Telling my family I was visiting a friend, I invested part of my pocket money in a return ticket to Cambridge, setting off at seven in the morning. By the

The Outbreak of War: My Career Plans in Jeopardy

time I arrived at Cambridge Station (via March and Ely), I was extremely hungry. Walking the long distance to the city centre, I passed a café, but while the smell of coffee was extremely inviting, I hadn't budgeted for such luxuries as food and drink on the day's outing. So I eventually sat down on a bench in a park very near to Jooss's house, mustered my strength, and resolved to do my best to succeed.

The door was opened immediately after my knock, and it was obvious that I had been expected. I was shown into a room where I could change, and told that Jooss would be along shortly. A little later there was a knock at the door and Kurt Jooss entered. I recognised him straight away from the photograph I had pored over in that library book: a little older, perhaps, but there was no mistaking the mop of unruly black curly hair that surrounded his gentle, kindly face. After a brief chat about my previous dance experience, I performed my audition piece.

He seemed quite pleased with what he had seen, even suggesting that I join his dance company as a student. This would, he said, involve daily training and a life on the road with his travelling company. I thanked him, and left to tell my family. Unlike my journey out, the trip home fled by. I was on Cloud Nine, walking on air. My father was sympathetic, but at the same time – and understandably – concerned for my safety and welfare. The war was going through a very bad patch for the Allies, after all, and there was a real fear of invasion. At the same time, I was then just seventeen, studying to complete my Higher School Certificate, and he felt that I should complete my education, by which time the international situation might have improved, and Jooss's own status become much clearer. Then he would help me. While I entirely understood, and was grateful for, my father's advice, I was disappointed to have to tell Jooss of my decision not to accept his generous offer. I don't remember if the letter included my promise to return to his door the following year, but that was certainly my intention. For the time being, I was still on Cloud Nine at having been made the offer in the first place.

The dance studio was meanwhile still running classes, and after taking my final exam there, my picture actually appeared in the local paper. A friend of my mother's approached her to pass on her congratulations, but my mother hadn't seen it herself, and I don't think she was aware of my success, preoccupied as she was by her nursing work at the hospital. I helped to teach at the dance studio, while at the same time busily working on my Higher School certificate. One mother asked if I might give her daughter a private ballet lesson. I wasn't that keen, but after the offer of half-a-crown, plus the bus fare, I agreed.

I had gradually come to realise that there was more to dance than just classical ballet, and while I loved performing in lyrical dance, I was drawn to dances that had a dramatic content, and which were frequently improvised. This interest grew with my experience at school with drama itself. As was the fashion of the time, I went to elocution lessons for a while, with a few of my friends, and at around the same time my teacher persuaded me to enter the drama competition being run by the Lincoln Festival of Art. I had prepared my piece, from 'Alice in Wonderland', and arriving with time to spare on the day, I was suddenly warned that the judges were ahead of schedule, and that I was next on. With no time for nerves, I went on, and was astonished to discover later that my performance had been awarded first prize. I hadn't anticipated this at all, and was delighted to have put paid to my early history of stammering. The adjudicator said he could tell I was a dancer by the way I moved. A very talented violinist about my own age won his musicians' class and later I seem to remember we performed at a local school. For a while we kept in touch. His name was Neville Marriner.

Throughout my childhood I had worked my way through all sorts of dance, including folk dance, tap, Greek and character dance. I still possess the red Russian boots that had cost my father the then princely sum of four pounds! I had only one class, in Nottingham, in modern dance. This was not a great success, and the gymnast who took the class, when confronted by a whole group of us ballet specialists, elegantly poised and ready to begin, lost all credibility with me when she asked us to 'jump about like cats on a hot tin roof'. I was always open to new ideas, but this struck me as ludicrous, and I was resolutely unimpressed. In fact, I felt I could

The Outbreak of War: My Career Plans in Jeopardy

take a better class in the subject myself – which, before very long, I did.

This was a series of recreational classes for office workers, held in the local church hall, which over the next few weeks became so popular – the hall was packed – that I started seriously considering starting another course. Unfortunately, however, one or two of my 'students' saw me in my school uniform one day, and word must have got around that the teacher was still a schoolgirl, and the numbers dropped off. This was probably no bad thing, since it allowed me to concentrate on my school-leaving exams, and other activities.

One of these was an invitation to sixth-formers to help out on our school's Open Day, in the summer of 1940. I offered to choreograph a modern dance composition, in which I eventually performed a ballet solo. My offer was accepted, and I auditioned my dancers from across the school's ages, adapting the movements to the abilities of those taking part (many of whom had never had a dancing lesson). I worked on the choreography at home, arranging regular rehearsals with different groups in the gym and the hall as and when they were free.

Of the schoolgirl dancers I selected, some were more naturally talented, more obviously able to learn the steps, than others; but even the less graceful movers were so shocked and flattered at the novelty that they worked doubly hard to pass muster to appear before an audience. The music I chose for the piece was the 'Summer Days Suite' of Eric Coates, whose work I had been introduced to by an early admirer (a young RAF pilot officer, one of the many regular visitors at my parents' home) but my own solo was to the 'Valse Triste' of Sibelius. Not a bad soundtrack to this period in my life, in fact – the wistfully jaunty melodies of Coates's summer, the brooding melancholy of Sibelius' dance with death. In any case, the event was a great success; so much so, in fact, that parents asking for their daughters to join the school's dance class had to be told that a sixth-former had devised it.

Shortly after this minor triumph, word went round that the wartime authorities were planning to organise a Girls Training Corps (G.T.C.) in Lincoln for young girls still at school, too young to be called up. I learned that they were looking for a physical training instructor, a post for which a number of gym teachers were already applying. After the success of my Open Day choreography, I was urged by the girls to put my name forward. How could I refuse? After warning them that I was utterly unqualified to teach gymnastics, I was offered the opportunity of a sort of audition, taking a class of would-be dancers. Closely observed by a gymnast, a Miss Swales, charged with recruiting for the post, I taught a Scottish dance in a hall packed with G.T.C. recruits. If the truth be known, my dance was unknown north of the Midlands – but who cared? 'Well,' said Miss Swales, 'you've certainly got them on your side.' She gave me the job on the spot, and I became a P.T.O. (Physical Training Officer) in the G.T.C. (Girls Training Corps).

During these years boy friends came and went. In those days we could go to the cinema, watch a hockey match or visit the Usher Art Gallery on a Sunday, not very exciting when you had seen the collection many times. Tea at Eastgate Court was a luxury if you could afford it and there was a chance of small cakes but my suitors were all aware that I was serious about my career. One, a pilot officer, introduced me to Eric Coates's music which I used for my choreography. We also enjoyed painting and sketching. Another young man some two or three years older than me, from Westport in Ireland was working as a surveyor's apprentice in the county and we had a light-hearted relationship, with much mutual teasing. He spent that first wartime Christmas with us. I was to meet them both again later in my life.

Immediately after leaving school, though, in 1941, I worked in my father's office for a few weeks, with two other employees, both of whom were far more competent than me, helping with accounts and stocktaking.

Meanwhile, however, I had continued to nurture my dreams. By the spring of 1942, I could console myself with the reflection that my enthusiasm for dance had found an appreciative audience both among my peers, and that I had had the privilege of actually meeting one of my great heroes, Kurt Jooss. When I finally picked up that brown envelope, I could not have dreamed that it would directly lead to my meeting Jooss's own teacher, the great Rudolf Laban himself.

Chapter Three

The Dream Comes True

1942

So there I sat, at the breakfast table in Lincoln in early 1942, opening the brown envelope addressed to me, assuming it contained a circular about a forthcoming evening class on recognizing enemy planes. Pulling out the piece of paper, I then noticed the words 'Dartington Hall' at the top. That name rang a bell.

I already knew a little of what went on at that country house in Devon, having sent off for a brochure on the Jooss Dance School there just before the war. I had read that Leonard and Dorothy Elmhirst, who owned the estate, ran it as a sort of collective 'commune' where artists were welcomed from all over the world, and offered the facilities to carry on their work. I imagined it to be a sort of Utopia – which indeed, for many years, it was: workers on the Elmhirsts' estate, for instance, were entitled to send their children to the Dartington school, where they were given the opportunity to learn a musical instrument free of charge. Jooss and his company had found a home at Dartington as early as 1935. I read on, with increasing excitement.

The letter was from the trustees of Dartington Hall, who were seeking 'a suitable candidate to take charge of the three hundred women workers on the estate', adding that the successful applicants would be required to take regular movement classes with them, following a period of three months' training under Rudolf Laban. **The** Rudolf Laban.

Laban's name – stressed on the first syllable, as I came to learn, to rhyme with 'carbon' – was one I had first come across, almost by accident, while working my way through the 'Dance' section of my local library at home in Lincoln. This had been an entirely self-imposed reading course, since I knew there were no official curricula for what I had dimly in mind for my future career. Traditional ballet training prepared students for teaching, or, with luck, entrance into a ballet company, or cabaret. Like many of my contemporaries, I had specialised in ballet, but had also learned some Greek national and tap dancing, and attended a rare 'modern dance' class which had not particularly interested me. When I had first read about the new dance-movement system that this man, Rudolf Laban, had devised – no tutus, no blocked ballet shoes, no exaggerated turn-out of the lower limbs – I couldn't believe my eyes or my luck. After investigating further, I also knew that Laban had been Kurt Jooss's teacher, that he was both a dancer and choreographer; that his movement theories included elements from crystallography and dynamics; and above all, that the whole Laban system was based upon an underlying harmonic structure. This was very different from anything that I had learnt in my years of studying dance – but it had struck a lasting chord with me, and I was willing to learn.

Laban himself, an artist and scientist, as well as an influential teacher, had arrived at Dartington in 1938, hounded out by the Nazis from the theatre where he was working and the dance schools in Germany he had founded. Ill – mortally ill, some said – and depressed, he had been granted a temporary British visa, subsequently extended following the outbreak of war, by which time he had regained his strength, thanks both to Dorothy Elmhirst at Dartington, and his companion Lisa Ullmann. My teenage self knew little of this arduous history, nor all that much of the unique mixture of philosopher, mathematician, artist, actor, dancer, and architect that was Laban. Subsequent historians have increasingly celebrated his achievement as a movement choreographer and dance designer of colossal vision. To me personally, he became a father-figure of immense charisma; to others, he changed the course of twentieth-century dance; to the world at large, however dimly this has been recognised, he revolutionised the study of human movement.

And now, in the early months of 1942, and in the middle of a catastrophic war, the chance of a lifetime had casually dropped through my letterbox. I applied for the job – of course I did! Yes, I could drive a car (a slight exaggeration); and yes, I did have sixteen years' dance experience; and yes, I was an experienced teacher. I saw myself as the perfect candidate, and sent off my application by return. To my absolute delight, I was later notified that I had qualified for the shortlist, and was invited to come down to Dartington for an audition and interview.

Finding overnight accommodation in nearby Totnes, I first of all checked the bed sheets with a mirror. I had read somewhere that if the mirror clouded, it meant the sheets were damp. I was taking no chances. Reassured, I went out to enquire about buses to Dartington. The next morning saw me, with my training kit in a small bag, sitting on the local bus, as it wended its way along the narrow country road. I was put off at some gates, and followed a long winding drive up to the main Hall. Dartington was in full splendour. The sun shone under a blue shy and the beautifully tended grounds gave off a variety of smells – the perfume of flowers, damp earth, and a hint of bracken further away. Trees lined the drive, many of a great age, to judge by their size. The house came into view, astonishingly beautiful in its setting. This was a perfect English early summer morning with only the murmur of bees and wood pigeons calling to each other. The war seemed a very long way away.

I barely remember presenting myself at the Hall but I was expected, and politely escorted to a room where I could change into my dance tunic. When I was ready, I was asked to go through to the next room where Laban was waiting. I saw a man of about sixty years looking at me intently with bright blue eyes. I recognised him from the photograph I had seen in my library book. Today he was smartly turned out in a darkish grey suit. His hair and moustache were grey and well trimmed. His aristocratic features stood out in a very pale face: I got the impression of a man recovering from an illness which he sought, by his bearing and demeanour, to hide before strangers such as myself.

I was later to learn how he and his work had been banned by the Nazis and his ration-card confiscated. He had somehow managed to get out of Germany, and eventually Kurt Jooss and the ballet mistress of the company, Lisa Ullmann, had travelled to Paris, where they found Laban ill and starving, bringing him back to Dartington with them in 1938. Had they not done so, there is little doubt that Laban would never have survived the coming of war, whether from ill health or the Nazi invasion.

Knowing nothing of these harrowing events, I saw a dignified man with a certain charismatic charm. He greeted me politely, with a strong accent that sounded German to me, though I knew he had been born in Hungary. He asked me if I would dance for him and I went through the piece I had practised. A woman came in at some point towards the end and, when I had finished, Laban introduced her to me. She was a woman in her mid-thirties with short, black hair and dark, luminous eyes. This was Lisa Ullmann. She listened deferentially as Laban spoke to her briefly in German, and then asked me to do some working actions such as swinging an imaginary hammer and lifting a heavy load. Rather nonplussed, I did so with gusto, and thought Laban looked pleased with my attempt. He thanked me and said that he must now meet the trustees and would I go and sit in the courtyard when I had changed. Someone would call me.

To find myself sitting in the very same courtyard I had seen in a brochure Jooss had sent me just a few years earlier fulfilled a dream. I sat under the warm sun and imagined the dancers working on the lawns. I thought the audition had gone quite well – but had it gone well enough? I could not envisage the possibility of failure. I think I sat in a kind of 'suspended animation' for about an hour before someone came to tell me that the trustees were now ready for me.

I followed him into the building, and was led to a room situated at the front. Opening the door for me, he showed me into a large room where several men were gathered at the far end, all looking in my direction with a mixture of undisguised curiosity, smiles, even a few grins, on their faces. I was introduced politely but informally to everyone and asked to sit down. The spokesman for the group began by explaining that the trustees thought I was too young to be in charge of three hundred women on their estate, which was, after all, the advertised job I was applying for. This should have been disastrous news, but the party spirit, obviously unexpected and openly expressed, reassured me. I sat quietly, waiting for him to carry on. However, he continued, Mr Laban had been very impressed by my audition, irrespective of my age. He thought I would make an excellent pupil, and after a period of training with him, he wanted me to become his assistant. I would work with both Laban and a colleague of his called Mr Lawrence, as part of their project to introduce their work into industry. The spokesman repeated that, unlike my rival candidate, who would now be offered the advertised job, I would not be restricted to three months' study with Laban but would instead be working closely with him for the foreseeable future. Would I, he finished by asking, be interested in accepting this role?

I think my delighted smile was sufficient answer. Everyone seemed to be laughing, and Laban meanwhile took the opportunity to introduce me to Mr Lawrence himself, a slim, angular man with a craggy face and a delightfully warm smile. Various trustees also came up to me, happily explaining that they had only intended to offer a single post but that Laban had eloquently forced their hand, and wishing me well for the future. Arrangements were made to write to me, we all said our goodbyes, and then, after picking up my small bag, I left Dartington Hall and started waltzing down its long drive in a rapture of excited happiness to catch my bus to Totnes. Momentarily aware that someone was watching me, I turned my head to look back, to see everyone crowding round the windows, leaning on each other's shoulders, smiling and waving to me – Laban, Mr Lawrence, assorted trustees, and Lisa, too, squeezed into a corner. I gave them all a final wave before turning the corner and losing sight of them.

Rudolf Laban 1944/5

Letters passed between my father and Lawrence and Laban over the next few weeks. It was agreed that my father would pay for my training, but they in turn, I think, guaranteed my paid employment thereafter. Because Lawrence's home and business were based in Manchester, Laban and Lisa Ullmann had recently set up home there themselves, and I was asked to get ready to join them as soon as Laban contacted me. Meanwhile, though, the trustees at Dartington proposed a meeting in London to celebrate the 'deal'.

I set out for London wearing what I considered to be not only an appropriate but rather stylish costume. It must be remembered that I had until very recently been at school and I had very little if any spare clothing coupons. Fortunately, my American relatives in Ohio (with whom I had so nearly gone to live) had sent a parcel of second-hand clothes, from which I had selected a short-sleeved, pale pink cotton bouclé sweater with tiny blue beads decorating the front. My brother Pip had meanwhile sent me a patterned blue silk skirt with a fringe, along with a pair of grey canvas wedge shoes, which although extremely uncomfortable were, I thought, incredibly smart. I'm not sure I took a coat with me, but the sun was shining on that summer's day too. I tied my hair back with a small ribbon, revealing a pair of earrings made from tiny coils of flexible wire hidden behind the tiniest of fabric flowers – they may have been second-hand, but as far as I was concerned they were pure 'haute-couture'. And so this dizzying apparition stepped forth onto King's Cross station at eleven o'clock that morning.

I made my way to Soho and wandered around window-shopping until it was time to make the appointment, which was for lunch at The Gay Hussar, the famous Hungarian restaurant in Greek Street – a suitable cuisine for the Hungarian-born Laban. The manager said I was expected, and took me to an inner room where all the Dartington trustees, together with Lawrence and Laban himself awaited me. Everyone was in party mood and we chatted easily as we found our seats; I think mine was in pride of place between Laban and Lawrence. A group of Hungarian gypsies came and serenaded me on their violins before handing me a red rose. It was a magical event, but not just for the personal excitement I felt at the glamour of it all. For this was a serious business meeting too, energised by the understanding, by all those of us present, that we were engaged on an enterprise that was both utterly new and of potentially invaluable use to the war effort.

F.C. Lawrence, a Manchester industrialist – I only ever knew him as 'Mr Lawrence', and don't even remember his first name – was an accountant who had worked with the trustees of the Dartington estate since 1938, and only recently met Laban himself. Lawrence had recognised the practical application of Laban's theories to existing 'Work Study' methods, together pioneering the system of 'Industrial Rhythm' at just the time I had joined their team. They made an unlikely pair of friends – Laban the unworldly, unconventional aristocratic aesthete, forever questioning establishment norms; Lawrence a pillar of that same establishment, a decorated Army officer and now a respected professional manager, accountant, and industrial engineer. 'Can you imagine,' as my friend Warren Lamb recently put it, 'two more contrasting characters? But they had one thing in common: vision.' Lawrence's respectability, combined with Laban's more exotic profile, had finally won my father's approval for the course I had decided upon, and from then on he always took a keen interest in the development and progress of our work.

Our lunch eventually broke up amidst a chorus of goodbyes and shaken hands. A taxi was found for me, and I travelled home in a state of some euphoria, with Mr Lawrence's words about 'seeing me in Manchester' ringing in my ears. I had left school the previous year with nothing but a dream of what I might do with my life. I had hoped to meet my heroes, Kurt Jooss and Rudolf Laban, after the dreadful war that threatened us all was over. Now here I was, with my hopes transformed to an amazing reality, sooner than I could ever have imagined possible. Just a few short months before, Laban had been a photograph in a library book and an inspiring idea; now I was making my arrangements to work by his side. Fortune had smiled on me.

I arrived in Manchester with a large suitcase and even bigger hopes. I had found myself a bed-sitter on the city's outskirts, quite near Palatine Road in West Didsbury, where Laban and Lisa had their flat.

I vividly remember this introduction to bed-sit land because of the first, extremely uncomfortable night I spent there. I had woken up in the dark to the terrible sound of scuffling, and scampering, and tearing of paper. Then I felt something run over the end of my bed, just beyond my toes. Unwilling to get out of bed to switch the light on, I reached for my torch, and to my horror saw in the beam of light a rat – a rat! – nestling under the grate of the empty hearth on the other side of the room. After a more or less sleepless night, I tentatively mentioned this fact to my landlady the following morning, hoping of course that she might offer to do something about it, or at least move me to another room, she blithely replied, 'Oh yes, I know. You're not frightened of them, are you?' It didn't take me long to find some other digs nearby, where life developed into a much more pleasant routine.

I walked towards Laban's flat to report for work on my first day wearing my Girls Training Corps uniform, simply because the rest of my wardrobe still largely consisted of school uniform. However, instead of my standard G.T.C forage cap, I was wearing a bright multi-coloured beret, which seemed to attract the attentions of a lorry driver, who tooted me as he went by. For the next week he would pass me at exactly the same time and always give me a welcoming toot on the horn. When I told Laban about this, he came to the window one morning to see for himself.

My first session with Laban was memorable because he had laid out a number of his three-dimensional models on the table, though at that time I didn't know how these mysterious objects related to his theories. On that morning, he simply asked me to pick out the one I found most interesting. This was a difficult exercise, but I eventually chose the figure-of-eight known as the 'lemniscate', because there was an obvious fluidity to its form. It was then that he started to explain to me how this shape was endless, an emblem of infinity. After this introduction we talked very briefly about the other shapes before getting down to the ground work of my future training.

I would be studying with Laban himself and much of the work would be applied to women workers in the factories, researched and selected by Mr Lawrence. I would be required to introduce the new Laban–Lawrence Industrial Rhythm programme ('L.L.I.R') into these factories, the object of which was to increase production and to relieve stress among the work personnel. I was also going to study dance movement with Lisa Ullmann. (Most of my early training was based on that given to the Jooss ballet students, though this gradually changed over the years.) On that first morning Laban also mentioned my previous dance training, saying that he found most classical ballet dancers had what he called 'stiff' backs, by which he meant that they held their backs in a rigidly artificial upright manner. He suggested that in my spare time I should improvise a dance which would overcome this problem, and I worked on this piece of homework for the next few weeks, to his eventual satisfaction.

From now on, my days were very full, typically starting with warm-up exercises with Lisa in the early mornings, followed by sessions with Laban introducing me to the two key strands of his vision of human movement, spatial harmony, and dynamics: in other words, I was introduced to his 'movement scales' and 'effort actions'. And as well as having to prepare Laban's work for the following day, I also regularly attended a series of evening classes run by Lisa in Manchester and the surrounding towns. These were often held in schools, mainly for teachers as the educational world became increasingly interested in Laban's work. Lisa worked incredibly hard to establish Laban's work in Britain, and I know that their relationship comprised the utmost mutual respect and affection. I would often travel back with her, on some darkened train, eager to discuss the particular class we had taken, or else the work in general. Lisa always did her best to answer my questions, while often failing to disguise her utter exhaustion: being an artistic pioneer in a foreign country in time of war can scarcely have been easy. It is true to say, though, that without Lisa Ullmann, Laban would never have exerted the lasting influence he achieved.

Where Lisa went into painstaking detail, Laban would constantly explore and test the validity of his work in a broader way, encouraging me to do the same. I was now living as part of the 'family', as Laban called us, and he led me into a world infinitely more exciting than ballet or anything else that went by the name of dance movement. We got on famously, and while I had the greatest of respect for him, revered him even, I was never in the slightest awe of him, and would occasionally pull his leg. Going for a walk one day, we saw an abandoned bath in someone's garden. It was mid-winter and there was snow on the ground. He remarked on this strange phenomenon. I told him it was the habit of the English to bathe outside in cold weather.

Looking back, I think my gentle teasing was probably good for him. When I first met him, he had lost most of his possessions for the third time, following the disasters of the First World War, the outbreak of the Second, and the Nazi persecution in between. Most of these were either destroyed by bombing or dispersed in safe houses around Germany. I remember him once mentioning Lisa's bravery when she travelled out of Germany with some of his papers, and having to hide while the train was searched. I'm sorry now that I didn't question him more about this bleak period of his life but the present was exciting enough for me.

The rigours of these last years had left him with stomach ulcers which continued to plague him from time to time. Yogurt was good for his condition, but in those days was in very short supply. He liked me to go to the local dairy because I always managed to come back with a few cartons. The Woodbine cigarettes he smoked were certainly not so good for him. When people remarked on the poor quality of cigarettes, he would always reply, 'Woodbines are so bad they can't get any worse!'

He was also very conscious that I had come straight from school, and took the time to widen my education, introducing me to the work of the artists and philosophers who had informed his approach, and in particular to the work of the Nobel prize-winning poet and playwright Maeterlinck, whom he had known personally. He also encouraged me to carry on with my drawing, in this respect taking over the role of mentor from my father. Himself a gifted artist, Laban showed me his own sketches and wickedly funny cartoons. I also remember seeing his drawings for the design of a revolutionary new theatre – they had won a prize – in which every seat had carefully been positioned to be approximately the same distance from the stage.

I also spent a great deal of time working in the garden (where there was more space), practising with a mallet as a means of studying natural working rhythms. After a while I could swing it in any direction with confidence. Laban told me that I had 'a real talent' for movement observation and analysis, and I suppose this was something to which I had learned to pay attention from an early age. Driving with my father, my eyes and mind were often directed to 'Look over there – by the tree: see it?', or to contemplate the shape or angle of some plant, flower, or building ('See where the light hits it?'). I remember his outrage at one particular row of exceedingly ugly new houses: 'How can an architect,' he said, 'make the same mistake so many times?' Our conversation was always punctuated by such observations – simply noticing the world around us. And now I was being asked to level the same critical eye at human movement – the way people moved in the street; how they used space, time, and energy in the 'flow' of their actions; and what the rhythm of their movement might reveal about them.

In addition to my morning and evening classes with Lisa Ullmann, and my daily work with Laban himself, two or three times a week I would also attend classes by another deeply influential teacher: Sylvia Bodmer. Sylvia had once had her own dance school in Germany, which she had had to flee, with her Jewish husband (a doctor) and their three young sons, under the Nazi regime in the 1930s. Eventually arriving in Manchester, she and her family now lived a short distance away from Palatine Road. Sylvia had trained with Laban; not only was she a good mover, she also had a finely tuned mathematical brain, and it was she who developed Laban's theories in greater detail, I learned to move harmoniously through the crystalline shape of the twenty-sided 'icosahedron', one of the so-called 'Platonic crystals'.

Studying with Sylvia was never particularly easy. For one thing, her English was not yet fluent – especially when she became excited, as she often did, by the ideas she was trying to explain. On one occasion, I remember, I was precariously balancing on my right leg, stretching and moving my arms and my other leg in different directions, only to hear Sylvia issue the instruction, 'Now lift your right leg into a horizontal position'. Well, I naturally obliged – and collapsed in a heap. Sylvia immediately saw her mistake, and burst out laughing. But I soon learned to see beyond the comic barriers of language, and concentrate instead on the wordless language of movement itself. After a while, we developed a mutual understanding of movement awareness, and I gradually became aware of the goals she had in mind. Indeed, my sessions with her often formed the perfect link between Lisa's precisely detailed analysis and Laban's own, more broadly philosophical disquisitions. After all, one can only learn by doing and experiencing the movement for oneself, and I began to understand from within my own body the theories I was processing in my mind. Laban always insisted that people could never fully understand his work intellectually. They needed to experience the actual efforts and shapes involved – hence the terminology of what he defined as the 'art of movement'.

As my understanding grew, I would sometimes practise my teaching techniques on Sylvia's youngest son Walter, then aged eight or nine – now Sir Walter Bodmer, a leading pioneer in the field of human genetics (so it doesn't seem to have done him any lasting harm!). When Walter was unavailable, Laban himself took over his role as trial pupil for me. 'Good, that's right,' I would exclaim, 'Good, that's the way,' whenever he effected a movement I had instructed, but as the 'lesson' went on, I was surprised to see his actions become ever slower and less accurate. When I pointed this out to him, he shot back, 'But you keep telling me I'm good, so I don't have to bother!' It was a useful lesson for me to learn – and I never made the same mistake again.

Chapter Four

Laban's Assistant Hits the Road

1942–1943

Established in the bosom of my new 'family', I was soon travelling as far afield as Yorkshire and Lancashire with Lisa, acting as her assistant on the courses for teachers that were by then becoming very popular, and before long I was running my own classes in Bolton and Doncaster. The one at Bolton was held in rooms above a 'British Restaurant' – the popular government-subsidised canteens where decent food could be had at reasonable prices.

The elderly principal of the Evening Institute where I took my recreational movement class had a very comfortable room as her office, with an open fire and a large arm-chair. She sat at an enormous oak desk, and her door would always be standing wide open when I arrived. Then she would shut the door, stoke the fire, and insist on my sitting in the arm-chair which she now heaved nearer to the flames. That done, she would imperiously ring her bell whereupon minions from the kitchen arrived with a silver tea service and a variety of daintily cut triangular sandwiches (thin bread-and-butter with jam); a plate of biscuits, and another of cakes. My eyes would glaze over – and my stomach rumble – at this display, for to me these were luxuries from a by-gone (or at least a pre-war) era, already half forgotten.

I would vainly protest that I wasn't so very hungry, but she would sit there smiling, shaking her whiskery chins and knowing best. In the end I would drink the tea, accept a sandwich or two, and a slice of cake, and maybe take another for later. Sometimes my train would be delayed, and I would arrive in a panic, really not having any time to spare – but she would have none of it: my class could wait for me. This was all very well, but our high tea was accompanied by a steady stream of very mature teachers tapping nervously on her door as they arrived to collect their registers. So while I sat there, roasting by the fire, filling my face with sandwiches and cake, and trying to express solidarity with a half-hearted smile in their direction, my gracious hostess would issue severe reprimands to her staff for late time-keeping or untidy registers. Remembering their forlorn faces as they stood in pathetic silence being 'ticked off', it's a wonder I didn't get a knife in my back!

Probably the only reason I didn't was my youthful appearance. Although by now I was nineteen, bus conductors always gave me change and a child's ticket, which made me feel quite cross. But there were other drawbacks, too. I remember being met off the train at Rotherham, to give a demonstration class to a group of teachers, and being driven out to the school. When we arrived and I got out of the car, the headmistress rushed forward and impatiently pushed me out of the way, calling to the driver, 'Where is Miss Newlove?' Laban always enjoyed the tales I brought back. I remember on one occasion when he had been quite ill, sitting on the edge of his bed and regaling him with the characters I had met – the formidable principal with her tea and cake, and the friendly vegan in my class who turned up in her swimsuit (very daring in those days).

Of course, all these evening classes meant travelling in the blackout, at the mercy of train timetables that were frequently disrupted, and hoping to escape any air raids. In some ways the danger added to the excitement of the time. We were pioneers in the field, and Laban's work was gradually becoming recognised and appreciated, especially by industry. One day Laban told me that Lawrence had requested that his team of industrial engineers should have some understanding of the art of movement and its relationship to industrial rhythm. It was decided that I should take regular classes over a period of six weeks with these engineers.

Although one of them had been an Olympic skater it was hard work at first. Hoping to free up their bodies a little, I asked them to take off their jackets and waistcoats, ties and shoes. They were a very self-conscious bunch, though, and it took a while for them to agree to such a strange request, especially from a nineteen-year-old girl. Nevertheless we eventually began to work on the 'efforts', and linking them to their own specific work. When this started to make sense to them, they were more willing to experiment and by the end of the classes, while they could hardly be called dancers or even particularly good movers, they had a much greater understanding of what the art of movement was all about, and how it could complement Lawrence's own work.

Lawrence was a visionary figure who recognised the great opportunity of linking his own work on 'time and motion studies' to Laban's revolutionary ideas on increasing output through physical well-being. The theory was based on the important premise that any employee should work in the most 'harmonious' manner possible, based on the careful analysis of their work, and a programme of devoted training. So-called 'effort studies' were also implemented to make sure that the right person was assigned the right job.

Perhaps surprisingly, the first factory to welcome our services was the Mars complex (as in 'Mars Bars') in Slough, and a meeting was arranged with the directors in their boardroom. The importance of the occasion was spelled out to me over dinner, when it was impressed upon our delegation – Mr Lawrence, Laban, and myself, and three of Lawrence's engineers – that no one must be late for breakfast the following day. We had a train to catch and cars waiting. The next morning, however, at this crucially timed breakfast, Laban was late; very late. It turned out that the doors in the hotel were self-locking, and he had locked himself out of his own room. There were smiles all round, and no harm done. I then excused myself, saying I was going to fetch my case – but my private fears were confirmed: I too was locked out. I managed to get a porter to help me break into my own room, and eventually arrived in the lobby where the others were waiting. (I never told them.)

Lawrence and his team went off to another part of the factory while Laban and I went to see women working in two separate areas: the kitchens and the assembly-line conveyor belt where they sat packing the Mars Bars for the troops overseas. For this I was politely asked to wear a set of white overalls and a cap over my hair. Laban waited outside the storeroom while I put them on. When I came back out, and stood among the group of identically dressed women, Laban looked straight through me when I smiled at him. So I stood there for a while, and the next time he looked in my direction I winked at him. He looked surprised – until I winked again and he at last recognised me, and burst out laughing.

It became obvious to us both during our preliminary tour where help was needed. Those women working in the kitchens, for example, had to carry the same large and heavy trays formerly carried by the factory's male staff. A few of these would need to be transferred to other duties while the majority could be taught better methods of handling the trays. Those on the assembly line, we observed, developed a nervous shaking of the hands after a couple of hours' work, and required regular breaks in the rest room. On my second visit I learned to do the job of wrapping and packing the bars myself, and here I knew I could be of help, both to increase production and eliminate the symptoms of 'shaking-hand syndrome'. The crucial factor was the speed of the operator's movement: it was far more important to establish a steady and regular rhythm than a fast and therefore stressful rate; the belt may be slower, but there would be fewer breaks required. A room was eventually set aside for my classes, and 'compensatory exercises' would also feature in the training sessions. In these, the 'conveyor women' would be given the opportunity to limber up and restore their muscular balance by employing large, swinging movements. The kitchen staff joined in these exercises, but were also shown how to lift heavy weights safely and without strain.

Arrangements were set in place for me to start my work at Mars immediately. I had been formally introduced to the boardroom that morning as 'Miss Newlove, Mr Laban's assistant, who will be in complete charge of the training programme'. Seeing the 'chaps' back to Euston Station after our tour, Laban asked me in his broken English, 'You can do?'

Momentarily overcome by the enormity both of the commission itself and the degree of faith being placed in me, I replied simply, 'I'll try.'

Laban immediately looked worried. 'But you always say, "Of course I can!"' he said.

'Well, of course I can!' I replied, and we were both laughing delightedly as he and the others waved me goodbye.

Left to my own devices in London, while Laban, Lawrence, and the others made their way back to Manchester, I returned to my digs just off Baker Street. These had kindly been found for me by another member of the 'family', Lilla Bauer. Ten years older than me, Lilla had been one of Kurt Jooss's dancers until the outbreak of war. I didn't know at the time that Laban had asked her – and her husband, the Hungarian-born composer Mátyás Seiber – to 'look after' me, and would probably have felt rather peeved if I had, but I was certainly grateful to her for her hospitality and kindness during this busy time.

I kept a careful record of all my expenses, which were enormous since they included daily trains and taxis to and from the factory in Slough, as well as my accommodation in London and a weekly return ticket to Manchester. At the same time, I was having to live as frugally as I could, usually eating at the Quality Inn, where a raw root salad was the cheapest thing on the menu. (I have never been able to touch turnips since!) This wasn't entirely Lawrence's fault, since I did save some of my pennies for occasional trips to the cinema. Every Thursday night I would catch the train back to Manchester, along with all the travelling 'reps'. The restaurant-car menu proudly offered sausages or rissoles. (The shape was different but the contents identical.) After a few weeks of this routine, the reps began to regard me with some curiosity, but while they accepted me as a 'regular', I never enlightened them about my work. I would report to Laban on the Friday morning, then go on to teach in Doncaster in the early evening. Saturday was my half day off; Sunday saw me returning to my bed-sit in London.

This tough routine had been well established, and I had been successfully teaching my classes for getting on for a year, when I came home one evening, in March 1943, to my Baker Street digs feeling distinctly off-colour. Looking in the mirror, I was alarmed to see that my neck was swollen on either side. I rang my mother to seek her opinion, and she correctly diagnosed a case of mumps. I also phoned my near-neighbour (and secret benefactor) Lilla Bauer, who offered to notify the factory staff at Mars, as well as the evening dance class I taught in Charing Cross that she had organised for me. I gratefully took to my bed. When I woke up the next morning, I was in a very sorry state indeed. Not feeling well enough to fetch more water, I was carefully rationing what little I had when Lilla kindly dropped in to see the patient bearing a bunch of violets – which she immediately dumped into my half-full glass of water!

That evening London suffered one of the worst air raids of the war. My full-length front windows were shaking so badly from the bombing that my landlady insisted on moving me to a back room for greater safety. I also remember that, in the absence of a proper hot-water bottle, she gave me a glass lemonade bottle, filled up to the top with hot water. It was a kind gesture, but I felt I was more likely to be scalded to death than killed by a direct hit.

Then, later that night and at the height of the raid, my mother suddenly appeared. After our phone-call the previous night, she had decided to come and nurse me in person, arriving in London from Lincoln more or less at the same time as the Luftwaffe's bombs. Hailing a cab (which the driver later abandoned to take to the shelters), she had had to finish the journey on foot, armed only with a small torch. I felt rather better for her unexpected company. In the morning we learned how very bad the night's raid had been. There had been a terrible disaster at Bethnal Green Underground station, where nearly two hundred people had fled from the bombing for shelter, only to die falling over each other on the stairs leading to the platforms below.

Laban's Assistant Hits the Road

*

Enduring and surviving both the Blitz and the mumps, and after a few days at home in Lincoln to convalesce, I was soon back at work at the Mars factory – where the workers' output and productivity had soon increased dramatically, despite the fact that they had taken their classes during their normal working day. The principle of Laban and Lawrence's 'industrial rhythm' was really taking off. I even took the opportunity to design my own outfit: a short-sleeved, silky-blue Aertex shirt, worn under a pale-beige set of dungarees; the blue of the shirt matched that of the hand-embroidered badge on the front of the dungarees ('L.L.I.R.', for 'Laban–Lawrence Industrial Rhythm'). I made my own dance shoes – from chamois leather, usually sold for cleaning windows.

It is strange to think now how very much I enjoyed my work during these busy and difficult years. I was young, lucky to be doing what I loved, while at the same time assisting the war effort by increasing factory production. My thoughts were often for my brother, by now posted in the Middle East, preparing for the invasion of Italy, but my parents kept me informed of his welfare and, after all, everyone had the same worries for family members on active service.

The local education authorities were also becoming increasingly interested in our work. One of these held an open day in the gymnasium and we were invited to come along and see the work of the teachers (none of whom were yet 'doing Laban'). The gymnastic display had seemed endless, and the schoolchildren were now hanging by their arms, with their backs to the wall-bars, occasionally lifting their knees to set their feet on a lower bar to ease their tiring arms. The Director of Education sat with his honoured guest, Laban, in the front row of the seats that had been assembled. I leaned over to ask Laban in a whisper what he thought of the wall-bar activities. He replied that he felt sorry for the children: 'They look like a lot of artificial monkeys on artificial trees!'

On another occasion, the 'British Drama League' got in touch. A voluntary organization founded in 1919, and an early champion of a British 'National Theatre', the League, already supported by some professionals, had heard that Laban was now working in England, and wrote to ask whether he might be available to run a weekend class. Politely declining due to pressure of work or ill health, he instead sent Lisa – with me as her assistant. It was arranged for the opening session that I should arrive first and start the programme, and that Lisa would take over after two hours. All went well in this introductory class, but briefly pausing for breath I happened to look out from the stage into the body of the hall, only to see Lisa's grinning face in the middle of the audience: I had been so absorbed in the work, I suddenly realised, that nearly three hours had gone by. As it had been going so well, she had decided to leave me to it!

All this was invaluable experience for me, and I blossomed under the régime, going on to take further drama courses across the country as the months wore on. One of the most memorable of these was held in my home county of Lincolnshire, run by its drama director, 'Marckwald', who had been a devotee of Laban in pre-war Germany. The most junior among the students was a young Joan Plowright, who had come with her mother. On the first night we were all sitting at a long table for the evening meal. I had taken some pains to make myself look older and more sophisticated than my nineteen years, successfully, it seemed – at least until an exotic woman in her sixties suddenly entered the dining room, wearing a Greek tunic and sporting a headband. Taking one look at me, she cried out, 'Why, it's little Jean!'; and there was the redoubtable Miss Harrison, whom I had last seen tapping out the metre of 'Ta-tay, ta-tay, taffa, teffi, ta-tay' on the blackboard, a decade or so before. I remember feeling slightly mortified at this reunion, while at the same time thinking that there was something timelessly English about her indomitability.

It was always a very busy time, learning and teaching in equal measure. A typical example of the sort of work I did is the series of movement classes and lectures I gave in Hereford to the so-called 'Land Girls' – members of the Women's Land Army, or W.L.A., who were drafted into agricultural work to replace the male workers then serving in the Armed Forces. I began with a few introductory remarks about Laban's work, then demonstrated to the assembled Land Girls in the hall how it was possible to make heavy manual work less tiring, and also to prevent strain when lifting or carrying heavy objects. In order to illustrate this physically, I now asked for a volunteer from the audience to come out: her job was to use her bodily strength to prevent me from lifting the wooden mallet I used to represent a working tool. They looked at each other for a moment, then all eyes focused on one particular girl in the front row. By far the heftiest girl in the group, she also looked the strongest. Without a word being said she tacitly acknowledged her colleagues, stood up, and stomped heavily towards me.

I asked her to hold the mallet down, at waist height, with two hands around its handle, and to keep it down while I tried to lift it against her pressure. I also took hold of the mallet's handle, manoeuvred myself beneath it and, bending my elbows, tried to lift it up. Nothing happened. This girl seemed an immovable force. I thought I had met my match. Then I remembered something Laban had told me – that one's movements are always strongest when made nearer to the body. So, shifting my weight closer under the mallet and grasping it from underneath, with my hands near to my chest I started to press upwards. As I did so, I moved completely underneath it, and slowly straightened my body into an upright position, with my arms holding the mallet aloft. My muscular assistant had had to let go: trained technique had overcome solid strength. There was a shocked silence for a moment, and then an outburst of clapping. My partner was gracious in defeat and nearly broke my fingers with a hearty handshake.

When the time came for me to return to Dartington from Manchester, Land Girls were also frequent members of the classes I held on the flat roof of the Central Offices situated some distance from the main Hall. This was also the venue for my classes with the office staff working there. As usual, in addition to general movement training, I gave attention to the specific problems arising from particular jobs. There had been a number of complaints, for example, that the cherries harvested from the outlying orchards by Land Girls were being picked when still unripe. It turned out that after several hours' work, the girls were suffering from disturbances to their colour vision. To rectify this, I demonstrated a series of eye exercises – focusing on near and far objects, with resting in between. The same exercises eased the tired eyes of the women workers employed in the textile mills who hand-wove the ends of the wool into herringbone patterns, for whom I also recommended a routine of recreational activities, such as encouraging them to move around freely, and to get a feeling for space, in order to compensate for the fatiguing and sedentary concentration of their work.

Another W.L.A. group I found extremely interesting to work with was the Forestry Corps. They were clearing copses and it was my job to teach them how to use a long-handled, ten-pound axe efficiently. I had of course expertly practised the actions of chopping and slicing imaginary branches with my trusty wooden mallet. Now for the first time I had a real axe in my hand, and was about to show the girls the correct way to use this formidable weapon. I felt confident that I knew how to align my body safely. Watched on all sides, I elegantly demonstrated the action, swinging the handle easily before me – before suddenly remembering, as the blade skimmed within an inch of my toes, that this was no mallet! I think I successfully disguised my relief at not having crippled myself, and after a while, with careful practice, we all acquired an impressively fluent skill – moving in a long line, working with our axes through the brushwood in a swinging rhythm.

All this was important work in itself – 'war-work', after all – but so, too, was the more obviously 'cultural' or 'artistic' dimension of our educational and industrial techniques. The German-born conductor Hans Oppenheim, for example (himself a member of the Arts Department at Dartington), regularly attended my classes on the lawn. Both he and his wife Cissie enjoyed the dance compositions I prepared for these classes – Cissie often leaving them, I remember, with a beatific smile on her face that I imagined her floating off into the surrounding tree-tops. On another occasion, the local girls' school sent word, asking me to give a talk on Laban's work and begging for a short dance performance. Now, I am a 'middle' or 'medium' dancer – which means I tend to lead with the trunk– in contrast to 'high' dancers (who like to leap) or 'low' dancers (who are more down to earth in their movements). Medium dancers are happiest in waltz-like rhythms. With this in mind, I rushed into Totnes, the nearest town, where I knew of a second-hand shop with some old records in stock, hoping to find a suitable soundtrack for the performance.

Riffling through the 78's, however, the only remotely possible piece of dance music I could find was Liszt's 'Hungarian Rhapsody' – not ideal for a waltzing type! Arriving on my bike to find the whole school waiting agog in the gym, it seemed to me a very short time since my own school days. After finishing my talk, I improvised to the 'A'-side of the Liszt record. Basking in the applause that followed, my triumphant mood was slightly dented by a request from the audience: when I recovered my breath, could I, possibly . . . do it again? This was becoming a bit tricky: they hadn't realised I had improvised the whole thing! Thinking on my feet (while I took a little more time than usual to recover my breath), I replied with the generous suggestion that I would improvise to the other side of the record. I was in my element, transported back to the days – not so very long before – when I had taken requests to improvise lunch-time 'performances' in my old school library. My second performance went down very well – so well, in fact that the school Head offered me a job to stay on. I politely declined – I was having far too much fun where I was.

I was continuing to give my various classes, and also helping the marvellously named Winsome Bartlett, who had taken over the job I had originally applied for. When I returned to Manchester, Laban told me he had an important job for me. The Catholic organization The Holy Grail had asked for someone to choreograph a performance of their Passion Play, to be performed at the Royal Albert Hall. Although Lisa had attended their first briefing with me in Blackpool, I was subsequently left in sole charge of the movement, which was a major part of the whole production, including the grand spectacle of Christ's procession with the cross. Although a daunting assignment, it was an enjoyable experience, working with several hundred people, as I travelled round the country preparing each group's activities within the framework of the entire play. Visiting Nottingham, one of my rehearsal venues, I took the opportunity to see my mother, and arranged to have lunch with her. It had been a long time since we had got together, and I know she was looking forward to spending a day with me, having come prepared for a shopping expedition and a gossip. Unfortunately, our lunch was a hasty affair, and I had to dash off back to work afterwards – much to her disappointment.

A major part of this production was the staging of the cosmic war between Good and Evil, the angels and the devils. The formidable Baroness G., who was in charge of the Grail's activities, sent me a memorable card during rehearsals. 'Dear Jean,' it read, 'The devils are marvellous but the angels still need some help.' It is always easier to be inspired by devils. In the event, I missed the play's final performances at the Albert Hall, though both Laban and Lisa went. Apparently, it was something of an 'event', with special trains being laid on to transport performers and spectators from all over the country – including a delegation of representatives from the Vatican. When I asked Laban what he thought of the show, he said the processional entrance into the Albert Hall of the Vatican hierarchy comprised in itself an entire rival production. Even so, he was pleased with my part in its success. But there was no time to rest on my aesthetic laurels: the factories beckoned. Our initial projects, such as the one at the Mars factory, were still bearing fruit.

Before coming to England, Laban had already begun devising a system of notation for dancers ('Kinetography Laban'), which Albrecht Knust, a former pupil, secretly continued to develop in war-time Germany. Laban now wanted a simpler version, which could be written rather like short-hand while observing a working operation, for the purposes of analysis, and he and I developed an 'industrial notation', which evolved into a serviceable temporary wartime system.

Towards the end of 1943, Laban asked me to teach at a 'Christmas Modern-Dance Holiday Course' to be hosted by Sheffield University. Since I was still so young, and students would include H.M.I.'s (His Majesty's Inspectors), as well as lecturers and teachers, Laban told me he had deliberately made my classes voluntary, members of the course being invited to sign up for classes in movement observation and analysis leading to a choreography. To my astonishment – and probably his, too – everyone signed up. Laban looked at the long list of names and turned to me. 'You can do?' he asked. 'Of course,' I replied. One of the things I devised for this course was an enormous human 'machine'. The class became the many levers, cogs, handles, and wheels, using a variety of 'efforts' – in other words they were the machine itself. This industrial 'monster' (as I called it) quietly stirred into life with a series of isolated and apparently insignificant little movements. Gradually, other parts came alive, each with their own rhythms and sequences, the whole thing eventually building into a sort of rhythmic cacophony – before slowing down, then repeating itself, before coming to a complete stop. Laban was very pleased with my 'monster', and brought the visiting Mayor and Director of Education to see it.

Meanwhile, as the war dragged on, it seemed that most days brought new requests for our work. And although the industry of the national war effort was paramount, I was also beginning to learn the equal importance – to national and individual 'morale', perhaps – of drama, and of dance, and of art. Back in Manchester, as well as teaching the students at its Northern School of Music, I still held regular classes in Yorkshire, Lincolnshire and Lancashire, ran a weekly evening class for teachers at Doncaster, and even assisted Laban with a pantomime at the Civic Theatre in Bradford, then run by the actress Esme Church.

During these busy years I realised how hard Lisa worked, not only to further Laban's work but also to help earn a living for them both. He was deeply indebted to her – but in Bimbo she had a rival for his affections. It had been love at first sight – and it was mutual. A stray itinerant cat, of indeterminate colour and even scruffier habits, Bimbo came and went as he pleased, something of a guttersnipe promoted to luxury living. After a week or so's absence, Laban would express his concern – and a sentimental reunion inevitably ensued. Sneaking up from the cellars, the cat would fly into Laban's sitting-room, leap into his accustomed position on the arm of his chair, and immediately set up a purring rhythm, while Laban greeted him joyfully with the words, 'Why, Bimbo, you old devil, where have you been?'

The arrival at my family home in Lincoln of another of those official buff envelopes brought this exciting period of my life to an abrupt end: my immediate presence was requested at the Labour Exchange. Lawrence managed to delay the bureaucratic process by explaining my increasingly useful role in industry, but the relevant authorities didn't understand our pioneering work. But there was no way out, and Laban and Lawrence were very upset at my enforced departure – not least, over and above the personal wrench, since there was no one ready to take over my work, and other factories were lining up to be part of our programme. After all our hard work, and the successful increase in production it was beginning to generate, the whole venture was in jeopardy. We tried to cheer each other up as best we could.

Of course, I would have joined up far more willingly had there been a greater choice of jobs that I felt I could usefully do. My brother Pip had fought in the North African campaign after Dunkirk, and was now serving in Italy. But by this crucial stage in the war, the W.A.A.F. and the W.R.N.S. – the Women's Auxiliary Air Force and Naval Service respectively – were full to capacity. And so despite my far more useful contribution to the war effort with the Laban–Lawrence Industrial Rhythm programme, the A.T.S. (Auxiliary Territorial Service) merely required cooks, clerks, and – domestics by another name – 'orderlies'. But the bureaucratic machinery was intransigent – it rolled on, and on, flooding the training camps with more and more recruits who then found that there were fewer and fewer jobs left to be done.

Did my country really need me to be a cook, clerk, or orderly?

Chapter Five

My Country Needs Me

1944

While awaiting my final papers to arrive in Lincoln, in the early days of 1944, Lisa prepared a farewell supper for us with Mimi Eckhertz, who had served as Jooss's housekeeper for many years and was now Laban's. It was a rather melancholy occasion, and although everyone was still hoping to persuade the all-powerful bureaucratic government officials to waive my call-up for the greater good, we all realised it was probably a futile effort. Lawrence promised that my job would be waiting for me; Laban and Lisa wanted me back as soon as possible. Even so, our work continued to a daily schedule.

It was during this very difficult time that Laban told me he was going to take 'the family' – meaning Lisa and myself – to visit Jooss, whose ballet company was then performing in Manchester. This was tremendously exciting news for me: I'd still been at school when Jooss had invited me to join his company as a student dancer, after our meeting in Cambridge a few short years – and what seemed a lifetime – before. The production we now went to see was a revival of Jooss's magnificent ballet 'The Green Table' – the revolutionary anti-war piece he had premièred in Paris in 1932. Its title referred to the green-baize tables of the diplomatic conferences that had followed the First World War, but this ballet was a 'dance of death', its delegates eventually pulling guns from their pockets and firing in the air. There had been cheers and wild applause from a great section of the audience at its première; but an equally vociferous chorus of boos, hisses, and catcalls – some from pro-classical balletomanes, outraged by the innovation of the piece, some from those who objected to its overtly pacifist politics. It was an early warning of the Nazi threat – Hitler came to power in Germany a year later – but the piece remains a profound masterpiece, its message all the more vivid at this performance in wartime Manchester.

There was an impromptu party afterwards, with Jooss and his cast – Ulla Soederbaum, Hans Zullig, and Rolf Alexander among them – all greeting Laban with great affection. Sitting in the train on the long journey home, Laban teased me about which of the young men had taken my eye. I admitted to a mild interest in Hans Zullig, who as well as being an impressive dancer, also seemed incredibly handsome. Laban laughed – it was usually Rolf who attracted the girls, he said. I only discovered later that Hans's proclivities lay elsewhere – but even if he had been available, I soon wouldn't be.

For despite our best hopes that Lincoln Labour Exchange had forgotten all about me – or even decided that my work was of national importance – the dreaded letter finally dropped onto the mat in February 1944. I had been given my marching orders, and I was devastated, both depressed and indignant that I was being forced to leave a job that I could see with my own eyes was so important: after all, production had increased considerably in the factories whose workforces we had trained. I suppose we were genuinely ahead of our time, and the bureaucracy of wartime officialdom did not recognise our pioneering contribution. I could only hope that Mr Lawrence might pull some strings to get me back to this vital work. But with a heavy heart, and everybody's goodbyes ringing in my ears, I returned home to Lincoln, and reported for service as instructed.

Lincoln Labour Exchange had been temporarily housed in the local Drill Hall, though its temporary status had now entered its fifth year. The large, dreary room was flanked on two sides by trestle tables piled high with government forms, each to be duly read, noted, acted upon and filed. There was a long queue, which I joined. Most people had, by now, developed a 'queue' mentality. Those who had the time would only have to see a queue to instinctively join it. It didn't really matter what it was for. In

Lincoln High Street, some of the longest queues formed outside tobacconists' shops. Rationing being in full force, it was very unusual to come away with a pack of ten, more often than not being limited to five, which, for non-smokers like me, could be bartered for extra sweet coupons or, perhaps even a clothing coupon. At least in those queues there was something to look forward to at the end of it. This one was altogether more depressing.

Finally arriving at the desk in the Labour Exchange, I handed my completed form to the clerk. Without a word, and barely a glance in my direction, he reached for a file and after searching through a mess of ill-assorted papers, pulled out the relevant vital scrap. After a cursory read, he reached for another form, which he now started to fill in – or at least hoped to.

'Surname of employer?'

I was suddenly aware of the ears of the queue behind me. They had nothing to do but listen, after all.

'Er . . . Laban.'

'I beg your pardon?' What he really meant was: 'Pull the other one!'

'Laban,' I repeated, a little louder this time.

'How do you spell it?'

'L – A – B – A – N.'

His pen hovered like a hawk over the blank form. Although the clerk kept his head down, he couldn't disguise the animosity I felt emanating towards me. From the slight stir I heard behind me, they had sensed trouble brewing too. He sighed briefly. Obviously this girl either had a speech impediment or was illiterate – or simply an idiot. With his luck, perhaps all three. Suddenly, his face brightened, and his movements became positive.

'Oh, Layburn!' he said, clearly delighted with his powers of deduction and relieved to have cracked the code, and busily wrote the name down on the form. Like a lamb to the slaughter, he asked his next question. 'What's his Christian name?'

The queue was by now agog; I like to think they were one step ahead of him. I was obviously brightening their day no end. I looked over his head and fixed my eyes on the poster on the wall behind him, warning us all that 'Careless Talk Costs Lives'. In as dead-pan a voice as I could muster, I replied, 'Rudolf Jean-Baptiste Attila . . . ahem . . . von Laban.'

A small explosion of shuffling feet, coughing, and disbelieving giggles erupted behind me, but I sensed they were on my side. Overcoming a momentary paralysis as the blush drained from his cheeks, he smirked in the direction of his colleagues as if to enlist their sympathy. It was just bad luck, after all, that I had happened to land in his catchment area. I could see that he wasn't even attempting to write down the names in full, and without another word he swivelled the form round and handed me the pen to sign on the dotted line. I noticed that for my employer's Christian name he had simply written 'John'. When I returned the signed form to him, he briefly looked up at me. 'You'll be notified,' he said curtly. I wasn't sure if that was a threat or a promise.

I turned to go, but his rudely dismissive tone had rankled. Halfway to the door, I put on what I hoped was a dazzling smile, swivelled round, and announced to the room, 'His full name is Rudolf Jean-Baptiste Attila de Varalja von Laban.'

With the laughter and applause of my fellow sufferers in the queue ringing in my ears, I waltzed out feeling much happier – and somehow more in charge of my own future – than I had felt coming in. (To be on the safe side, however, I have never been near an employment office since!) What rankled even more with me was the ridiculous demotion I was being asked to accept – from helping to pioneer the use of movement theory to improve industrial production in Britain's wartime factories, to a post as cook, clerk or orderly in the A.T.S. (the 'Auxiliary Territorial Service'). My sense of outrage wasn't helped by the abounding rumours that the A.T.S. was in any case full up with 'recruits' – and so were the 'Wrens' (the W.R.N.S, or 'Women's Royal Naval Service') and W.A.A.F.s (the 'Women's Auxiliary Air Force').

The day before I left to save my country, I heard from a school friend. Both she and her elder sister had diplomas in cookery and catering. The elder sister had duly joined the A.T.S., and on the strength of her qualifications was made a Lieutenant within a year. My friend had suffered from this rather bossy sister for all her life, and when the time came for her own call-up, she wrote to tell me she had decided to do things a little differently. So when she in turn eventually joined the A.T.S., she signed up for work in the cookhouse without mentioning her qualifications. When I met her later on, she told me she had – unsurprisingly – sailed through her basic training in mass-catering. I shall never forget her words: 'They think I'm a genius, and I've been made a Junior Commander!' That was the equivalent to the rank of Captain – and one rank higher than her sister!

My own turn to report for service came on 4 February 1944; I was ordered to report to barracks in Pontefract in Yorkshire. Perhaps the worst thing about it all was the upset and frustration I felt at leaving behind the work – the factories where our training schemes had increased productivity and morale; the success we had achieved with the Land Girls and the Forestry Corps; not to mention the new requests for our help that were coming in from all over the country.

These had recently included a new and exciting commission from the Army to work with trainee parachutists – no doubt in advance of the D-Day landings. As Laban discussed with me, the 'stress factor' among these brave young men was (understandably) very high, and it was thought that he might arrange a programme of exercises to help relieve their tension, and somehow deal with their larger 'anxiety factor'. This was an important job – to put it mildly – requiring a full-time operative, and one willing even to join these men on their training flights, and jumps, in order to monitor their reactions. Laban asked me if I might be interested. Needless to say, I immediately agreed – but my impatient wait for lift-off was abruptly brought down to earth by my call-up to Pontefract barracks. As things turned out, I would have to fight my own little wars.

Reporting for duty there on that gloomy morning, I felt almost as disoriented as those brave parachutists I wasn't helping. Abruptly separated from my adoptive family and home – where my talents had been nurtured, and such tremendous responsibility laid on my young shoulders – I was suddenly just another name and number. Dartington Hall suddenly seemed a lifetime away, and I felt quite empty inside. I found the cultural shock enormous.

We were, it must be said, an extremely unpromising bunch of recruits. One girl, of Italian extraction I think, sobbed hysterically non-stop for three days, and received her discharge papers. Like other depressed spirits, I sourly believed that the tears would dry up the moment she climbed on to the London train. But I admired the performance. Unfortunately for me, the Girton ladies teaching at my old school would never have countenanced such a lack of moral fibre. Because of the stiff upper lip they had instilled in us all, I was not to make my official escape for almost another two years. After swearing the oath of allegiance, we went on to the stores to collect our kit. This included a gas mask, in a case also containing some bits of tatty material looking like dirty cotton-wool. Someone suggested that it might be for cleaning the goggles, but most of us felt that was too simple an explanation and, in any case, the rags looked none too clean. We never did discover what they were for. About to follow instructions and change into uniform in our allocated hut, we were reminded to pack our civvies and post them home as soon as possible. Above the din of voices from this mish-mash of non-starters, a plummy voice came over loud and clear: 'Who does our packing for us?' A deafening silence ensued. Up to now the behaviour of the stores personnel had been one of rather bored contempt. Suddenly they froze in disbelief. We all turned to view this creature from another world in our midst. Let us call her 'Joanna'.

Joanna was pretty, and a natural blonde; but from then on, she was a marked woman. Stores deliberately issued her with shoes that were two sizes too big, an overcoat that reached below her ankles, and a hat that perched rakishly on the top of her head. Every Tuesday, recruits were allowed to exchange ill-fitting kit; every Tuesday, without fail, we would watch Joanna walk across to Stores in her extraordinary outfits, only to mince back in even more outrageously unsuitable garments. Even though she had my sympathy, it was hard not to giggle at this vision passing before us.

My Country Needs Me

Through it all, however, she kept her good manners intact, almost as if it were happening to someone else. Word would race around the camp that Joanna was on her way back from Stores and everyone would rush to view the latest creations thought up by the sadistic stores personnel.

Joanna was different, and she was being made to pay for the privilege. Seemingly unable to defend herself, she went on paying for it until our ragbag platoon of misfits realised she needed protection. The problem was partly brought on by her own upbringing, of course, but at the time we were not aware of this. She never volunteered an opinion: if Stores said it fitted, she was totally acquiescent, even though it was patently obvious to the rest of us that if – heaven forbid – she ever found herself in the front line, she was never going to be able to advance or retreat particularly effectively under that tent of a coat or in those enormous shoes. As time went on, she was gradually introduced to the real world by the self-appointed 'minders' from the group. One of these girls, the eldest of nine children, was so aghast watching Joanna's attempts to wash herself in the morning – wearing every single piece of kit except her hat – that she took charge there and then, and from then on assisted her in her ablutions. It was simply an impossibility for her to get up, wash, dress, and be out for roll-call in the allotted time without assistance.

I later discovered she was the daughter of a brigadier and had spent her entire life abroad. Keeping the flag flying in these distant outposts, surrounded by servants, had left her completely out of touch and utterly helpless. And yet there was a stoicism about her behaviour that one had to admire. She took every knock to her dignity in her stride, with enviable equanimity. Never once did she complain. Whether this reflected her stubbornness, stoicism, or stupidity I am still unable to say, but she intrigued me – and I warmed to the strangers who took it upon themselves to protect her.

I did notice, on one occasion, a native cunning on her part which I felt augured well for her survival. Waking before reveille – the blaring alarm call that started each day at some ungodly hour – I tiptoed across to her bed to wake her, thinking she might need a little extra time to get ready. The weather was bitterly cold, so anyone keeping the squad waiting outside in the dark became very unpopular. We were not allowed to wear our greatcoats or tunics, only thin overalls, and the roll-call was not taken until everyone was present: which to my way of thinking made the whole business superfluous. Joanna responded to my shakes by throwing back the blankets to reveal herself fully dressed – even down to her shoes! Throwing on her cap, she rushed outside before anyone could stop her. The duty sergeant almost died of shock to see this lone figure standing to attention under the wintry stars just as reveille sounded.

On my first night under these depressing circumstances, I prepared to make up my bed, bleakly surveying my 'biscuits': this was a mattress divided into three parts – for no obvious reason that I could fathom other than to make life still more uncomfortable – all of which were extremely hard, and none of which formed an even surface. (Much later on, one learned how to 'swap biscuits' until one acquired a more even mattress.) I put the worst biscuit under my pillow, since that way I thought I wouldn't feel the lumps. Two thin regulation army blankets followed the two single sheets, and my bed was ready. No one was very talkative, each of us lost in our thoughts of what and whom we had left. As I gingerly climbed into bed, some kind soul came round, sharing out some sticks of chewing gum. There was a tacit understanding growing among us that we had better all stick together to survive. Chewing gum was a small luxury, and I gratefully accepted the gift. Dog-tired, I fell asleep almost immediately, only to wake up several hours later to discover that the chewing gum had meanwhile migrated from my mouth, and was now stuck firmly to my hair. No amount of frantic combing could remove it. In the end I had to root out my nail scissors and snip the worst tangles out in the dark, before falling back to sleep. In the morning, I resembled an early version of a punk rocker. Not the most auspicious start to my new career.

What had actually been achieved in those first weeks of our basic training? We had been vaccinated, and shown how to use our gas masks in case of gas attack; we had been lectured on the variously arcane aspects of Army life, such as how to make our bedding and kit acceptable for inspection. We had also been initiated into the equally arcane practice of drill parades . . .

About ten days into my six-week training course with the A.T.S., I was sent for by the Junior Commandant. This could hardly be promotion already, could it? Or, better still, had they discovered they didn't really need me after all? The bubble was soon burst.

'So you play hockey, Private Newlove?' she asked. 'I see you were Captain of your school First Eleven and occasionally played for the county.'

I nodded modestly.

'What position do you play?'

'Centre forward.'

She smiled like the Cheshire cat, then said, 'Would you like to play for us?'

I thought for a moment or two – long enough, at least, to become aware that she was holding in her hand my application for a weekend pass. One learns fast in the Army. 'Yes,' I replied, 'I'd be pleased to!'

She handed me the signed pass.

It was therefore with some amazement that Lisa saw me arrive at Wakefield that weekend to assist her on the dance course, just a few short weeks since the 'family' had thrown their farewell supper for me.

Appearances in hockey matches weren't the only thing I traded for weekend passes, though. It was obvious from my C.V. that I had other talents. I was duly asked to choreograph the musical made famous by Jack Buchanan, Goodnight Vienna, for our battalion 'spectacular' in return for my next signed pass. This was a musical production put on by the battalion for everyone, including the local people. Indeed, I seemed to have so many 'extra-curricular' activities that one officer once remarked, not quite jocularly, that she thought that the A.T.S. was, for me, a part-time occupation. As far as I was concerned, she was right. I had been working much harder in Civvy Street, and to greater effect. It was also obvious that there were too many recruits being called up at this stage in the war.

Because I was usually so busy elsewhere, I nearly always managed to miss the regular marching drill on the vast parade ground at Pontefract. This was driven home to me when I found myself on parade one day in the position of 'marker' at the head of the squad. This meant that everybody else 'levelled off' by stretching out their right arms, sideways, shoulder high – to be equidistant – before dropping their arms and standing to attention. Orders came thick and fast. Half-turns and quarter-turns followed in quick succession. Unfortunately, with no one on my right, the squad and I had long since parted company, marching off in different directions. I was unaware of this shambles, of course, since we were strictly ordered to keep our 'eyes front' while marching. 'Atten-shun! – Right turn! – At ease! – Atten-shun! . . . By the left, quick march . . .' My concentration may have soon begun to flag, but at least I was putting on a good show of marching forward purposefully. It only struck me a little later that the drill sergeant's voice was a shadow of its former self, and that I could now hear no other feet than my own. I risked a hasty look over my shoulder – only to see a set of dots doggedly disappearing at the far end of the parade ground. By the time my squadron of recruits had returned to join me, we had all managed to stop laughing.

'Postings are up!' When the cry went up after six weeks' training, we flew to the notice-board. Who were the lucky companies that were going to enjoy our expertise in the 'Three C's' – cooking, cleaning, and clerking? And where was my name? Ah yes, there it was, at the bottom of the list. I was promoted to 'Acting Lance-Corporal (unpaid)', and attached to 'Holding Company'. I had no idea what any of this meant, but it didn't make me very popular with my peers, who seemed to think Churchill had personally wangled a stripe for me. This was soon forgotten, however, in the excitement of going off on our very first extended leave before reporting to our new companies. It turned out that the inscrutable wording next to my name meant that I was the only one of us all to have been selected to return to Pontefract. Much as I disliked the place, I had already discovered that it was usefully situated – a good centre for travelling to any courses that had been arranged by Laban and Lisa at the weekends.

I had planned to take the first part of my leave in London, with Laban and Lawrence of course, who were then leading another factory-inspection with a team of engineers. The plan was for me temporarily to resume my work with them, and to explain my role to the management. I arrived in the middle of the blackout, just as an air-raid alert was sounding. Anxious to get to my hotel in Eccleston Square, I quickly made my way to the Underground. The station was already packed, the nightly exodus to the nether regions being in full swing. Those of us who were bona fide passengers picked their way over the recumbent figures with difficulty. They lay stretched out along the platforms, blanket-covered and anonymous. Some had more sophisticated accommodation, in the form of rough wooden structures providing tiered bunks. The air was fresher near the mouth of the tunnel, and many tried to establish themselves there, though the deafening noise of the approaching trains made it difficult to sleep. The heat in the middle of the platform was oppressive and fetid; young children soon became fretful, and toilet arrangements were rudimentary. Everyone appeared to have brought their ubiquitous gas masks – though what good they might do was beyond me.

We heard the deep boom of the ack-ack guns as the bombers came in, the deep thuds shaking the ground above us and prompting a clattering down the stairs – more human flotsam of the night to join us. Jokes became earthier, I noticed; the nightly comradeship was springing to life. Sandwiches and flasks appeared out of old shopping bags, and were shared round. In the distance I heard a mouth organ start up 'Roll out the Barrel', in which a chorus of voices soon joined. Now an accordion took over the tune, and the sing-song was in full swing. As I stood there, taking in the scene, I suddenly became aware that there was one thing I knew for certain – I remember it as clear as crystal to this day, and it never ceases to astonish me: my total lack of fear. (I was to experience it later in my life.) Trapped underground during an air raid as I was, I wasn't at all frightened or nervous in my predicament. This, I am sure, had little to do with bravery. All I felt was my determination to arrive safely, and do my job well. I remember thinking how absurd it would be to get myself killed before I'd seen Laban and the others – and I was damn well not going to let that happen. I had wasted so much time over the last six weeks – or so I felt – that a sort of grim determination, a contained anger, had taken over. I wanted to do this job because this was what I was good at. And no one – not even the Luftwaffe – would stop me.

A train at last rattled in and, skirting the sleeping bodies, I jumped aboard. It remained motionless for some time, allowing me to catch some of the running commentary between the songs. 'Such-and-such are getting it tonight . . . That was near! . . . They're probably aiming for so-and-so's factory . . . The bastards have hit the school . . .' My train at last moved off on its nightmarish journey. Almost immediately, though, the initial speed slowed down to a crawl, and we ended up at a standstill, in complete darkness. Sound was distorted and the continual reverberations of the bombardment were unnerving. I had the feeling that if only we could keep moving, we'd have a better chance – which is pretty silly when I come to think about it now.

The All Clear was sounding as I finally left the Underground after I don't know how many minutes or hours. It was good to feel the fresh air on my face, and to see the night sky above me. Even the search lights, beaming across it for more bombers, felt reassuring. At the hotel, I was greeted like a heroine returning from the front line by Laban and his party, all of whom were delighted at my sudden appearance. We hoped to get our new collaboration off the ground during the next few days, and I looked forward to working intensively with the team once again. The 'boys' were glad to see me.

After a welcome meal, I was told how important this new job was, and what they wanted me to do. I was to observe, and notate in the industrial short-hand we had devised, several of the jobs being undertaken by women. I was also to write down any impressions I might have for improving conditions and increasing production. Laban and Lawrence had been asked by the Lyons company to help adapt their factory lay-out to wartime needs, while working with the women employees on the factory floor. I was given a tour, shown the different jobs the women were required to do (much of it quite physically demanding), and returned later to a meeting with Laban, Lawrence, and the management personnel. Our initial impressions were very favourable, and we agreed that the factory could swiftly be adapted with very little disruption, and the women workers shown ways of increasing production without strain or injury.

The next few days passed in a flash, and we managed to achieve a great amount in the limited time available to us. Both Laban and Lawrence fulsomely expressed their gratitude, and as for me it was a joy to be working again with my old friends, at something worthwhile. Lawrence and his engineers were able to come up with new lay-outs after consultation with Laban and myself. I completed the notations, and sorted out an area where movement classes could take place. This would make life simpler for my successor, Gerda Rink, who had joined Laban just a week or so before I left to join the A.T.S. She was in her mid-thirties, married and the mother of a young son. She had moved to the country with a housekeeper, who was now taking charge of her son while she came to us to help the war effort. Her husband, an anaesthetist, was serving in the Middle East, and was one of Churchill's medical aides when he caught pneumonia. Gerda had been working as a movement coach with the French actor–director Michel Saint-Denis at his drama studio in London. Like me she had hoped to work with Laban one day.

We finished at the Lyons factory around lunchtime on my last day. After very little consultation the management accepted our ideas, and we were delighted at our success. Building on good reports of our methods, Lawrence had now gone off to visit another factory. Laban and I, and one of Lawrence's engineers, Mr 'Y', were the last to leave. I had always found Mr 'Y' rather dull company, and I privately hoped he would disappear so that Laban and I could spend a little more time talking shop together before I went for my train. To my delight, I now realised that Laban felt the same way. We had already peeled off the obligatory overalls after our final tour of the factory and, after a moment's silent indecision, we both began making for the main doors. Out of the corner of my eye, I saw Mr 'Y' hurrying to pick up his briefcase to follow us. What had started as a dignified walk for the two of us, now developed into a mad dash for the exit. We fell into a taxi outside, and the obliging driver moved off at breakneck speed, no doubt imagining we had urgent business elsewhere. I looked through the back window and saw the breathless and puzzled Mr 'Y' looking up and down the road after his quarry.

Laban took me to a good restaurant, and over supper listened patiently to my complaints about the uselessness of my present A.T.S. plight. The success of our Lyons project merely emphasised the absurdity of my position – did the Army really need me to be a cook, clerk, or orderly when I was helping to increase the national war effort? As well as welcoming his sympathy, I was also flattered to discover that he and Lawrence were doing all they could to secure my release. They had contacted 'people in high places', it seems, and it was simply a case of 'Now we must be patient, and see what happens'. He then told me of his plans for the long-term future, after the war, and the role he wanted me to play in it. I felt immensely cheered. In the meantime, he said, I should learn all I possibly could, observe behaviour, dance whenever possible, maybe take some classes – and always remember that they were doing all they could to achieve my discharge from service. After supper we went to the cinema, and saw The Magnificent Ambersons – Orson Welles's monument to the grace of a passing world.

When the time came for us to part, Laban insisted on coming with me to King's Cross, and hailed another taxi. I remember that the evening was cold and grey. A slight drizzle was falling. We walked the length of the platform together and he waited while I reserved a seat with my duffel bag. I came back out, and stood with him in the fading light. We were each of us lost for words, both now possessed of an extreme melancholia. Somebody shouted something, and doors began clanging shut along the carriages. It was time to go. But I had to lighten the mood. Remembering his attempts to teach me his 'native' German, the lingua franca of our spoken French, and the few words of Russian I had since picked up, I reached up to embrace him, kissed him on the cheek, and trying as best I could to smile, told him, 'Ya vas lublu avec tout mon coeur, mein Gott Vater.'

There were tears in his eyes as I got on board the train and stood leaning out of the window. My own eyes started to sting as the forlorn figure in grey mackintosh and trilby continued to stand there in the rain, waving sadly at me as the train moved off and we lost sight of each other.

My visit home to Lincoln was pleasant and uneventful. Well, almost. The house was so full of service personnel being given hospitality that I truly believe my parents were responsible for the entire Second Front. I still have the visitors' book: Poles, Americans, Free French, and British came and went and, if they were lucky, came again. Many of them were flight crew, and we often felt it personally when 'one of our aircraft was missing'.

When my mother went to visit relatives in the States after the war, our American relatives were amazed to see an enormous crowd of ex-GI's and their families waiting to greet her as she came down the gangplank. Unfortunately for the rest of us, my mother was generous and impulsive to a fault. Things had a habit of disappearing: my father 'lost' his evening suit, my brother his gramophone. And now, as I came home on leave, I saw from the top of a double-decker bus, a girl crossing the road who was wearing a dress identical to one of mine. This was all the more surprising because I had bought the material specially from Liberty's in London before clothes rationing, and it was the first dress I had ever made. After greeting my mother, I told her of this extraordinary coincidence. I looked at her face. 'Oh no, you haven't!' But one look in my wardrobe confirmed that she had.

'But you never wore it,' she said as I started to object.

I told her I had no intention of wearing my uniform when on leave. Realizing my problem, she did her best to put matters right and surprised me by running up a dress almost overnight. I was delighted and immediately tried it on. It fitted beautifully – except for the armholes, which in her haste she had stitched in back to front. I walked around for most of the day with my arms held stiffly behind my back. It took a while for her to realise that it was not my army training that caused this curious deportment.

Returning to camp was not a happy experience. I had sewn my lance-corporal's stripe to each of my sleeves, but I still felt very much like a rookie, so when I was told, 'You're duty N.C.O. tomorrow,' I didn't have a clue what it meant. When I asked, it transpired that I would have to accompany the duty officer throughout the day, acting as his assistant. I would also be required to wear a red sash. I looked at myself in the small mirror. A stripe and a sash after only six weeks! I felt like a general already.

The day after parading importantly with the officer, I dropped into the company office to see how they were getting on without me. It proved to be a great mistake.

'You're to take your kit and move into Barrack D. You've been assigned to help Corporal G.'

I trudged over to my new quarters and found Corporal G. packing. 'It's all yours,' she said. 'I'm off on ten days' leave.' And off she went with nary a backward look in my direction. I was now left in charge of a bunch of raw recruits. I made up my bed and sighed, thinking of the 'good old days' of hockey matches and Goodnight Vienna – all of four weeks ago. The gaggle of recruits returned, exhausted from whatever training they had been doing, and flopped noisily onto their beds. I entered the vast dormitory and introduced myself. A sea of faces looked up and as I rattled on, it gradually dawned on me that few of them seemed to understand a word I was saying. It seems that the Army, in its infinite wisdom, had seen fit to put me in charge of a large number of Polish recruits, none of whom appeared able to speak English. Momentarily fazed, I somehow managed to get them outside and lined up, waiting patiently as I desperately tried to remember the proper commands. It was partly a case of stage fright, and partly the result of my previously sporadic presence at drill parades.

'Please turn right,' I announced. This didn't sound quite right, so I showed them what was wanted, and the front row eventually obliged, amidst a few giggles. From the others, however, who hadn't seen my demonstration, there came a heated multilingual discussion and argument. Five minutes later, we were all facing in the same direction. 'Well done!' I said (though again, I don't remember anyone on the parade ground saying that to me). I gritted my teeth, and we set off at a steady pace towards the mess for the evening meal. Then in the corner of my eye I saw an officer approaching from the right: crisis! She would expect a salute, so I immediately issued the command (I remembered this one), 'Eyes right!' This was ignored by everyone but me. Also, fixing my eyes to the right and saluting put me at a great disadvantage: namely, my inability to see either the wall looming up at us, or the front lines of my platoon piling up against it. It took a little time to sort ourselves out, and when I looked at my watch I realised that if we didn't get to the mess-room soon, we'd have to wait outside to be seated, and by then the food would be cold. The squad sensed what I was thinking . . .

It is (literally) drilled into every soldier, very early in their training, that the parade square is sacrosanct. I still have no idea why this should be so. All personnel going about normal camp business must walk around the perimeter. All squads being trained upon it must always march across it in formation. No one – but no one – must ever run across it. Bearing this in mind, I lined my lot up as best I could, and we started a brisk march across the square. Unfortunately, a rival squad now suddenly hove into view from the right-hand side of the perimeter. The language barrier disappeared as my platoon instinctively hastened their step. Then a second rival squad appeared behind us on the left. Ignoring all these rules, my squad abandoned all pretence of military professionalism, broke ranks and ran. This tactic demoralised the rival squads who, as unwilling as we were to eat a cold supper, also broke into a run – though we had a few hundred yards over them. Somewhere in the distance I heard the bellowing voice of an irate sergeant-major, but his intervention only served to put the fear of God into everyone, and the gallop became a stampede. I am pleased to report that my Polish team arrived first. By the time the sergeant-major entered the mess, I was engaged in an animated conversation, talking fluent mock-Polish gibberish to an influx of latecomers, with my arms folded in such a way that my hands covered up my lance-corporal stripes.

As a footnote to this escapade, I must record that I became immensely popular with the girls temporarily placed under my command, all of whom quickly realised that when it came to Army ways, I was almost as green as they were. They trusted me – and I was touched by the confidence they placed in me when they asked me to keep an eye out for one particular girl, who walked in her sleep – and tended to make for open windows. I was also amazed, a week or so later, to be approached by a very pleasant and quiet girl who now confessed in a whisper that she was actually from Yorkshire, but had soon decided that it was simpler to merge into the group and keep her mouth shut. Life was much easier this way, she said; and in any case, there were few people she could speak to.

Looking back, I suppose the 'powers that be' actually thought they could make something close to a useful soldier out of me. I was being treated like a member of the recruitment-training personnel, in charge of the welfare of my squad until the corporal returned from leave. I was also expected to join in the drills of the residential training staff. Word had obviously gone round that I was pretty good on the hockey field, and also very useful when it came to musicals. I was now obviously being considered as a suitable candidate to join the resident training establishment. Unfortunately, my first drill parade with the resident staff was also my last.

Our female sergeant-major, whose pursuit of perfection was relentless, had a habit of addressing many of her remarks to me while studiously looking in the opposite direction. She had trained a crack contingent of experienced personnel who knew all the marching orders and performed them to perfection. I did my best – and even managed to improve considerably when I discovered I could make the proceedings less boring for me by humming a suitably march-like tune under my breath. But I can't say I was particularly surprised when I finally met my Waterloo on the drill ground.

There was a snap inspection on parade, and no fault could be found with anyone's uniform. But the ordeal didn't stop there. We were then each turned round, and ordered to lift our feet up – like horses for a blacksmith – one at a time. The sergeant-major wanted to see if the small section of leather separating the sole from the heel of our shoes had been polished. It seems that everyone had burnished theirs – except me. I was told that if I wished to continue as part of this élite team, I would have to remember the importance of such details.

I was unable to disguise the look of utter disbelief that must have spread across my face: I was, at any rate, asked to see her afterwards. The outcome of this solemn conference was that we politely begged to differ over the relative value of polishing a sliver of leather on the sole of a shoe. Unsurprisingly, she discerned in my attitude something close to moral subversion. And as for me, I had never wanted to join the élite of Training Personnel in the first place. Fortunately for all concerned, my first posting duly appeared on the company notice-board: I would go to Heckfield as a private and a member of the 'S.D.T.C., R.A.S.C.'.

For the uninitiated, I had joined the Specialist Driver Training Centre for the Royal Army Service Corps.

Chapter Six

I Seem to be Surplus to Requirements

1944

Firelight flickered from the dying embers of the small round coke-burning stove in the middle of the Nissen hut, making the fur of the dead rabbits ranged limply beside it glow in the semi-darkness. As I lay gazing at them from my bunk, my thoughts roaming to what the future might hold for me – I suddenly saw one of the rabbits move! Ridiculous, I told myself, I must be over-tired. The journey from Pontefract to my new posting near the Berkshire village of Heckfield had certainly been a long one, and I had finally arrived in this camp, partially hidden in the woodland, several hours late – to the obvious displeasure of my new housemate Doris, the only other inhabitant of the hut.

Doris made it clear from the start that I was an unwelcome guest, granting her 'permission' to move in only grudgingly. I felt rather like an awkward evacuee being dumped on a resentful housewife. It was not until later that I realised that her isolation – the Nissen hut was designed to accommodate three or more people – was a matter of mutual consent throughout the camp. An eccentric, red-headed woman of about forty, Doris worked as an orderly in the Officers' Mess, from where she retrieved (or scavenged) any tasty morsels she could find. These would accumulate in the Nissen hut until such time as she had a weekend pass, when she would set off, laden with these ageing titbits, to an elderly aunt of hers, on whom she doted. It had not been the warmest of welcomes.

I Seem to be Surplus to Requirements

There! Something did move! I padded past the rabbits and switched on the light by the door – and stood hypnotised by the sight of armies of maggots leaving their hosts, in full battle order, heading away from the heat of the fire and dispersing in all directions. Overcoming a strong desire to throw up, I gathered up the rabbits and flung them outside, stamped on as many maggots as I could, and staggered off through the woods to find the shower hut to clean up.

Doris returned later that evening, by which time I had taken the precaution of moving to the spare top bunk. Since our previous meeting had not been a conspicuous success, I felt at an immediate disadvantage as to how to approach the subject of her rabbits. I opted for a conciliatory tone, mentioning that I had 'just put the rabbits outside' because of the maggots crawling over the floor. But Doris took great exception to this, and became very disturbed. Rushing outside, she collected up the bloody carcases and returned them to their position by the stove, which she then refuelled, with much banging and swearing. When I questioned the advisability of such actions, my junior position was immediately made clear to me: the rabbits had pride of place, Doris told me. If I didn't like it, I knew what I could do. My self-esteem – somewhere below a maggot, apparently – reached a new low that night.

Despite this unpropitious start, I had a very happy time at Heckfield. Arriving on a beautifully sunny day in the midst of a heat wave in the late spring of 1944, I had quickly fallen in love with the rural setting. It was an isolated camp with a relatively benign regime – certainly by comparison with the Pontefract barracks I had left. Nissen huts were dotted throughout the woodland and the whole place seemed idyllic to me. And my mood improved even more when, soon afterwards, I reported to the Education Officer. He looked dumbfounded when I cheerfully quoted the 'Company Orders', which stated that he was willing to help all personnel take up study courses. I don't think anyone had been in to see him for months.

But, yes, he could help. What exactly did I have in mind? I suggested a course in Philosophy, Ethics . . . something along those lines. A degree course, perhaps. He sat down very suddenly, and looked at me intently. Was I pulling his leg? When he realised I was in deadly earnest, he promised to do all he could – and he was true to his word. After a few months, I found myself enrolled as an external student at nearby Reading University. I had heard that transport was available, and I was looking forward to attending the classes.

In the meantime, however, while waiting for word on my application to the university course, I asked the Education Officer whether it might be possible for him to arrange a language class for the camp. What language did I have in mind? German. German? To his lasting credit, a notice duly went up on the board. There was only one applicant for the course: myself. And so it was that I came to meet a very nice old-fashioned German professor, who travelled out to the camp to give me private lessons. My intention in all this was of course to surprise Laban with my sudden and miraculous command of the German language, and letters flowed from my pen. I remember my teacher most of all for his nostalgia for 'the old Germany', but also for teaching me two old songs, 'Das Gibt's Nur Einmal' ('You Only Live Once') and 'Du, Du Liegst Mir im Herzen' ('You Belong in my Heart'). In the event, though, our lessons came to an abrupt end when, just before I could start my course at Reading, we broke camp, and the entire company of the Royal Army Service Corps Specialist Driver Training Centre was relocated to Blackdown in Surrey.

Before then, however, it seemed to me to be only fair to do something in return for the obliging Education Officer, and I suggested to him that I should run an evening of classical music. There was a spare hut with a gramophone which would be an ideal venue. The notice was duly posted up – and duly taken down without exciting any interest at all. But there was one useful consequence. Army bureaucracy being what it was, a driver appeared from the men's camp with orders to run me into Aldershot once a week, for the express purpose of exchanging records for these non-existent classes.

My driver on these weekly jaunts was Paul, a former member of the Hallé Orchestra, and a cellist by profession. To my young mind he was definitely 'elderly', though he was probably only in his late forties. Nevertheless we shared many things in common. We both knew Manchester well; both of us ached to return to our own professions; and we both struggled to survive in an alien environment apparently unable to find a use for our respective talents. One day he turned up looking even more depressed than usual and he warned me this would be our last trip together into Aldershot. Totally lacking in aggression, with a wry sense of his own inadequacy as a 'fighting man', it was all he could do to exist in the Army's daily life. I doubt if he even knew how to hold a rifle. It was painfully obvious that he didn't feel he would come through. We talked and talked. I tried to encourage him. The war would soon be over, I told him, and he'd soon be back with the Hallé. I'd be back in Manchester, too, and would come to see their first performance. He gave me a sad little smile, and promised to write as soon as he could. Although I had given him my address, I never heard from him again.

Meanwhile, the records I borrowed during my trips with this kindly man in some ways laid the foundations for my subsequent career. Most of my evenings would be spent alone in the empty hut with the gramophone. I would hurry through the darkness, clutching a small torch in one hand and my dance kit in the other. Then, curtains drawn, and the latest record on, I would start to limber up. I continued to work from Laban's notes, and to keep myself flexible. In fact, working alone in this way became a way of life for some time to come.

Of course, there was also work, of a kind, during the day, and my temporary post – while they figured out what to do with me – as Keeper of Company Records certainly enhanced my knowledge of human behaviour. As I was filing records of our newcomers, the door of the Nissen hut burst open to reveal a truly 'larger-than-life' character. Corporal 'S' was back from leave with a bulging suitcase. ''Allo, me darling, you new?' he asked me. Staff gathered round excitedly as this fifty-year-old cockney sparrow opened his battered case to reveal a glittering array of cosmetics, nylon stockings, perfumes, laces, nail polish, shampoos, soap, hair-grips and so on. And out came his little, well-thumbed notebook in which he ticked off his transactions. And then, as quickly as he had arrived, and after a hurried warning, he and his suitcase vanished in a trice.

My colleagues in Company Office included a spotty young corporal with enormous pebble-glasses who appeared to be in charge (probably in the absence of an officer on leave). An unprepossessing young man, when he announced that his girlfriend was going to attend the next dance, there were a few unkind jokes voiced behind his back by the girls in the camp. But when he did proudly present his girlfriend – his fiancée, in fact, by the beautiful ring she sported – both sexes were literally dumbstruck. I noticed the incredulity on the girls' faces and the open admiration of the men. She was a 'stunner' in the best Hollywood tradition – a dazzling mixture of Jane Russell and Anne Baxter. Her dress clung in all the right places, and she wore nylon stockings – kindly supplied by Corporal 'S'. (She was also – unforgivably – an extremely nice person!)

Even more surprising, though, than the hidden attractions of that spotty corporal in the pebble-glasses, was my transfer soon afterwards to the Pay Office. I tapped at the door of yet another Nissen hut. Silence. I went in and was confronted by three khaki backs crouching over a small box. The Pay Office staff were examining some new-born mice – though whether in the interests of breeding them or locating the source of an infestation I wasn't sure. After their curiosity had been satisfied, they turned their attention to me. I think we each liked what we saw.

Sergeant Harding, Corporal Ernest Broadbent and A.T.S Corporal Joanna Pollock welcomed the arrival of A.T.S. Private Jean Newlove with great warmth. The very efficient Sergeant Harding had been entrusted with the smooth running of the office by Captain 'T', a regular Army officer, promoted from Sergeant-Major at the outbreak of the war who had married soon afterwards, and was now the rather surprised father of a baby daughter. Since he was coming up for retirement, and this was his first marriage, he seemed to be in a constant state of shock at the enormity of what had happened to him. All he wanted was a quiet life – and that was what Sergeant Harding provided, ably assisted by Corporal Jo Pollack. Jo had a twin sister, but had lost out to her when the recruiting powers, debating which of them should be called up, realised that 'J' for Joanna came before 'P' for Patricia. Corporal Ernest Broadbent – Ernie – was a musician who had played the Wurlitzer – the 'Mighty Organ' – in Blackpool before the war. We were destined to make a great team.

Obviously, the Pay Office, like the Company Office, was overmanned – or 'over-womanned' in the case of Jo and I. Of course, many A.T.S. recruits were doing extremely worthwhile jobs throughout the services, but few of those jobs were open to latecomers like me, and in the camps I went to, the A.T.S. essentially served the Army in a more menial capacity – as cooks, clerks, and orderlies, irrespective of their individual talents. Speaking for myself, I found the work utterly boring and devised activities for myself to stop depression setting in. These sometimes took a childish form, but those of us who perpetrated such antics saw them as a way of keeping our sense of humour – and with it our sanity.

My first full day in the office was a case in point. There we all sat, at separate trestle tables, scribbling away. Glancing to my left, I saw Ernie looking at me. He gave an ingratiating smile, I flashed a brief smile back, then looked around at the others, who seemed in an oddly edgy mood. I carried on working. After a few minutes, I caught Ernie looking at me again, still wearing the same idiotic grin. His behaviour was very odd. His body was turned away from me although he continued to look in my direction. And his shoulders were gently heaving up and down. At that moment, the heavens opened, and I was drenched from above. Looking up, I saw a Heath-Robinson sprinkler system fixed to the ceiling directly above me, from which a hose snaked its way down the far wall, attached to a stirrup-pump sitting in a bucket of water next to Ernie's chair. Welcome to the Pay Office!

Jo told me how I might get my own back on the culprit. There was a creaky old chair in the office which tended to collapse when anyone sat on it with any force. (It was kept for visitors, apparently.) Rushing back to the office after a hurried lunch, I switched it with Ernie's chair, awaiting his return with some satisfaction. Unfortunately, nobody had told me that today was pay-day, and that the Captain, who always presided over these transactions, always used Ernie's desk. Before I could say a word, he gently disappeared under the table in a flurry of sparks – as the metal caps of his boots scraped across the concrete floor. The men queuing for pay tried not to snigger; Ernie was sobbing into his handkerchief near the stove; and Jo – that Jezebel – studiously avoided my eyes. I rushed to help the poor man up. He took it in good part: he was later seen cycling through the camp to the Officers' Mess with a large 'L'-sign attached to the rear mudguard of his bike. Helpful personnel cheered him on his way.

Needless to say, my transfer to the Pay Office had not been calculated with a great deal of attention: I knew absolutely nothing about family allowances, deductions, increases, different rates of pay . . . And so Ernie (when not soaking me in water) taught me to write out the relevant names, ranks, numbers, and rates of pay on long spools of pay-rolls, while finding the time during this mechanical work to write new tunes and transcribe music. Whenever a visitor entered the office, he hid his work under the pay-roll. In the early days of this new regime I asked Captain 'T' if there was anything else I could usefully do after finishing each of the pay-slips. He looked a little bewildered, thought for a moment, then handed me an exercise book, and suggested that I might usefully draw margins on every page with a pencil and ruler.

It was at times like these that I seethed with anger and frustration, thinking about where I could have been – far more usefully – employed. After all, I was by now used to working much harder than these pen-pushing exercises – though I must admit my work for Laban had never seemed like hard work. There was no point in blaming Captain 'T' – he didn't have enough work to do either, and we were all victims of the system. Following Ernie's lead, then, I worked on my own notes, drawings, and diagrams given to me by Laban.

My technical expertise in dance and movement studies kept ahead of my office skills, which even a week's course at Aldershot failed to improve – though at least it increased my weekly pay (by

I Seem to be Surplus to Requirements

Physical Training Course, ATS 1944/1945

about a shilling). The sergeant-major charged with teaching us the rudiments of pay and allowances was very charming and gave me considerable help, without exactly telling me what the exam questions were. I scraped through.

I remember one interesting encounter during this course. Allocated a downstairs room in a supposedly empty married quarters' house, I became aware of the unmistakable sound of a sewing machine being used in the room above. I decided to go upstairs and introduce myself. An A.T.S. girl was busy turning army blankets into dressing gowns. She was very friendly and told me to find a space and sit down. The room was filled with piles of blankets in one corner, and of finished garments in another. As she chatted to me, an Army sergeant made a fleeting visit, dropping some more blankets on the pile and picking up a batch of completed dressing gowns. When I asked her where her company was stationed she just laughed. They had moved out a long time ago, she told me: she'd been overlooked and left behind. I began to worry as to whether or not she was still on the Aldershot pay-roll – but it didn't seem to matter very much. She and the sergeant obviously had a pretty lucrative business going. I refused the offer of a dressing gown for myself.

Unable to get home to Lincoln and back on a weekend pass, I often spent the time with old friends in nearby Reading, keeping a few spare civvy clothes at their house. So an overnight pass would see me racing for the station bus, and changing out of my dreary uniform into a dress as soon as possible. This was, of course, strictly against the rules. The next morning I would go to Reading Station and wait for Jo to arrive to meet me from the camp. The forecourt of the station would be crawling with 'Redcaps' – the dreaded military police ('M.P.s'), of both sexes, who tended to work in pairs. Jo, in uniform, would be horrified to see me dressed up in a summer-dress and sandals – she thought it was terribly risky. I used to watch the police single out a victim and then pounce, checking identity cards and passes. The women M.P.s were particularly aggressive in their manner and this made me very angry. But there was nothing I could do about it. Only once did I feel that I might have been rumbled, when a Redcap stood staring at me suspiciously for an uncomfortably long time. I thought I would brazen it out. Smiling broadly, I walked up to her and enquired about the time of the next train to somewhere or other. It worked! My problem was, of course, that I sometimes used the station wearing uniform and, therefore, could never be sure if I wouldn't be recognised; on the other hand, I passed for younger than my age when wearing civvies.

One particular expedition to the nearby idyllic village of Sonning still stays in my memory. Jo and I had packed a few sandwiches and a bottle of pop and were prepared for a heavenly day on the river. We rowed the hired boat gently downstream, one of many such small craft. Family groups enjoyed themselves on the river bank and for a while, one could pretend the war didn't exist. It was hot and sunny with a faint breeze. I was getting quite brown in my sun-dress. Jo was in uniform although she had removed the jacket. Then I noticed something.

'Jo?'

'Yes?'

'Aren't we getting rather low in the water?'

She stopped rowing and looked around. 'I think we are . . . maybe it's the picnic things?'

'Jo, there's water in the bottom of the boat. It wasn't there before.'

'So there is.'

'We'd better keep an eye on it.' But before she could answer, the water gushed in, filling the boat to within a few inches of the top. The cushions started to float away on the current. I swam after them, leaving Jo trying to hang on to the oars and the picnic. We dragged the boat to the bank but could not lift it out of the river. It sank next to us, in the clear water, as we lay exhausted and hysterical on the river's edge, having no idea what caused our shipwreck.

Eventually we recovered our wits. We were feeling cold and very damp. This part of the bank was in shadow and the sun couldn't penetrate the overhanging trees. It seemed a good idea to eat our modest picnic and share out the lemonade. If we had to walk back, it would be one thing less to carry. Just then a boat rounded a bend in the river, manned by a team of public school Sea Scouts and their coach. They were rowing splendidly and wearing all the right gear. I even caught the sounds of a sea shanty. Saved!

Jumping to my feet, I waved and smiled to attract their attention. This rather upset their synchronization, but I called out that our boat was damaged and could they help us? Seeing two bedraggled damsels in distress, to a man they changed direction and steered their boat towards us.

'Where's your boat?' one of them asked, looking vaguely around the river. I told them they were almost directly on top of it. They stared at our sunken vessel lying on the river bed in some stupefaction. But they were men after my own heart: no challenge was too great.

We watched admiringly as they salvaged it, revealing a hole you could put your hand through in its side, and a smaller hole on the other side. The coach said the boat was rotten and should never have been allowed out. Improvising on the spot, they cut the cardboard of a cigarette packet to shape, fixed a piece of waterproof backing over it, and tacked the whole makeshift patch into place over the larger of the holes. With that they saluted, jumped into their own boat, and disappeared to the strains of 'The Eton Boating Song'. Three cheers for the public schools!

Not wishing to risk a return journey in such a fragile craft, we walked back to report our loss. The boatman wasn't helpful. It was a good day for business, and he was hiring out everything he had – as we had discovered to our cost. We had to fetch it back. He was under the impression it was completely repaired. Could he at least supply us with a serviceable rowing boat to tow it back? Impossible! We must take a punt.

Punting is an art form which we had never tried. We got in not quite knowing how to cope with the pole. The boat circled and dipped with our efforts, and it was hard to take it in turns because we were never both inside the boat at the same time. Then I stuck the pole in the water and pushed. At first, nothing happened. Suddenly, the boat shot forward taking my feet with it and leaving me suspended diagonally, hanging grimly to the pole. It didn't help our progress that we both saw the funny side of it, particularly as we became the butt of much good humour, passing the same stretch of water for a second time. Jo's damp uniform tended to impede her own punting efforts so it was left to me to battle on, ignoring her witty remarks as best I could. We arrived about an hour later, tied a rope to the beached boat and set off again on the final leg of our journey. By now we were probably the best known boaters on that stretch of the river, and the picnickers waved and cheered as we limped past them, hoping to get back before the boat sank again.

We just managed it – but the boatman was still not satisfied. When he saw the smaller hole he almost burst into tears, immediately demanding compensation. I saw no way of that happening on my nine shillings a week. I told him there was a bigger hole on the other side, and that we'd been told he had sent us out in a rotten boat. It was lucky for him that we could both swim. He was silenced for a moment, before spitting out that he didn't want to see us again. The feeling was mutual.

That evening, after I'd changed back into uniform – and looking decidedly smarter than my colleague – we cycled back towards camp. Very soon, however, we were lost along the country lanes. The night was coal-black. In those days, fields and heath-land were often surrounded by barbed wire. Signposts had a tendency to disappear. This was to confuse the enemy in the event of invasion. It certainly succeeded brilliantly in confusing the transient population, many of whom had never in their lives travelled so far south. Arriving at a crossroads, one had to trust to luck. It seemed that whichever road we took, the 'blasted heath' was in our way so we decided to lift our bicycles over the barbed wire and trudge across the bumpy terrain, directly, as the crow flies.

As the first glimmerings of light crept up on us, after an hour or more, we reached the far side and saw a major road ahead. We threw our bikes over the wire and helped each other across. A large sign attached to a pole caught my eye. A signpost at last! Better late than never. We stood in silence as the message sank in. 'Danger. Keep out. Unexploded Shells – War Office'.

If my skills with a pencil and ruler were surplus to requirements in the Pay Corps, let alone my boating or navigational expertise, the Army had at least noticed my interest in physical movement and training. And so, to my great surprise, following my return to Heckfield, I was asked if I might like to take on the job of a part-time 'P.T.I.' (or Physical Training Instructor) at the camp. 'Where's the catch?' was probably my first thought. But then I remembered how useful my appearances on the hockey field and my brief role as the choreographer of 'Goodnight Vienna' had been for securing myself a few extra weekend passes, and agreed.

My colleagues were less sanguine. It seems that, prior to my arrival at the camp, the compulsory P.T. classes had been so extremely unpopular with the girls that they had quietly been dropped by our largely sympathetic junior commander. But an inspection by a visiting martinet of a P.T. Officer had recently changed all that. So there was a catch, after all: with a 'trained' N.C.O. (a stripe and a bit of extra pay was part of the deal) at the helm, classes would be reinstated, order and discipline would be seen to be restored – and I would probably end up as the most disliked A.T.S. lance-corporal on the camp.

In order to be initiated into the mysteries of teaching P.T, I travelled up to South Wigston in Leicestershire, where a hearty female explained to me that we must 'encourage and inspire' our class by a 'lively intonation of the voice'. She then proceeded to give a practical demonstration to our group of trainees. Jumping into the middle of the gymnasium, right arm outstretched like some demonic traffic policeman, she twirled round on the spot shouting, 'This way round . . . RUN!' We all dutifully ran in the direction indicated – all except one poor girl, who remained on the spot like a chicken hypnotised by a rattlesnake. 'Now . . . the other way . . . CHANGE! . . . Four walls and back again . . . Jump – and high crossed legs and . . . SIT!' Like Pavlov's dogs, we obediently ran to the four walls, then rushed back to our places, springing into the air before sitting cross-legged. All in all, it was not a happy or particularly enlightening experience.

Now, I'm not actually blaming the tutor for my indisposition, but it is a fact that, that same night, I became quite seriously ill. The M.O. (Medical Officer) immediately arranged a bed for me in C.R.S. (Casualty Reception Station) – but how was I to get there? That was obviously not her department – at least to judge from the bicycle that arrived in lieu of an ambulance a little later. I was helped on to it, while a couple of medical orderlies, one steering the bike, the other carrying my toilet bag and towel, propelled me through the camp. That night I had a high temperature, apparently, and a doctor was sent for. I have no idea what ailed me but, just to be on the safe side, I have never attempted 'a high-crossed leg jump' since. My convalescence was a very pleasant affair, though. I enjoyed cups of tea at all hours, occasional chocolate biscuits, and the luxury of decently served meals. I was certainly in no hurry to leave. But at least when the time came to return to my quarters in Heckfield to demonstrate my new-found skills, it was with the new rank of '(Part-time) P.T. Lance-Corporal (Paid)'.

Unsurprisingly, P.T. was as unpopular as ever – even Jo asked me to sign her in and out in her absence – and I could easily see why. Exercising by the roadside at 7.30 in the morning, with the men gathering to watch on the other side, calling out words of 'encouragement', left the girls feeling angry and ridiculous. Matters improved somewhat when I found a clearing in the nearby forest, away from prying eyes, and introduced a system of more dance-like routines. Needless to say, however, this break from official guidelines eventually came under scrutiny, and censure, from the more hidebound senior N.C.O.'s. At the same time, though, there was apparently even talk higher up of my becoming a P.T. Officer. But was I 'officer material'? Along with Toni Wagstaffe, another up-and-coming recruit in my unit, I was dispatched to a weekend Officer Assessment course to find out.

Chapter Seven

I Exchange Bombs for Doodlebugs

London, 1944

Toni Wagstaffe and I presented ourselves at the portals of a large house, set in its own grounds, somewhere in Hampstead, North London. This was the War Office Selection Board (or 'W.O.S.B.'), and it was here that we would be assessed as future officer material. Toni, also stationed at Heckfield and a full corporal, had already been in the services for over two years. Her husband was a major, serving overseas. I thought of her as quite old but, looking back, I think she must only have been twenty-eight.

As we waited for someone to answer the echoing bell, we were acutely conscious of coming from 'wildest' Hampshire and being flung into an altogether more sophisticated environment in the posh part of London. We arrived for our weekend visit with our regulation shoulder-bags, gas masks, and duffel bags. I remember thinking how incredibly smart Toni looked. Her uniform had worn smooth over the years, and the brass buttons gleamed with a silvery finish, their insignia half-buffed away; her shoes were 'boned' until they were as smooth as mirrors. Many 'old timers' like her had learned to steep their khaki shirts in bleach until they achieved a more delicate pale-biscuit colour or, if they were very clever, the palest shade of pink. Being Government-issue, no one in authority could complain. Female N.C.O.'s whitened their stripes with 'Blanco' (the stuff used to whiten tennis shoes) and pressed a knife-edge crease down the centre of each chevron; their Army-issue skirts had a similar inverted pleat, carefully pressed on either side – in itself a small work of art, since there was very little spare material to work with. Their cap-badges shone, their narrow shoulder-straps gleamed; but it seemed to relative rookies like me that we would never achieve such distinction. Indeed, I, for one, never did: while admiring the end result, it always seemed to me that most of their spare time had been taken up with 'spit and polish' – and I had better ways to fill it. My own uniform, by contrast, was distressingly new. Despite all the pressing, I could never get rid of the surface fluff and achieve the much-coveted 'threadbare' look; my buttons remained a brassy yellow, which quickly dulled after every polish; and my leather shoes were hard and new and grainy where they should have been smooth. Of course, another two years' service would undoubtedly correct all these problems. Two years! It was unthinkable. I consoled myself for the moment with the thought that I had done my best.

Someone eventually answered the door, our names were ticked off from a list, and we were shown to our sleeping accommodation. The atmosphere was rather like that of an upmarket boarding school. After settling in, we were called to an informal meeting, briefing us on what to expect over the coming weekend. As far as I was concerned, the news that no ranks would be used for the period of our stay made the most impression. We were given white armbands to hide any existing stripes: we were all temporarily made equal before God and the Selection Board. In the relative privacy of the small dormitories, however, the more senior N.C.O.'s were having none of this malarkey, one particular staff-sergeant easing her armbands down a smidgen to allow a glimpse of the chevrons underneath. Toni didn't; perhaps that's why I liked her. In any case, it would take more than a subtle shuffle of my armband to reveal any part of my single lance-corporal stripe.

After a snack lunch we were to report for a written test – 'Nothing to be alarmed about' – that would identify our various aptitudes. A psychiatrist would analyse the results and select certain candidates for interviewing on a one-to-one basis. Although this would have absolutely no bearing, we were told, on the ultimate selection for officer training, she – the psychiatrist – was particularly interested in the candidates' answers to certain questions. On the Sunday, we would all be going into the garden for some exercise, where an assault course had been arranged. We were to work in small groups, and although not followed around by the Staff, our progress would be timed. The names of these groups were then read out, and though the rest of our team was an unknown quantity, Toni and I were pleased to be together.

The exam turned out to be an early version of I.Q. testing. Understandably, given my training, I found the spatial puzzles easy. As I recall, there was also some sort of word-association test, and an exercise in which we were shown a picture and had to use our imagination to write a story about what we thought it represented. At the end of the exam we were told that we were now free until dinner at seven o'clock. The gong would sound at 6.55 p.m. Toni and I grabbed our caps and made our escape down the hill to Hampstead Village. We weren't used to shops and pavements and took great pleasure in window-gazing. All too soon, the time came to turn back. We walked up the hill deep in conversation. I have never been too sure about what exactly happened next.

There was a momentary black-out on my part, and then I found myself lying in the street several yards ahead of Toni. I had a few scratches, but was otherwise unhurt, though my uniform was looking rather the worse for wear. Toni was meanwhile busy picking the contents of her handbag out of the gutter. I don't remember us discussing the incident much; our main concern was for our uniforms. In retrospect, I imagine we encountered the after-effects of a 'Doodlebug' – the terrible rocket-propelled V-1 bombs that had begun to fall on south-east England that year. We certainly heard no whine, which probably meant that the engine had cut out. It became common knowledge that you'd be all right so long as you could hear the engine, but if the noise ever stopped you were in deep trouble. We were lucky.

I cleaned myself up in reflective mood, and was lying on my bed in the dormitory, waiting for the dinner gong, when a loud, slightly aggressive voice interrupted my reverie. 'Ah, there you are!' I looked up to see, with sinking heart, the bossy staff-sergeant who had monopolised the conversation on arrival. The one I had seen primping in the mirror, giving that little downward tug to her white armbands. 'I think you are in my team. Are we ready?' So she had already appointed herself leader, I thought, and was even using the royal 'we'. She looked me over critically: I was obviously a rookie, and far beneath her usual notice. I felt irritated by her behaviour but before I could think of a suitable reply, the gong sounded. 'Follow me,' she announced, then swivelled on her heels and led the way, like a general at the head of his troops, down the corridors to the main staircase. I had no choice but to follow her – I would have got hopelessly lost otherwise. It was patently obvious that she had spent her afternoon's free time doing a 'recce' of the house. No window shopping for her.

Arranged into our teams, we waited with all the other cadets outside the dining room for the Staff to appear. They led the way in order of rank. (I couldn't help thinking that the 'democratic' atmosphere would have been more successful if they had hidden their pips and crowns under the ubiquitous white armbands.) To Toni and me, the dining room seemed splendiferous. I had quite forgotten what comfort – let alone luxury – was like. Dark polished wood, subdued lighting, paintings on the walls; silver plate on the tables, a plethora of cutlery, glassware and . . . napkins! After the brief cultural shock, I looked around me to see the expressions on the faces of other guinea-pigs. They made me want to giggle – all those personnel from the 'out-back' of the Army, hicks from the sticks, desperately trying to remember their manners and control the primitive urge to reach across the table and snatch a bread roll. Then I turned my gaze on the Staff. Our table-manners were being delicately scrutinised: etiquette was obviously important for lady officers.

There followed another interesting piece of role-playing, when various members of the Officer Selection Panel struck up a cheerful conversation with us. Their bonhomie approach, however, seemed calculated and unnatural. It struck me that to reply in the same 'jolly-hockey-sticks' spirit of badinage would be to risk sounding presumptuous; but if, on the other hand, you politely answered only when spoken to, you might come across as a dull or introverted sort, and not leadership material at all. On this last score our team had few worries, since the staff-sergeant put on a great performance, wasting no time in explaining how she had volunteered for active service, and detailing her subsequently rapid promotion. She laughed delightedly at the mild jokes of the Staff, answering their follow-up questions with a self-deprecating smile that hid her ruthless ambition about as efficiently as her white armband hid her stripes.

By now we were drinking our after-dinner coffee. Or rather, not drinking it, since although the coffee had been served, no one wanted to risk appearing rude by drinking it during the Head of Staff's opening address. This formidable woman was probably in her fifties, short and thick-set, with close-cropped hair like a man's. Her skirt was almost indecently short, and she spoke with a cigarette constantly hanging from her lips. The buttons and button-holes on her jacket strained in an uneasy partnership. Lacking stature, she had walked to the front of her table. Then, in an endeavour, I suppose, to keep the informal atmosphere, she gave a little upward jump and tried to sit on the table immediately behind her. This was rather a dismal failure, though, since her legs were too short. At the second attempt, she changed tactics and manoeuvred sideways, hoisting one buttock on the edge of the table, followed by a thigh, and then a knee. She left her other leg on the ground; presumably for stability.

Perched on the table, cigarette still dangling from the corner of her mouth, she looked like some cartoon character from the pages of Punch. Then, without removing her fag, she announced in a clipped and husky voice, 'We model ourselves on the men!' She went on to explain to us 'gels' how that proposition would affect our training this weekend. Most of her audience appeared shell-shocked – even the staff-sergeant was taken aback at this extraordinary performance. I didn't dare look at Toni, who seemed to have suddenly developed a nasty cough.

*

Sunday was going to be a very busy day. Following the close analysis of our psychometric 'I.Q.' test, I'd looked on the notice-board to see my name heading the small list pinned to it of those candidates required for interview by the psychiatrist. Toni's was the second name. Well, at least we were 'interesting'. It couldn't be that bad . . . could it?

'Why did you leave home?' This was getting incredibly boring. It was the fourth time I had been asked the question. I politely repeated that I had finished my schooling, taken my Higher Certificate, and then met Rudolf Laban, who wanted me to study with him prior to becoming his personal assistant. I considered it a great opportunity. Another long pause, and a little note-taking. 'Were you unhappy?' This woman obviously had a one-track mind. On the contrary, I told her, I had been thrilled at the prospect, since this was what I had always wanted to do, and my parents, who always believed I had some talent for this work, had been delighted for me. Then, in my youthful enthusiasm, I explained the 'efforts' of Laban's methodology, and described the significance of the Icosahedron, along with the importance of observation and the analysis of movement. My interrogator's hands flickered a little, her fingers picking and stroking her skirt constantly. She seemed at a loss; I wasn't enjoying it much either. I don't think the interview was going according to plan. So I tried to ease the situation. 'After all,' I said, 'everyone has to leave home sometime if they want to follow a career . . . even to join the A.T.S.!'

But my little joke fell flat. I wanted to add that – not to be too dramatic about it – I had been engaged on work of national importance in some government quarters, but since it was advanced and uncategorised, I had ended up in the services drawing margins in a book with a pencil; that I was hoping this weekend experience at W.O.S.B. might rescue me from that pointless morass into something more truly worthwhile; that it was the excruciating boredom I couldn't stand . . . but I must confess that I kept silent. It was not a good start to her day, and I didn't want to make it worse. And then . . . Coffee break! I certainly needed it; and so, I think, did she.

All the assembled candidates were now briefed for the rigours of the assault course in the garden that afternoon. The idea, it seems, was to get round it in our teams, surmounting its many obstacles in a spirit of true and collective camaraderie. We were 'on our own'.

'Off you go!' Our turn. The staff-sergeant, as always, led the way, exhorting us all to 'get on with it'. The first thing we saw was a huge canvas lying stretched across the first lawn. Underneath this we had to crawl. 'You two, hold the ends!' She meant Toni and me. Two others were delegated to hold the other ends. We struggled to lift the corners, nearly collapsing under the weight. As the last members of our team wriggled beneath it, it suddenly occurred to me that once they were all through, there would be no one left to help us. Would we lose marks if we didn't go underneath ourselves?

Staff-Sergeant Bossy-Boots now launched herself under the canvas. Toni and I smiled as we assisted her to the middle – at which point we dropped the canvas onto the flailing lump of her body, and hared after the team like bats out of hell. I thoroughly enjoyed the rest of the course, swinging on a rope ladder, walking along a tree-trunk across a pond, and climbing up netting. There was only one flaw: I had no idea where the rest of the team were. Nor could the team explain the absence of their staff-sergeant at the end of the exercise. For all I know, she may still be there . . .

We left the following morning to return to our units, resuming our public ranks by handing over our white armbands. Was it my imagination, or did the Staff regard some of us rather differently as we said our farewells? Well, possibly. For shortly after returning to Heckfield, I was called to Company H.Q. It appears that, after due consideration, the Board had recommended that I apply to them in a few months' time, when I had gained more experience of service life. As I had by now organised quite a busy schedule for myself, I was more than happy to stay put.

Joanna, my old friend from our training days in Pontefract, had since been posted back to London – rather luckily, we all thought, since it meant she could live at home. We had exchanged a few vague letters, but when I mentioned in one of them my forthcoming weekend appointment at the Selection Board in nearby Hampstead, she had invited me to 'afternoon tea'. This was too good an invitation to refuse, partly of course for the opportunity to meet up with her again, but also as, hopefully, a blessed relief from N.A.A.F.I. catering – the Army cafeterias that offered tea, coffee, and a strangely black sticky 'cake', the ingredients of which no one ever seemed able to determine. Arriving at Joanna's address after the surreal events of my Officer Selection course, the Mad Hatter's tea party in which I found myself that afternoon has never left my mind.

Goldhurst Terrace was full of drab-looking houses set back from the street. The frontage of iron railings and gates that had once kept the occupants at a safe distance from passers-by had now all been unceremoniously wrenched out for the 'war effort'. Gaping holes left in the brickwork and concrete allowed the weather to do its worst, and the low garden walls had collapsed, giving the whole area an atmosphere of decay and genteel squalor. The rubble was only partly hidden by a wild profusion of nettles and weeds. A long, narrow path led to the front door of Joanna's house, bounded on one side by a sea of mud, with only an occasional tuft of grass to show that this had once been a fine lawn.

The bell didn't work, so I knocked at the door and waited. From inside I heard the murmur of voices coming from a front room. I knocked again. The door was eventually opened by a woman who appeared to be in her late forties. She wore a floral dress in the style of the early 1930s and brandished a silver tea-pot. Her hair was extremely untidy, giving her a slightly rakish look. She smiled at me in my uniform.

'You must be Joanna's friend. I believe you're the first one of her group to go up to OCTU,' she said, referring to the Officer Cadet Training Unit. 'Come in, we're all in the sitting room.' I suppressed a giggle: she sounded as if she expected all of us to 'go up to OCTU', but we were scarcely the most suitable candidates and I was none too sure of my own standing. 'Perhaps you'd like to tidy up first?' she continued. 'Use the bedroom on the left. The door's open. Don't mind Daddy.' She led the way, laughing gaily. I found myself laughing too, for no apparent reason. She laughed again and wafted a hand in the direction of the staircase as she turned to rejoin her guests. Climbing the stairs, I had time to reflect that her mannerisms reminded me of Joanna's. She had the same unworldliness, which gave the impression of extreme vulnerability. Certainly, neither of them seemed equipped for the rough and tumble of everyday life.

I entered the open doorway of the bedroom, glad to take off my hated A.T.S. cap. Shaking my hair loose, I threw the offending cap onto the foot of the bed – onto the top, I now saw, of a pair of highly polished men's shoes. Containing feet. On further inspection, the feet were connected to a pair of legs, and I was amazed to see a man lying on top of the counterpane. So this must be 'Daddy'! He was in the full-dress uniform of a brigadier; his cap lay beside him. I paused stock-still . . . he didn't move. I thought he was dead. Perhaps they had laid him out? More than a little unnerved, I crept a little closer and saw that his eyes were wide open and unseeing. Nonplussed, I was not sure how to behave. If he were dead, everyone downstairs was taking it very lightly. Sounds from the tea party carried up to me and it all seemed very jolly. I backed to the dressing table in a sort of reverence. Well, I reasoned, if the family was not too upset, I could hardly mourn him. This was our first meeting, after all, and we hadn't been properly introduced. I combed my hair and in my most sang-froid manner looked at myself in the mirror as I applied some fresh lipstick and did my best to ignore the inert figure reflected in the background. Time to go down and join the other guests.

As I turned to leave, curiosity overcame me and I walked quietly to the top of the bed. I thought if I spoke to him and he didn't answer, I'd know the worst. Hesitating, I was about to ask him if he was all right but that seemed rather facetious in the circumstances. 'Can I get you anything?' I whispered in my best Florence Nightingale voice. There was no response. No flicker from those staring eyes. Dead? I looked at all the medals proudly displayed on his chest, and thought I saw a glimmer of movement. But, no, I couldn't be quite sure. I remembered going to Madame Tussaud's as a young child and pinching a lifelike waxwork of an old lady who had fallen asleep eating an apple. I had wanted to make sure she wasn't real. But I didn't like to pinch the brigadier.

After all, I was only a lance-corporal, and still making my way in the Army.

I went downstairs and entered the sitting room from where the sounds of laughter and rattle of crockery had come. It was the very picture of gentility. Ladies in mid-calf-length floral dresses and floppy hats were standing or sitting, balancing cups of tea and plates with minute sandwiches, and conducting animated conversations. There were constant references to 'the hills', 'the heat', 'ayahs', 'polo', and 'home leave'. Mrs R swept round the small room, introducing me to each little group of guests, and lastly to Clare and Elizabeth who turned out to be Joanna's sisters.

Clare, the eldest, worked in an office. Her hair was black and wavy and she was extremely good-looking with classical features. Elizabeth was still at school. She had very curly auburn hair that fell below her shoulders. Her figure still showed traces of puppy fat and freckles covered a very pretty face. With Joanna, the middle sister, a natural straight-haired blonde, they made a striking trio. As we discussed our present activities – army, office, and school – I noticed that they, like Joanna herself, never offered an opinion about anything. There was a curious detachment, a fatalism, almost, about what life had in store. I put it down to spending their entire lives up to now in far-flung outposts of the British Empire. War torn Britain, with its bombs, shelters, food rationing, clothing coupons, and uncertain climate, must have been a far cry from a hot sun, croquet, servants, and a life of unending leisure. They seemed to accept their newly straitened circumstances with exceptional good manners and good humour, though.

I was beginning to wonder where my friend was and, excusing myself, went in search of her mother. 'Joanna's in the kitchen,' she laughed 'to fetch more hot water.' I volunteered to help fill the jug.

'Straight through the door on your left!'

I grabbed the jug and, exiting the crowded room, pushed the kitchen door open to find myself, quite unexpectedly, in the back garden. I was dazed. Then I saw Joanna tending a boiling kettle on a Valor oil stove. She smiled, and said how delighted she was that

I could come, but offered no explanation of her present predicament. I looked around, and saw dust and rubble everywhere. Fragments of curtain flapped under the fine drizzle that had begun to fall. A smashed cooker lay on its side. The broken sink had fallen behind the door, and twisted pipes sprawled like iron snakes over the broken tiles. My eye caught sight of a charred mattress on the lawn, leaning against part of a dressing table with a smashed mirror. Realization dawned. Looking up, I saw an overcast sky where once a bedroom had been. A chair hung precariously over the void. Joanna followed my gaze and smiled.

'We were bombed in the early hours of this morning. The back of the house caught it – it's disappeared. Luckily,' she added practically, 'Mummy had another tea service in a cabinet in the sitting room.' She filled my jug and poured some more water into the kettle from a bucket. She looked cold and the rain dripped down her neck. Her blonde hair was now plastered to her head.

It didn't seem to be the best time to ask, but I had to know. I plucked up courage.

'What happened to your father?'

She smiled. 'Oh, don't mind Daddy! He has severe concussion.' I was relieved to know that he wasn't dead. Later I had a sneaky feeling that the women in his family had perhaps shown more staying power than the head of the household. I looked again at the yawning gap above me and noticed for the first time the half-open bathroom door. I'm glad I hadn't looked for the bathroom. One mistake and anyone opening that door a little further would have fallen straight into the garden.

I have since wondered what the brigadier was doing in full dress uniform in the early hours of the morning. There wasn't a speck of dust or dirt on him. Maybe these ladies weren't too sure that Daddy would pull through, and dressed him up . . . just in case? Surely they didn't dress him up for the tea party? One thing I am quite sure about now. For all their unworldly air, they were certainly not vulnerable people: they were survivors. The Luftwaffe may drop its bombs but a tea party had been arranged and a tea party would go ahead as scheduled. They took it all in their stride.

Chapter Eight

D-Day: A Night to Remember, and Grim New Circumstances

1944–1945

It was truly a night to remember. The noise was deafening. I listened, still half asleep, expecting the racket to cease at any moment, but it was to continue non-stop throughout the night. Eventually throwing on my greatcoat, I rushed outside and looked up. The early morning sky was completely filled with planes for as far as the eye could see, wave upon wave of Lancasters, and Halifaxes – as well as types I couldn't immediately identify, presumably American. Our camp in Heckfield must have been a designated spot on their flight path, since they all turned at a sharp right-angle, directly above us, and headed for the Channel. Some of the planes gave a victory 'wiggle' with their wings. We waved back wildly. It was a truly awesome sight, wave after wave, darkening the dawn sky like avenging angels. Along with the rest of the camp, I joined in the noisy cheering of our long-awaited Second Front: D-Day had come.

After a while, I wandered away from the crowds to stand alone and reflect, wanting to remember this night, knowing that I would never see anything like it ever again. I wondered how many of those bombers would not be returning to base. Some of the planes were for parachutists. How many of them would survive? I feared for my friend Paul, my cello-playing driver, who had already left the camp with a contingent of tank transporter crews. I feared for the endless stream of servicemen who had passed through my parents' front door in Lincoln. And I also felt a renewed pang of guilt over one of those men in particular.

I had still been at school when 'R', a flight officer in the R.A.F., had first been welcomed to our home. Sharing common interests in the arts, we had spent some time sketching, painting, and listening to music, and it was he who had introduced me to the music of Eric Coates, whose 'Summer Days Suite' I had used for a choreography at school. I liked him well enough, but there was never any hint of romance – at least from my point of view. In fact, I remember once seeing his sports car pull up outside, and tossing a coin with my grandfather as to which of us should entertain him: my grandfather lost – and I was away before the doorbell rang. So it had all been rather awkward when 'R' turned up at Heckfield, eighteen months or so later. He had used his leave to travel down from his aerodrome base at Scampton in Lincolnshire, to come and see me. Well, to be more precise, he had made the journey in order to propose marriage. I refused as gently as I could, shaking my head when he asked whether there was any possibility of my changing my mind. It seemed kinder to be brutally frank now than keep his hopes alive, but I hated the feelings of guilt accompanying my decision. At the same time, my hackles had risen slightly at something he had said – that he 'wouldn't mind' if I wanted to continue with my dancing. I am sure he meant it in good faith, but it was bad tactics. I was damned if I needed anyone's permission to carry on with my career once the war was over, and absolutely no one was going to stop me. I had a lot of time to make up.

There seemed nothing more to be said, and 'R' looked very miserable as he slowly climbed down from the gate where we'd been sitting, said, 'Goodbye,' and turned despondently away, walking away down the long, dusty country road. I felt very sorry for him – not least since he had missed the last bus. He didn't look back. And now, watching the endless columns of aircraft pass high overhead on that morning of D-Day, 6 June 1944, I hoped he was sharing some of my elation and relief.

Since all the tank transporters had now left for the Normandy landings, leaving our numbers drastically reduced, and since they had been the reason for our presence in the first place, the vague and disquieting rumours turned to a dreaded reality towards the end of that summer. Official: Heckfield Camp had outlived its usefulness, and we had to split up! We were ordered to tidy up the area, and prepare for our removal to the old barracks area of Blackdown Camp in Surrey. The remaining male personnel of the Royal Army Service Corps spent weeks ferrying our equipment to the new camp, each time returning with increasingly dismal stories. We would be amongst thousands of Army personnel billeted there; the place itself was grim: very regimental, with daily parades and poor food . . . The list was endless. We were utterly downcast. I had rather liked my time at Heckfield – for its idyllic location, of course, but also because 'red tape' had been kept to a minimum, as had the ordeals of the parade ground. There had also been a great feeling of comradeship, between all ranks, among both men and women, which I'm sure came from the Commanding Officers, who were all extremely courteous in their treatment of other ranks.

It wasn't just me who felt this. Many of the A.T.S. girls had come to regard the camp as 'home', and were in tears as the first lorries moved out, one after the other tooting their horns and carrying the men away in full kit. I was also depressed, holding the pair of wooden sandals a friendly corporal had been making for me, which he had handed over to me before boarding one of the lorries. He hoped I'd like the colour; he had painted them green.

Now it was our turn to move out – along with an extraordinary collection of objets trouvés and souvenirs. It seems that, freed from the tyranny of the drill ground, the girls had spent their spare time making rugs or tapestries, knitting or embroidery, all of which now filled their duffel bags and backpacks to overflowing, a few carrying the more awkward and bulkier ornaments, bric-a-brac, and other breakables in their arms. Nothing of any sentimental value was left – including Bettina's cat. Bettina, I should explain, was a very smartly turned out A.T.S. corporal whom I had got to know quite well. Now she arrived, dishevelled and in tears, complaining that she couldn't find her beloved cat, which she had taken in as a stray a year or so before. Cats always sense a change in the air, and usually head for the most obscure corner under the bed to hide. A search party was organised – and to cheers all round, the animal was deposited into her outstretched arms. We were off.

The light was fading and a fine drizzle falling as we arrived in Blackdown Camp that evening. Our first impressions seemed to confirm the grimmer elements of earlier reports. This was, indeed, like a huge garrison town, and quite hideous with its rectangular barracks and offices, drill square, married quarters – there were straight lines everywhere. At least we had been warned what to expect... well, almost.

The tailboard of our lorry suddenly dropped, to reveal the squat little figure of an A.T.S. sergeant-major. She was looking at us with a mixture of undisguised shock and contempt. We descended awkwardly, helping each other with our luggage. But this was all too much for her. She screeched out angrily that we should 'Line up NOW'. I looked around at my colleagues doing their best to come to attention, and assemble into line. It wasn't a pretty sight. At least Bettina did her best to comply, standing upright, eye front – but unfortunately not eyes front, since her cat, taking an instant dislike to the gesticulating martinet in front of him, had clung on to the back of Bettina's head in terror, dislodging her cap over her other eye in the process. Joining the line, I tried to keep my own face as straight as I could. Then someone else dropped a bird-cage, and when the girl next to her bent down to help retrieve it, the rug she was carrying knocked a rather ugly vase out of her other neighbour's hand.

This was too much for the virago in front of us. Seeing before her an untidy bunch of dangerous layabouts who had been allowed to live wild, she finally vented her spleen. She shouted, pranced, and spluttered, calling us every name under the sun, and vowing to sort us out with regular drill parades. She was so ridiculous in her antics that I'm afraid I started to laugh. I couldn't control it. And it caught on. Soon we were all hysterical. The men from Heckfield now began beckoning to their friends, and giving the 'V'-for-victory sign (or something quite like it) behind the lady's back. That started a fresh paroxysm of mirth. Gradually identifying me as the main instigator of this insurrection, she finally looked in my direction: 'What's your name?' With some difficulty, I obliged. Among other things, she promised to keep a close eye on me from now on.

We gradually calmed down sufficiently to be directed to our future accommodation. I was allotted a room in 'married quarters'. On being dismissed, I had to pass the little virago.

'What's that?' She pointed to my own bundles.

'A pair of wooden sandals.'

'No, that thing – the cage.' I felt a rising hysteria again. She wasn't going to like the answer. 'Well?'

I managed a fairly matter-of-fact voice as I replied. 'Oh, that's my icosahedron.' I was right. She hadn't liked it at all. As I turned away to follow the others, her voice screamed after me in the darkness. 'I've made a note of you, Lance-Corporal. I know your billet . . . And you can stop laughing.'

The following days were spent collecting army bedding, setting up the pay office and . . . drilling. Our sergeant-major friend saw to that. It also transpired that our records hadn't arrived yet, so we had to go before the new company office staff to give details of our service life and state our religion. We had been warned that Sundays were pretty dreadful, blighted by regular church parades. To worship privately is one thing; to be drilled before the local congregation, then marched in and out of a house of worship, is another. My turn came.

'Religion?'

'Greek Orthodox,' I answered hopefully.

'Sorry, no can do. Put her down as C of E.'

Well, you can't win 'em all.

The 'missionary department' of Company Office now decided in its wisdom that the new girls should spend their Monday evenings being educated. I went along to the first meeting rather half-heartedly, hoping it would be a valuable way to spend the time but having serious doubts. 'Well now,' said the officer to us all,

D-Day: A Night to Remember, and Grim New Circumstances

'what would you like to discuss?' Silence. It was quite obvious that most people wanted to go and do their own thing. 'Come along now,' she persevered, 'you must have some ideas.' After another excruciating silence, I volunteered the information that I would like to learn more about Jung. The officer licked her lips, gazed into the middle distance, and ignored me entirely, vainly waiting for someone else to speak. The meeting broke up early. I went 'home' to my own study evening.

I began to take great pleasure in making my small room neat and attractive. An orange-crate, covered in a piece of cloth, held my books; the icosahedron perched on the narrow mantelpiece; and a few of my better drawings graced the walls. When the bed was made up, it served as a sofa in the evening. There was no chair, so I acquired two more army 'biscuits' to sit on. During the day, when the bedding was folded up, I put the extra 'biscuits' neatly against the wall, like cushions. The dance classes were temporarily over, the German classes abruptly terminated, and the opportunity to take a university course lost. Never mind – I could at least concentrate on my own studies, working as best I could, and writing 'home' to Laban, who continued to send me every encouragement and news of the projects he and Lawrence were now working on. On one occasion I rang my own home, and an American voice answered. I asked for Mr or Mrs Newlove.

'Who shall I tell them is calling?' said the voice.

'It's Jean' I replied.

'Jean who?'

The winter of 1944 was severe. The tiny grate in our pay office barely threw out any heat. When we asked if we could at least have some more coal, the sergeant-major in charge of fuel distribution came in and announced that we could only have one small bag. He yelled something rude to his minion outside, who now entered, a young recruit covered in coal dust. He smiled very politely and asked whether we wanted our coal 'whole or crushed' – he could supply either. Very public school, he had obviously learned to survive the taunts of Army life.

The coal barely lasted two days. We foraged for wood, but of course everyone was doing the same thing. More than a few chairs disappeared. We attempted to write out the pay-rolls with fingers almost frozen to the pencil. The grate was full of cold ash. Not for the first time, my mother came to the rescue, sending me a pre-Christmas parcel containing a cake and a small bottle of gin. Very practical, as ever. Jo and I would do the pay-rolls as best we could, then rush back to my room for our break. We boiled the kettle, made mugs of tea, pouring a little gin into each mug. For a while we glowed right through.

The winter conditions worsened. One morning we woke up to a thick fog and hoar frosts that lasted all day – and still no heating. Sergeant Harding would send us out to walk briskly round the block and see if there was anything we could scrounge or scavenge for burning. By now there usually wasn't, but at least the walk kept our circulation going.

Just before Christmas, I received a long, creatively worded and spelled letter from Laban, which cheered me up enormously: 'If we would write you each time we speak or think of you, you would already have whole volumes of letters,' it began:

Your letters show me, that you are immerged into extremely simple problems . . . As far as your outer life is concerned . . . and though I regret for you the boredom connected with this and not only the boredom, but also strain of patience and lack of freedom, I think it has all a sense, so far as you will see in your later life, against what and for you are fighting. Because I think, the profession you are choosing will be inevitably a fight. People are only partly ready to see the beauty . . . and the usefulness . . . of movement, and even those who have a glimmering don't know exactly what is behind all that. You will also need a good deal of inner and outer fighting in order to make yourself ready for understanding and action.

Going on to comment on the playwright Maurice Maeterlinck, whom he knew well, he said that while Maeterlinck's belief was in 'the might of thoughts and ideas and their expression in words', Laban himself thought his friend's symbolist play Pelléas and Mélisande (1893) was full of 'exquisite shadow-moves'.

Maeterlinck liked sport (boxing, to be precise), he continued, and imagined movement as mainly a fighting business which had nothing to do with those finer sensations and tendencies, which he tried to capture in words. It is thus, that he looked at science partly with awe ... because they use words so cleverly to convince the brain ... and partly with disdain ... because scientific description gives only images of tiny shadows of reality ...

It is really a tragedy and most of contemporary people suffer under the charm and the disillusionment of thinking and pondering and so do partly also you. Besides your experience with A.T.S. girls and captains it might be that your experience with brain-mongering might also trouble you. It is however, not so bad for you, to find one day a way into space. (This is of course not the icosahedron, which is mainly a compartment of the train running into space and ether.) I see your capacity to get there, and should like to tell you this at the occasion when I am sending you my good wishes for the darkest days of the year (Xmas) when we must lit candles in order to believe in light, and for the change onto the increase of light (New Year) when hope is lit in us for the flowering of spring.

You see there are things, which people of old times have expressed in dances. Our contemporaries might also go to a 'dance' at the crisis days of darkness and light, but I wonder if their 'one step' will liberate them? In a certain degree and certain fashion: yes. But what are we calling 'dance' is still another thing: don't you think so? It is not that we should be proud or conceited with that: on the contrary, we must be very humble, if we shall become able to extend our inner security into our whole being, and then out of us at the service of other people. ('Services' would be a much nicer word if understood in this way.) ...

Things go on, and we do our best to spread our ideals. It is however up to the coming generation to do a good deal of that. And we are reckoning on you to the number of people who will count in this endeavour.

Sending you all my love and good wishes I will end this long Christmas letter with a cheerful 'space-ether' hoorah!

Yours,
   old Laban

*

In the first few weeks of my training with him, Laban had often teased me for being a 'transcendental idealist'. Without realizing it, I was indeed now being toughened up for the future, although at the time I believed it was only the drabness of 'Service' life that required toughness and a tenacity to carry on and not give up. Well, I would persevere, and try to develop this 'inner security'.

Although Christmas Day began well, it became a rather depressing occasion. Jo and I went for a long country walk on Christmas morning, and when the sun broke through for a brief moment or two, making the frost sparkle, the world seemed a much better place. By the time we retraced our steps, though, the sky was again obscured by fog. People celebrating the season in their own homes watched us pass by outside, but no one asked us in. It was all very different from the previous Christmas – I had still been in civvies then. And now, when we returned to Blackdown, there was a personal message waiting for me on the Company notice board. It seems the virago sergeant-major and the C.O. (A.T.S.) had made a surprise inspection of the married quarters, finding particular fault with my own room: 'The extra biscuits must be returned to stores immediately. Everything must be put out of sight. I am not satisfied with this N.C.O.'s room.' Rightly or wrongly, it was widely believed in the camp that of the two, it was the sergeant-major who really wielded the power. So she was now getting her revenge.

I returned to my neat little room. The drawings came down and the two offending biscuits were taken back. I removed the cloth covering the tea chest. The whole room now looked bare and characterless. I couldn't believe that we were expected to live like that. So much for Laban's 'space-ether'! Perhaps it was the empty gin-bottle on the mantelpiece that had upset them. I had been saving it for spring flowers.

D-Day: A Night to Remember, and Grim New Circumstances

*

'P', whom I had got to know when I was still at school, came over from the Irish Republic to visit me the following weekend. He stayed at the local inn, and we had a couple of very happy days. I was free on Saturday and again on Sunday from lunchtime until 11 p.m. Our relationship was always full of fun, and that was what was needed right now. My colleagues in the pay office joined us for drinks on the Saturday. It appears in retrospect that P. had actually come down with the intention of proposing to me, but was continually interrupted by friends joining us. Regaling him with tales of army life, I mentioned my friend the cellist, and my concern for his well-being. That, and the fact that a mutual friend had warned him about my continuing passion for dance and the unlikelihood of my wanting to be tied down, gave him cold feet, I think. I was really sorry to see him go.

Some weeks later, in early 1945, a notice appeared in Standing Orders that really interested me: 'Personnel with a good command of French are needed urgently.' I signed up immediately. My French wasn't all that good, but if they were desperate, I thought, they might just take me on. After all, the Army often moved in unfathomable ways. Before long I was wanted in Company Office straight away! I rushed there, trying to practise my French in my head. The C.O. had a letter in her hand, and looked at me in some surprise: it was from a senior Commander Hawkes in Whitehall, asking me to attend an interview. I knew she was in charge of the Army's P.T. programme, and silently blessed Laban and Lisa for not giving up the struggle.

Commander Hawkes turned out to be a charming woman. She told me to take my cap off so I wouldn't have to salute anybody, and she called me by my first name. I began to feel human again. The outcome of our interview was that I should attend another P.T. course, after which I would become a full-time Physical Training Corporal, wearing the crossed-swords insignia. (At least I was escaping the ranks of the cooks, clerks, and orderlies!) She would also post me to Manchester as soon as a vacancy occurred. But the icing on the cake came last: she wanted me to introduce Laban's work into my classes. This was beyond my wildest dreams.

I arrived at Newton Abbot in Devon for my P.T. course under a warm sun and blue sky, and in high spirits. The girls were very friendly, and when they knew I was a 'dancer' they begged me to arrange a class after the daily curriculum. This proved so popular that it was held regularly throughout my course, and was very well attended.

One of the more difficult tasks was to take charge of a morning run involving the whole company. This wasn't a popular exercise, and no one had succeeded in getting anything like a full turn-out. I think the officers in charge wanted to see who had the necessary leadership qualities. The extreme reluctance of some of the students was through no fault of their own, since the run had previously been scheduled after a morning's strenuous exercise and just before lunch. So when my name appeared on the board, I knew exactly what I was going to do.

After making a phone call on the evening before, I went round all the 'spider huts' – so-called because they were arranged in different directions like the legs of a spider – telling everyone to be on time the next day because the run would start promptly. I also told them that they should each bring fourpence with them. They were all so intrigued that more or less the entire squad turned out in shorts and plimsolls, clutching four pennies in their hands.

We ran in silence for about twenty minutes, until we reached the pub on the other side of the village, where, as previously arranged, a trestle table laden with glasses of cider awaited us. I collected the money and settled the bill with the landlord. After about ten minutes relaxing over our very welcome drinks, we ran back in record time and full of good humour. The officers greeted us in some amazement, and I was congratulated on my success in improving the 'ésprit de corps'. To my knowledge, no one ever spilt the beans.

I returned to Blackdown a full-blown P.T. Corporal, and within days my posting to Manchester came through. The C.O. played the last little card from her pack of Army protocol: I would not be

D-Day: A Night to Remember, and Grim New Circumstances

allowed to sew my extra chevron or affix my crossed swords to the sleeves of my uniform for as long as I remained on the camp premises; but I had to arrive properly dressed by the time I reported at the next company office . . . which meant they all had to be sewn on during the journey.

I said my farewells to the pay office, and a young Lieutenant kindly offered to give me a strictly unofficial lift on the back of his lorry. As I jumped off at the station, though, I saw him blushing to the roots of his hair: a detachment of men from the camp had just marched up with their – and his – Commanding Officer, and were now standing at ease around us. He had always wanted to make the Army his career; I sometimes wonder how he got on.

The regimental sergeant-major who shared my train compartment was a nice old boy. Seeing me remove my jacket and start to fiddle with the chevrons as we moved off, he gallantly offered to take over the task. He got out his own 'housewife' (Army slang for 'sewing kit'), and stitched on the new chevrons quite beautifully. He even cut out a section of the leather cover of his diary to make a suitable backing for the P.T. crossed-swords insignia higher up each sleeve. Making two little holes in the sleeve and the leather, he told me this was essential – it would keep them firmly in position, and help when I came to polish them. Then he brought out his own cleaning materials, and proceeded to polish the swords until they shone. He even 'boned' my shoes – applying boot-polish and rubbing with a smooth bone to give a mirror finish. I couldn't thank him enough. Whether he took pity on me, or else merely wished to demonstrate solidarity against the widely unpopular A.T.S. sergeant-major and her C.O., I don't know; but this kind old gentleman, now quite pink with embarrassment as I thanked him effusively, showed me more kindness than I'd experienced from anyone else during my long stay at Blackdown Camp.

Chapter Nine

The Wanderer Returns

1945

My posting from Blackdown to Manchester was met with great rejoicing on the civilian front. I had deliberately kept my news from Laban – for the pleasure of being able to surprise him. Arriving early at his first-floor flat one Saturday afternoon, it was his housekeeper, Mimi Eckhertz, who opened the door to me and who, after overcoming her initial shock – she was an old friend – gave me a great welcome. I was on a weekend pass from the Army, and Mimi insisted I stay the weekend, and find my new 'digs' on Monday morning: Laban and Lisa had been taking a course, and were due to return that evening. Chatting to Mimi and catching up with the news while helping her prepare the evening meal, the time flew by.

Then I heard the front door open, and the familiar sound of Laban's voice as he and Lisa slowly climbed the stairs. I called out to him, and as he looked up, ran down the stairs, threw my arms around him, and gave him a kiss, knocking his hat into a rakish angle. The transformation on their faces, from weariness into laughter, and their unmistakeable delight at my appearance, made all the vicissitudes of service life momentarily disappear. Once we had all got over our excitement and were sitting upstairs in the flat, the first thing both Lisa and Laban wanted to hear about was my visit to Senior Commander Hawkes – the interview that had landed me back in Manchester. Having pioneered the 'Laban–Lawrence Industrial Rhythm', they said, I was now pioneering Modern Dance in the services. We agreed that we would fit in our own classes as soon I knew my schedule the following week.

Meanwhile Laban rang Lawrence to say that I had arrived back in Manchester – he was happily surprised, and said that he'd let the team know. Although it was tacitly understood that I was still a member of His Majesty's Forces and would not be able to travel for them just yet, optimism reigned. This was early 1945, and everyone knew that the war was nearing its end. And now, as Laban said, 'The family is back.'

The Army's welcome was a more muted affair. In fact, my arrival on their doorstep on Monday morning occasioned some confusion among the guards, who had not been notified of it, and were reluctant to let me pass into the factory-like building where I had been ordered to report. That was when I made my big mistake: I should simply have turned round and disappeared into the busy street for ever, but – poor innocent that I still was – I dutifully proffered the paperwork proving my identity and posting. Still showing some misgivings, one of the guards then led me up several flights of stairs to the A.T.S. Company Office. Here I caused another frisson among the otherwise laid-back office staff. They looked at each other in consternation: not another P.T. corporal? They already had four of these unpopular creatures, apparently, and I began to see that I was not exactly flavour of the month.

The building I found myself in was a huge dilapidated ex-factory commandeered by the Army for its main Pay Corps Offices – a far cry from the cosy little Nissen huts at Heckfield. This rabbit warren on several floors housed hundreds of army clerks, who would scuttle along its labyrinthine passages and abruptly disappear into the makeshift, partitioned wooden hutches called offices. With my new pass I was now, like them, 'officially attached' (a euphemistic term) to the Manchester Pay Corps as a Physical Training Corporal.

My P.T. colleagues were a jovial bunch, and quickly made me feel welcome, though our working conditions were pretty appalling. A tiny corner in a busy corridor served as an 'office', and our games equipment was virtually non-existent. Not that that particularly worried me since, as I went on to explain to them, I had been given permission to introduce dance into the sessions. To their credit, they were unfazed by this, merely offering the thought that this might cause problems at some of the venues. Having accepted an invitation to meet them at the local pub the following day, I realised that, unless any special army parades were planned, they were free from Saturday midday until Monday morning (they all had plans for Saturday night). After the grim conditions I had just left, my future did indeed look rosy, and I went off to check on my new billet some two miles away.

I was shown into a small terraced house by a pleasant lady who explained that she would provide a cooked breakfast twice a week. This was unheard of in wartime – and I think I managed to say that I'd be more than glad of just one, if that were possible. My bedroom was spotlessly clean – one bed, one chair, lino on the floor, and curtains: basic and simple. After I'd agreed to stay, we went downstairs, where her two teenage children had just come in. Introducing me, she insisted that we all sit on the small two-seater sofa while she made a pot of tea in the kitchen. Crushed on either side by her hulking children, I was all but unable to turn around to look at either of them to help open a conversation, and they were embarrassed into silence at being in such close proximity to a complete stranger. After a few excruciating minutes, the boy excused himself to make a quick getaway, leaving his sister to pass round the tea.

I couldn't drink it fast enough. After hurriedly unpacking my things, I rushed out to check the local buses, and found one that led directly to Laban's flat on Palatine Road, Didsbury; Birchfields School, where Lisa ran her evening classes, was just round the corner. Things were truly looking up – thanks to the lady in Whitehall.

There were a few surprises in store for me when I met up with my new Army friends at the local pub, where I was told there were now only four of us left: the colleague I hadn't yet met had been discharged. It seemed that my classes were to be held in several places, none ideal, and that I would need a bicycle. I was promised a map, marked up with the venues – after which they lost interest in my affairs and showed me some photos of the big wedding one of them had had a couple of months earlier. The only daughter of a local manufacturer, no expense had been spared. She was now pregnant and expecting to leave the services in the next week or two. I congratulated her. With hundreds, perhaps thousands, of A.T.S. in this enormous Pay Office, it was a good job I had come to help out.

Among my other colleagues, one fellow corporal was a single girl, and another, Liz S., was married to a civilian. The three of us were eventually left alone in the pub – only for the single girl suddenly to announce that she, too, was pregnant, and about to get married; and as for Liz, she was almost three months pregnant herself and was also leaving. She was generous enough to feel rather sorry for me. That night I lay in the dark of my Spartan room, counting off the P.T. corporals. I would very soon be on my own and, so far, I hadn't taken a single class or seen a single venue.

Next morning I went down to the first of the 'cooked breakfasts' I had been promised: a boiled tomato on a slice of waterlogged toast. I couldn't face the soggy toast and, seeing my hostess's son eyeing my plate, said I wasn't hungry and offered it to him. From then on he was always at hand on the mornings I was given a cooked breakfast. Borrowing a bicycle, I rode to the different venues and was shocked to see two were limited to a tiny area on a cobbled road. I couldn't find the last one. When I reported back, Liz said the Fire Brigade directly opposite our Pay Office had offered to lend us their parade ground when it wasn't being used. I walked over to see a vast space, and immediately arranged a timetable for my classes to fit in with theirs. As far as exercise was concerned, it was only the Fire Brigade ground that made our classes worthwhile. The cobbles were dangerous, particularly in wet weather, and dance would have been impossible. I wondered how the others had managed under such bad conditions. At least I was able to do some dance-like activities on the parade ground – though I had to use a whistle since the noise of passing traffic drowned out my voice.

The day finally came when I had to to say goodbye to Liz, and be left on my own, with hundreds of A.T.S. scheduled to take part in regular P.T. classes – only, in my case, it was dance. A few days later, the A.T.S. Commandant told me cheerfully that she had heard that some P.T. officers were coming to inspect the girls' training. In retrospect I should have taken them to the cobbled areas to demonstrate the poor conditions we all had to work under. Instead, I explained to those of my students who worked as clerks in the main office that I needed their help with my visitors, particularly as I was hoping to introduce dance instead of P.T. We continued with our movement swings and turns, but I was at a loss to know what to do in such a vast space until the conductor of the Fire Brigade band came up to me, who had noticed our change from P.T. to a more dance-like movement. I explained my difficulties and the imminent arrival of inspectors. To my delight he suggested the band should play for me! Now I could teach a couple of dances for the many taking part. The patterns woven by the dancers would look good, and from a gentle beginning, the dance might change into a lively Hungarian czardas and end with swirling round to the accompaniment of voices. Only one problem now remained: where would I find the music? I didn't: I could only sing what I remembered of the pieces over the phone, while the poor man at the other end tried to write it down. He told me not to worry too much: the band would practise it.

Two days later, my dancers were in position as the main gates opened to reveal a posse of A.T.S. officers and their assistants. I could not go over to greet them as the distance was too far. In any case, on their arrival the band of the Fire Brigade struck up, determined to do us justice, and the dancers responded in kind. The first part went well. But then came the dance, which we had not practised together. It took me a little time to recognise the tune, and the dancers a little longer to realise that they were meant to dance to it. But they made up for a slow start and managed quite well – though I did hear one dancer whisper, 'I'm a man – what are you?' The gentle mood changed dramatically and, as I had exhorted them, it now became a wildly passionate Hungarian czardas, with suitable cries to accompany the war-like actions and swirling ending, which stopped as abruptly and dramatically as I had intended. The dancers were sweating. So was the band. Even the band master took his hat off to wipe his forehead, looking rather pleased with himself. I looked eagerly across to the distant visitors. They seemed to be somewhat shell-shocked. Instead of walking over to the dancers to congratulate them, they stiffly turned on their heels and left.

That evening, the band and dancers met up at the local pub to celebrate the occasion. As far as they were concerned the co-operation had been a great success, and I even heard some of the girls say that they'd like 'to do more of this'. The next day, however, the A.T.S. Commandant said that her visitors had been expecting to see team games and physical exercises more in line with their official programme. I explained that I had been asked to run dance classes – and got the distinct feeling that she had rather enjoyed the display . . .

The cobbled streets were still a problem, though. On my next visit I looked around the adjacent house and discovered that the semi-basement was free, moderately large with a fairly decent floor, and completely empty. Beautifully suitable for my future dance studio! I 'commandeered' it for my work. No one ever questioned its use or came to see what was going on. I acquired a wind-up gramophone and some records, and brought my own drum. At the next class, I brought the girls down to this room and said that, starting there and then, we would be doing more dance-like movements. After the initial shock (considering none of them had taken part in the Fire Brigade performance), some said they preferred the change. No one wanted to carry on as before, so I hoped to win over the rest.

Back at the main building I was now getting requests from medical staff to help those with foot problems – flat feet and the like. Two of the girls had a sixth toe on top of the foot between the fourth and fifth toes, and I did wonder what I was expected to do in these cases. All of these 'patients' I took on at my newly acquired 'Treatment Room' (alias my 'dance studio') at the annexe. As the war in Europe was at last drawing to a close, and many A.T.S. leaving the service, the remainder, not yet due to return home, were understandably getting a little impatient. They could smell freedom was near. I don't think the girls expected me to change the position of their little toes, but a little therapy helped morale. So I decided to start a warm-up with everyone doing foot exercises (good for flat feet) and then carried on with a movement class. Soon, by choice, the movement classes and therapy sessions merged, and I was booked up with several classes throughout the week.

Senior Commander Hawkes would have been proud of the girls' response. The change was proving a great success, even if certain die-hards in the P.T. Officer world weren't ready for the change. Gradually, as word spread, more and more girls seemed to require 'foot therapy treatment' as a way into the dance class. After foot exercises it was all dance movement – and makeshift leotards started to appear among the 'patients', along with 'Health and Beauty'-style black satin pants. One Pay Captain, in charge of a department, asked me if any of them ever finished a course with me once they embarked on one. He had noticed that they never seemed to return to full-time work. This was obviously a warning, and one I took on board.

The facilities of my 'Treatment Room' had by now stretched to include the full casting of a complicated dance composition, and we decided to schedule the 'therapy' around office demands – and the system worked well. Pregnant or not, A.T.S. girls continued to be demobbed at a steady rate, but there was still far too much for a single Corporal to do in the way of Physical Training, but since many of the remaining girls had now eagerly chosen to become 'patients', we made quite sure that nobody was ever away from the office for too long. I was able to cope with the dance courses I had found myself conducting.

Living in civilian digs, as we all did, was a tremendous bonus, and I was lucky to have the evenings free. Well, 'free' in the sense that I was able to work with Laban (who always took a great interest in my stories of army life), and from time to time accompany Lisa to her classes, which she occasionally asked me to take over. Lisa was now preparing the ground for her Art of Movement studio, ready for when the war ended . . .

Which at last it did when V.E. Day arrived: Victory in Europe! That night, in May 1945, I was invited to a dance with all the Laban–Lawrence crowd. I rushed home to collect my dance dress, last worn at the Anglo-Polish Ball in Lincoln, some six years – and to me a lifetime – before. (Thank goodness, it still fitted!) That was a night to remember. We were a large crowd: all the engineers, Lawrence included, brought their wives; Lisa was there; and so too, of course, was Laban – my first dance partner of the evening, for an elegant waltz, and for many dances afterwards. I had plenty of partners that night, but none with more charisma and grace than Laban. Six years before, I could never have begun to imagine that I would be celebrating the end of the war dancing with Laban. Our time in London with the constant bombing, the trauma of being called up, and the poignant farewell at King's Cross station all seemed distant memories. The future welcomed us. Surely it wouldn't be long now before I was demobbed?

But the weeks dragged on into months, and by the time we celebrated V.J. Day (the end of the war in Japan) in August, I was still stuck in the same position. It was a long hot summer. Sometimes a young Lieutenant would take me out, on one occasion to see Donald Wolfit in King Lear during a heatwave. Impressed by his performance, we went into a pub and ordered a jug of iced lager. We were sweltering in our uniforms, and the frosted glass of lager was like nectar. I had no idea that this young man had serious intentions. All I knew was that he, like me, was anxious to get back to 'Civvy Street' as quickly as possible, and as far as I was concerned, that was our common bond. I was more interested – though not for those reasons – in two other young men I met later on that summer.

I met Howard Goorney and Gerry Raffles while attending one of Lisa's classes at Birchfields School in Withington (very near my billet). These were, as I soon learned, actors. Howard had been with the Army in Belgium, and Gerry was a 'Bevin Boy' (serving his country by working in the coal-mines), but both were now free to resume their theatrical careers. Of course, I was terribly envious. It seemed their producer was a fan of Laban, and had suggested that they come to Lisa's class. On hearing that I was still stranded with the A.T.S., Howard agreed that I should get out as soon as I could: he had returned to England within a few days of speaking to a sympathetic Medical Officer, and suggested I do the same. Before I could consider this suggestion seriously, however, a memo came through the usual channels, announcing that I was to be posted to Bury in Lancashire – a short rail journey away, but enough to make life more difficult for working with Laban. I felt personally disappointed, of course, but I also felt angry, since there was no one to take over all the classes I had so successfully set up in Manchester – so all that hard work went completely to waste. Whether my transfer was due to a deliberate attempt by the P.T. officers to thwart my efforts, or whether it was just another example of the Army's bureaucratic obsession with redeployment, I shall never know.

Chapter Ten

I Survive my Living Quarters in Barnsley

1945–1946

Barnsley Barracks made Blackdown look like the Ritz Hotel. I was told the Dickensian buildings had been condemned after the First World War. Then, during the Second World War, the Americans had refused to quarter their men there, on the grounds that they were considered unfit for habitation. Perhaps the A.T.S. were a tougher breed . . . or simply more expendable.

On my arrival, I was put in charge of a platoon of girls who shared a large room on the ground floor of a barrack block. From the large number of beds, it looked very overcrowded to me. There wasn't even enough space to walk between the beds without one's legs touching them on either side. My own 'living quarters' were up three flights of stone steps, in a tiny room containing an iron bedstead, a minuscule fireplace (which was in any case cosmetic since there wasn't any fuel to burn in it), and one dim electric light. The summer's heatwave had cooled, along with all the excitement about the end of the war, and my spirits had slumped into a chilly autumn. It was bitterly cold in the room, with such a smell of indefinable age and damp that I was always glad to get back into the open air.

Out all day from necessity and choice, it took me a little time to realise that the chilly atmosphere of my room was not entirely due to the ancient stone or brickwork, though I had noticed that my blankets had become very damp within a couple of days arriving there, and any clothing left out for any length of time swiftly became too damp to wear. Then I noticed the walls glistening with moisture; and the tiny rivulets running down the cracks. I would stand on the bed at night and wipe down the wall with an old cloth, but to little effect. Wrung out repeatedly, it did nothing to stop the steady stream of condensation . . . if that is what it was. Rather belatedly, I took to covering over my two blankets with my greatcoat and cape, getting dressed to go to bed, and keeping the rest of my clothes in my duffel bag. Not surprisingly, I spent as little time as I could in the room.

But if my nights were miserable, my days weren't much better. The weather was usually atrocious, and some of my scheduled P.T. classes were in the open air. These various outlying venues I was expected to reach by train, but they were generally rather futile affairs, since no one could tell me who was still available to attend them, and I even felt a sneaking sympathy for those frustrated P.T. officers back in Manchester. There was a sad little café in Radcliffe where I stopped off for an ersatz coffee. I seemed to be their only customer – which rather summarised the general mood.

A dank and gloomy winter had suddenly taken over from the dying autumn, and the cold, grey setting of the mill towns seemed hideously ugly to me in my misery. The classes were closing down, and the few trainees who bothered to turn up had mostly all disappeared by Christmas. Meanwhile, in contrast to this general apathy, I would travel back and forth to Manchester two or three evenings a week, to see Laban and Lisa, and to work. Quite often this entailed a further train journey with Lisa to a new venue. One evening, not feeling too well, I turned up at their flat to say that I really didn't feel up to going with her. But Laban greeted me with the news that Lisa herself had come down with flu, and was counting on me to take her class that evening. I said nothing, of course, and immediately agreed to take it – then returned to Barnsley, and my freezing room.

The best facilities I was ever offered, totally unexpectedly, during my 'day job' were the large sports hall and changing rooms at Bury Technical College. The hall was modern, and was sprung with an excellent floor. My A.T.S. colleagues in Manchester would have been thrilled with such luxury – especially the dancers in the basement room, who would have enjoyed the hot showers afterwards. In the event, however, I was the only one to enjoy them: I waited in vain. Not a single girl turned up – it seemed most of them were busily engaged in working as cooks and orderlies, and expecting early demobilization 'any minute now'. I decided to keep a low profile, and still turned up regularly to continue with my own training.

One day I saw that a lorry had stopped outside the college, from the back of which a group of interesting young people were manhandling what seemed to be theatre equipment, and ferrying it inside. I followed them through the main entrance and saw them disappear through another set of doors. Gingerly opening them, I found myself at the back of a large auditorium – to see the same interesting young people setting up on stage for a performance. Rather than introducing myself, I gave in to my sense of outrage that they (especially the men) were all 'free', while I was still stuck in uniform. After all, no one could say the A.T.S. were exactly in need of my services! So I returned to the empty sports hall to work without thinking to talk to them or find out when they were playing. This was a pity, since I learned much later that it was none other than Howard Goorney and Gerry Raffles, among others, who were setting up the stage, and that the newly founded company was called Theatre Workshop.

During this lean time, I would occasionally also travel back to Manchester to see my Pay Corps Lieutenant. On the last occasion, he gave me a small present – a beautiful silver compact, with my initials engraved on it. While thanking him profusely, I was also very concerned that he was reading too much into our friendship: we really knew almost nothing about each other, and I told myself I would have to let him down gently – and soon.

I suppose I should have realised that the solitary and unhealthy conditions of my damp and miserable quarters in Barnsley would eventually take their toll; in fact, it was only after I had been feeling off-colour for quite some time that I fell victim to them. I don't remember how long it was before I was found in my bed with a high temperature. I remember being helped into my greatcoat over my pyjamas, and the great efforts that we all made to put my feet into my shoes; someone thrust a toilet-bag into my clutching hand. Somehow I managed to negotiate the stairs with help and sympathetic murmurs from, so I imagined, the girls in the platoon. I stood woozily outside until my 'ambulance' turned up – an open lorry with a bench on the back. After several attempts I was deposited onto this back seat, in the open air of a winter sky. I was driven to Company Office, where the driver and her assistant had to obtain the requisite 'chit', and I was signed out – like any other piece of worn-out military equipment.

These bureaucratic negotiations seemed to take forever, and left to my own devices outside I found myself singing, quietly happy to see the first flakes of snow gently drifting down. By the time we left the barracks, the snow was falling heavily, and before long I was covered in it, hallucinating crazily, chatting, laughing, and shivering at this wonderful white world all around me. Feeling very happy, I sang to all the residents of Barnsley as we drove, slowly and carefully, to the A.T.S.'s Casualty Reception Station ('C.R.S.'). On arrival, with my hair plastered to my head and my hands and feet frozen, I was left to wait while the necessary papers were exchanged. After all, the driver had to have proof that her cargo had arrived in one piece – albeit a cargo (as the nursing staff later told me) completely covered in snow. The doctor quickly diagnosed pneumonia – for which a trip on an open-topped lorry in a snowstorm was not exactly the most effective therapy. I was eventually tucked up in a warm bed in a warm room – the height of luxury, and almost worth the illness in the first place. My meals were even brought to me at my bedside. I remember Lisa sent some dried bananas (an exotic treat), and my brother Pip wrote to me to say he was back in England. He had done rather better by his country than me, and was now a full Major – I felt that the Army had tested my reserves too, without my ever having had to leave the country.

As the first weeks of December wore on, I slowly began to recover – but the better I felt, the more I dreaded returning to my awful rooms in the barracks. When the time came to go back, however, there was a pleasant surprise in store for me. I can only think that my superior officers must have suffered a sudden rush of concern – or guilt – over my appalling accommodation, since when I reported back, I was issued with an immediate 'sick pass'. I don't remember returning to collect my things, but I suppose I must have; nor do I remember seeing anyone in authority, though a few of my friends in the platoon wished me well as I all but flew to the railway station – and, to my parents' delight, home for Christmas!

It was good to be home – even though my brother Pip was still with his unit, though thank God at last back in England. As my grandfather Charlie went off with my father to the golf club on Christmas morning to celebrate the season, and the end of the war, my mother and I set out the carefully saved bottle of sherry and bowl of nuts and raisins for visitors. (Rationing was still very much in evidence.) As I looked nostalgically across the common and golf course opposite the house, I privately remembered the glum walk Jo and I had taken the previous Christmas at Blackdown, when no one in the area had been public-spirited enough to open their doors to us. Returning to the present, I became aware of a small group of drab, hunched figures (prisoners-of-war from the nearby camp) passing aimlessly by our windows – and my mother suddenly announcing, 'I don't care if they are Germans. The war's over, it's Christmas Day, and I'm inviting them all in for a drink!' With that she rushed to the front door, opened it wide, and ushered everyone inside. Before long, the room was overflowing. They stood, rather awkwardly, in the hall, and sat on the stairs. Handing out glasses, she shared the bottle of sherry around, her slightly bewildered and grateful guests politely rationing themselves. The few nuts and raisins went the same way, and my mother brought out a few precious cigarettes for them to share.

Well-worn family photos were brought out from their wallets, and then, as one, they all started to sing carols as a 'thank you'. It was very moving. They left with smiles and 'Happy New Year', waving until they were out of sight. I remember noticing how the pace of their walking had changed: there was now a spring in their step, and the sound of scattered laughter died away as they went back to their camp.

Coming back indoors, I realised that two of our German guests remained: Herbert, who seemed to be in his forties, and his friend

Willi, around my own age, in his early twenties. My mother had invited them both to share our Christmas dinner, her only regret that she couldn't have invited more. They helped me tidy up while my mother checked on the cooking. Unable to get chestnuts for the stuffing, she had boiled some rice and was mixing it with peanut butter (surprisingly enough, it made an excellent substitute).

When Dad and Grandfather Charlie returned, they were introduced to our new visitors. The only comment my father made to me, when he saw the empty side table in the lounge, was that we were having friends over later and he didn't know what he would be able to offer them. The cupboard seemed bare, but he was quite philosophical about it. Then the doorbell rang.

'That'll be Andrzej,' my mother called, 'let him in, will you?' I opened the door to a Polish airman. We introduced ourselves; he seemed to know his way about the house very well, and carried a few small gifts for the family. Apparently he was a regular visitor, an ex-teacher, who hoped to return home before the end of the new year. As the day went on, I learned that Willi had been a member of the Hitler Youth in pre-war Germany. He looked little more than seventeen even now, whereas Herbert, an army conscript in the Wehrmacht, was old enough to be his father. Both had been captured early in the war and were, unsurprisingly, politically ignorant. On the other hand, I think Andrzej had some proper misgivings over returning to Poland, but was of course desperate to see what was left of his family.

Looking around the table of our Christmas lunch, I saw Andrzej taking a plate from my father and passing it to Willi; Grandfather was meanwhile thanking Andrzej for the pipe tobacco he had given him (and which must have come off his meagre service ration); while my father presided over the occasion, seeing that everyone was served. For one fleeting moment, on Christmas Day 1945, it was hard to believe that we and our guests had until very recently been trying to kill each other.

Returning in the new year to my solitary routine at Barnsley, my room was declared unfit for human habitation, and thereafter I shared the huge downstairs dormitory with my platoon. All these A.T.S. girls were either cooks or orderlies who, concerned for my health, generously gave me a bed in the prime position next to the stove. While deeply appreciating the warmth both of their kindness and my billet, I soon discovered a serious drawback. Returning to barracks in the evening, I would always find people lying on or around my bed, enjoying cosy fireside chats – the obvious place, of course, for such assemblies. Unfortunately, though, this arrangement gave rise to other assemblies – a nasty outbreak of nits, which I dealt with as best I could.

When not exterminating nits, my life went on pretty much as before – depressingly so: the war had already been over for nearly six months! – until an A.T.S. officer called me one day to suggest that the time had come for me to report back to the W.O.S.B. selection board. 'This would, of course,' she said, 'entail your staying on in the A.T.S. for another two years after your commission...'

Help!

Before any decision could be made, however, yet another notification came through, this time of my transfer to Preston, twenty-odd miles away. Since so many personnel were being demobbed, it was obvious that the A.T.S. had no use for me in Barnsley – but yet another new posting? This was too much. I told Laban miserably that I would now be too far away to travel back to him in the evenings, and resigned myself to my fate.

I only have vague memories of my sleeping quarters at Preston, so they must have been better than my damp cell in Barnsley. (Mind you, almost anything would have been.) As in my previous camp, however, what I was actually doing there remained a rather depressing mystery. P.T. was still in the agenda, but was gradually being phased out as more and more people were demobbed. In the first class I joined on my first day, a visiting Medical Officer, and a specialist in such things, apparently commented to the P.T. Sergeant in charge that I had 'perfect feet'.

It later turned out that the sergeant was the sister of my friend in the Pay Corps, Lieutenant B., who had told her of my impending arrival. Embarrassingly, however, she began to behave rather oddly, smiling coyly as she told me her brother was due to visit

Preston on Wednesday, in a couple of days' time, and grinning knowingly when she said he had 'something very special' to ask me. Being treated like a future sister-in-law by this perfect stranger was more than I could bear. I didn't want to hurt her feelings or her brother's, but we had only been friends, nothing more – and certainly nothing had led me to expect a proposal.

My mother had meanwhile written from home to say that my grandfather wasn't well, and since she still had 'evacuees' to look after, was finding things a bit difficult. I had decided enough was enough, and asked her to write for compassionate leave on my behalf. This was granted and a travel warrant was made out for Thursday – the day after Lieutenant B's threatened arrival. I spent Tuesday praying for fog – and sure enough, a pea-souper closed in towards evening, so thick that by the following morning, all traffic was at a standstill, and we were cut off. I breathed a sigh of relief. The fog began to lift on Thursday morning, and through it could be seen a spectral P.T. Corporal haring for the station at first light.

The civilian official who came to see me while I was on compassionate leave was very supportive. My mother had been ill during the latter part of the war after nursing my father, and looking after my grandfather had proved a strain. She was also looking after adult evacuees at the time. He had no hesitation, therefore, in at last recommending my demob. I returned to Preston within days, to collect my discharge payment (for a civilian outfit and a pair of shoes), and say my goodbyes. The only thing I took home with me was my P.T. tracksuit and a small 'R.A.S.C. S.D.T.C.' badge; everything else I left behind, folded neatly on my bed.

Within two weeks of my arrival home, two evacuees had left, and life became much easier for my mother. I rang Laban, who invited me to the summer school he was organizing at Bishop Otter College in Chichester. As my father had a business meeting to attend in Leicester, my mother and I decided to shop there for my demob outfit. Andrzej was invited along for the ride and to see something more of the country than his aerodrome before returning to Poland the following week. Willi and Herbert, still constant visitors, offered to do some gardening, and my grandfather was left happily sitting in the sun. Our day trip proved doubly rewarding. I bought myself a clerical grey Vogue-style tailored coat and a Moygashel linen dress; and after walking around Leicester, Andrzej could now say he knew two English towns. Arriving home that evening, we were met by our smiling German duo, who had not only weeded the garden and cut the lawn, but also prepared our tea. The table was set, the salad prepared, and the kettle on the boil.

The future looked good.

Chapter Eleven

Back to Civvy Street

1946

During the time that I was working with Marckwald on the Lincolnshire drama course back in 1943, I had been introduced to a friend of his, Geoffrey Mostyn-Lewis, who had now only just returned to normal life after a considerable spell in hospital, invalided out of the RAF after crash-landing on returning from a mission. Although traumatised by his severe wounds, he was making a gallant attempt to return to civilian life, despite the 'pipes' inserted into his nasal passages to help ease his breathing difficulties. Geoffrey had enjoyed movement classes with me so much on the Lincolnshire course that, despite his injuries, he joined us again on the summer course Laban was running at Bishop Otter College near Chichester, and we travelled down together.

Quite by chance we passed through the market town where I now remembered my erstwhile admirer from the Pay Corps in Manchester, Lieutenant B—, had said he would eventually return to work at his bank. Full of goodwill and the sheer joy to be out of uniform, I rather naively suggested we pay him a flying visit. His bespectacled but recognizable figure was there at the counter, staring at me as if seeing a ghost while I prattled on, eventually introducing him to my travelling companion. It didn't seem the time or place to explain about Geoffrey's accident, or that he was a happily married family man; nor, I must admit, did it cross my mind to do so; blithely euphoric, I was in love with the world, thrilled to be a working civilian at last, and naturally expected everyone else to feel the same. Poor B—! I don't know what he made of it all but however confused his state of mind, he remained ever the gentleman as we waved our goodbyes as abruptly as we had appeared.

On arrival in Chichester, Laban gave me a tremendous welcome. For me it was like arriving at an oasis after months of travelling through an intellectual desert. The Bishop Otter course had attracted H.M. Inspectors, Lecturers in Education, as well as others specifically interested in the study of dance and movement. This was a promising development, since none of the P.T. officers I had previously encountered had obviously benefited from dance training of any kind, and had indeed remained quite hostile to the discipline. Laban, Lisa, and Sylvia were all teaching on the course, but a new face to me was Joan Goodrich, who had been instrumental in developing Laban's work at Bedford Physical Training College. The course also provided very useful therapy for Geoffrey – so much so, in fact, that he later arranged to spend a year at the Manchester Art of Movement Studio before returning to his civilian job.

The Art of Movement Studio in Denmark 1948

Jean Newlove - Yum Di Dee Dah

At Elsinore Castle, Denmark 1948

I returned to Manchester after the course, back once again as Laban's personal assistant. Among my many professional duties, I was particularly needed for my yogurt-shopping skills – not such an easy one in late August 1946. Mimi Eckhertz had returned to Germany for good, and I also learned that Lisa had persuaded her ailing mother to leave Berlin, where she had been living in a bombed-out cellar with her housekeeper, and come instead to England to stay with them at their flat. Lisa's Art of Movement Studio was by now a reality with students from as far afield as Switzerland, Norway, and Germany itself. I had quite a busy schedule myself, giving private lessons and teaching during the week, joining in classes given by Lisa and Sylvia whenever I was free, and working with Laban on a number of projects, all the while staying at the flat he shared with Lisa. Classes were also restarted at the Northern School of Music, and I still often travelled to give classes to teachers in the evenings.

Before Lisa's mother arrived, we had a brief visit from André Perrotet. André was the son of Suzanne Perrotet, a dancer who had had a liaison with Laban and was now working as the regisseur of a theatre in Switzerland. André, a married man with three children, met Laban for the first time, I believe. I thought André was one of the most handsome men I had ever seen, and very French, it seemed to me, in his manners. Laban introduced us to each other before dinner: 'My son – my daughter.' I think André was a little surprised, but from then on, on the rare occasions we corresponded, we always jokingly addressed one another as brother and sister!

Since Mrs Ullmann had been through the worst of the Berlin raids, we were all rather concerned for her welfare, and before she left to pick her up, Lisa and I had prepared a very nice bed-sitting room for her. Within a week or two, though, we seemed to have integrated her into 'the family' and indeed she was very happy to take over the cooking, an arrangement with which the rest of us were very pleased. I would occasionally help out, and learned to make a few dishes. She would prepare the evening meal for us, which we would sit down to eat together. Laban's health was still fragile, though, and he would occasionally remain in his room, working from his bed when he felt really unwell. It was then that the yogurts were very welcome.

One day Mrs Ullmann asked me to tell Laban that supper would be on the table very shortly. He had been rather unwell, and had worked from his bed all day. A little later, when she told me she was now ready to serve the food, I gained the distinct impression that she was determined to make him get up and grace the table. Duly knocking at Laban's door, entering his room and delivering the message, I was a bit surprised to see Laban grasp the book he had been working from and hurl it with all his force at the closed door.

It was around this time that Laban received a letter out of the blue from Joan Littlewood, asking him if he could recommend someone to give movement classes to Theatre Workshop, the company she led. She was running a series of weekend drama courses, and needed someone to take charge of that part of the training. She added that the company also hoped to benefit from movement classes when they returned from a short tour. Their base was at Ormesby Hall near Middlesbrough in Yorkshire. It seemed that Joan had heard of Laban's pre-war work in Germany, had attended some Laban-based classes at drama school, and was full of admiration for his ideas. We talked over the proposal, Laban suggesting that since these classes were planned for the weekends, they might not interfere too much with the weekly schedule. His main concern was that I shouldn't try and take on too much work – at that time, Lisa also depended on me for several classes – but somehow we managed to sort everything out satisfactorily.

The Studio syllabus was becoming more educationally biased due in part to the enormous enthusiasm shown by the teaching profession. It was also where Lisa's main interests lay, furthering Laban's work in education in this country, and a safer course for her to steer than the very unpredictable life in the theatre. I have no doubt that she did the right thing, though it was a pity that Laban, essentially a man of the theatre, did not have an opportunity in his later years to work creatively with professional artists. Although at first I was visiting the company as Laban's nominal 'assistant', in practice he left me free to work quite independently of him. It was now I began to realise that I would soon have to make a decision. Laban recognised from my early days that, although I could teach, I was also a performer at heart. The war had put such careers on hold. Luckily for me, I had been fortunate to continue studying and working with Laban and Lawrence, adapting to the needs of wartime industry. With peace came new and exciting opportunities.

*

Optimistically swinging along the drive of their base at Ormesby Hall, I was eager to find out more about this Theatre Workshop Company. I had never seen them in action, knew nothing of theatre history (other than dance), and was a complete innocent as regards politics – well, I was anti-fascist, but so was everyone else. I was also looking forward to meeting up with Howard and Gerry again, having no idea that our paths had so nearly crossed that morning at Bury Technical College. I think that, somewhere in my subconscious, I felt drawn towards theatre life, but the war had sidetracked me, as it had so many others. Meanwhile, I was just looking forward to taking classes in a creative environment.

A grocer's van sped past me and pulled up in a flurry of gravel and dust in the courtyard ahead. The figures I had seen crossing the yard had all now disappeared. The driver tooted his horn and waited as I approached. No sign of life. He tooted again impatiently. Nothing. Having by now arrived on the scene, I felt that very odd. 'Dad's here!' he now bellowed, equally mysteriously. I looked at the young man in some bewilderment as he manhandled a huge box of groceries from the back of his van and looking up at the faceless windows, before desperately shouting again, 'Dad's here!'. It was only then that I noticed the name on the van: Dadd the Grocer's. He shouldered his way through a door, came out a moment later empty-handed before driving off at break-neck speed the way he had come.

Now what? I stood hesitantly at the half-open door leading into a vast kitchen and knocked. I was sure people were still around; I could hear peculiar little noises in the darker areas but still I couldn't see anyone. Then a face cautiously appeared from behind a pantry door. 'Has he gone?'

'Yes, I'm sorry. He couldn't make anyone hear.'

My words brought a number of further shadows from their boltholes. Between greeting me in a very friendly manner and speedily unpacking the groceries, they explained that they'd been hiding because they couldn't afford to settle the account. I thought this was a temporary embarrassment, a momentary hiccup. I was not to know that the company's poverty would last for years – though even if I'd known, it wouldn't have altered any of the decisions I made concerning my own future.

I was escorted through the door leading into a large refectory where a vast hearth displayed a complete upright tree-trunk, its base firmly embedded in hot ash and giving off a glowing warmth, while the upper part disappeared into the cavernous darkness of the ancient chimney recess. A gong now sounded, summoning a number of other figures from various doorways, one of which I noticed in particular, busily chatting to another company member. Of slender frame, he was wearing a rust-coloured cotton jersey and, although his hair was black, he sported a red beard! I felt I had been hit in the solar plexus. There was no logical reason for this, I knew it. Yet, for the very first time in my life, I seemed not only to be falling in love, but had already fallen, even before we had spoken a word to each other. Having simply come to do a job of work, this was the very last thing I had on my mind.

Howard Goorney then arrived, recognised me, and introduced me to the 'red beard', whose name appeared to be Ewan MacColl: he was the resident playwright. I remembered now that Howard and Gerry had mentioned something of all this long ago, at that class in Manchester. Sitting between them at supper, I was slightly overwhelmed by their joint attentiveness. Kristin Lind, the glamorous Swedish member of the company, entered bearing plates with a tasty concoction on each, individually wrapped in a large cabbage leaf. When most of us had nearly finished the meal, she rushed in with a pair of scissors and with large soulful eyes dramatically announced that she was very sorry but she had forgotten to remove the thread stitching up each cabbage leaf. I noticed a few pieces of thread on the plates as I helped to stack them – though not, I suspected, all the original strands.

The meal over, we gathered round the huge fireplace and I met Joan Littlewood for the first time. She was wearing a scarf, turban fashion, round her head, and a light tweed skirt and jacket. After giving me a warm welcome, she muttered the words 'Trinity at last!'. Howard interpreted this to mean that my presence as a Laban exponent completed her dream of an artistic trinity, working with Ewan and herself to develop this new theatre of ideas.

This visit was just to establish contact with the theatre company and view the facilities, and we discussed the future 'drama weekends'. Ewan was going to teach voice, and Joan direct, and they would share the Stanislavsky sessions. It was further agreed that I would start each day with a warm-up, followed by an introduction to Laban's principles of movement. I was shown the venue for these classes, a cavernous barn, which looked ideal. The theatre company itself would be on tour during these weekends, freeing up the accommodation space for the drama students on the proposed courses. By now it was dark, the fire was glowing and to common assent Ewan started the singing. Sometimes the young actress Isla Cameron, who had a sweet voice, would supply harmonies, and at others the whole company joined in, especially on the sea shanties. Then Ewan sang alone. The breadth of his repertoire was quite stunning to anyone who, like myself, was hearing it for the first time. But more than that, his voice seemed to fill the whole room by the sheer quality of its magic. In those days there was never any accompaniment to the singing, and it was not missed. One of the reasons Ewan made such an impact on his listeners, I think, was because, being also a skilled actor, he was able to put across the emotional content of each song. In Laban terms, he was able to cover a range of feelings. Some years later, having studied Laban's work with me in more depth, he was able to pass on a combination of his own skills with this knowledge of Laban's theory of efforts, to his newly formed singers' group.

The evening over, I retired to a small, sparsely furnished bedroom, and told myself that no one, but no one – certainly no one in their right mind – ever falls in love at first sight. And that had been before I'd heard him sing! Anyway, for some reason I had always vaguely assumed it would be a fair-haired chap who would eventually catch my eye, certainly not a man with black hair and a red beard! And besides, I was in no hurry to complicate my life right now. My new-found freedom was too precious. I woke the following morning, ready to report back to Laban to start another busy week. I liked the set-up at Theatre Workshop, I would tell him, and it was a refreshing change to be mixing with young people who were working as professionals in the theatre. I also now felt ready for new challenges.

Somewhat to my surprise, Ewan came to the station with me. The words flowed – the theatre company would have a great impact, I was essential to its development, and so on – and I slowly began to realise that he was simultaneously trying to impress and to woo me. Perhaps his was the more honest approach, but I gave nothing away; and brilliantly exciting as the weekend had been, it still all needed thinking about. One thing was for sure: I fancied seeing more of this singer–playwright, though quite how much he didn't know.

The next few weeks turned into heady weekend visits of theatre work and courtship with the summer sun continually shining from a cloudless blue sky, and every moment was precious to us. It seemed that there was nothing that could not be accomplished, that we had a lifetime to fulfil our dreams. Ewan would sometimes turn up unexpectedly in Manchester, snatching a few hours of freedom from Ormesby to meet me. Walking along the high street, I would be stopped in my tracks by a shrill whistle – and there he was, hanging precariously off the end of a bus by one hand, and holding out a small parcel in the other, a huge grin on his face. My present was quite ridiculous: a hairbrush that was specially designed to impart perfume as one used it! It was on one of these visits that Laban and Lisa welcomed and entertained him. I believe that Laban felt himself to be 'in loco parentis' – which was strange, considering his relationship with his own children. I do remember that Lilla Bauer (formerly of the Jooss Ballet Company) told me that Laban had asked her to look after me while I was working in

London. There is no doubt that this first meeting went well. Laban was particularly interested in Ewan's ideas on theatre, and arrangements were made for us all to see one of his performances in the near future.

On one of my weekend visits, Ewan took me to Staithes on the Yorkshire coast, where we spent an idyllic summer's day examining the contents of rock pools and looking for fossils. He seemed to be very knowledgeable about flora and fauna. After walking along the beach looking for shells, I noticed that the tide was getting uncomfortably close – Ewan said we would have to climb the cliff or risk being cut off. In retrospect, I think he wanted to show off his climbing ability – which he did, impressively, by expertly scaling the cliff-face with only an occasional backward look. Glancing upwards as the soles of his climbing boots disappeared, I reflected that in my red wedge-heeled shoes, with a shoulder bag hampering my every movement, I was at a distinct disadvantage, and already experiencing a lot of problems. I also found out, once embarked on the climb, that I had no head for heights. Turning to look down once, I was overcome with nausea as I saw the huge waves crashing against the rocks, their spray just missing me. But it's amazing what the combination of fear and the instinct for self-preservation can accomplish – and not just when stuck up a cliff in Yorkshire.

The Theatre, as I soon realised, could only infrequently pay a wage to its members. Even so, Ewan managed, at the very last moment, to give me a much cherished Christmas present of a Yardley lipstick. The constant financial poverty in Theatre Workshop was accepted by everyone because we all felt privileged to be part of such a ground-breaking artistic venture. We felt rich and, like everyone else, I was totally committed. Unfortunately for me, the A.T.S. had been unable to utilise my industrial experience, already proven in the factories, but had seemed to go on recruiting long after it was filled to capacity. It was inevitable that boredom set in. On leaving them all those years ago I have never been bored since. My Laban work still fascinates me and I continue to learn.

Chapter Twelve

The Best of All Worlds

1946–1947

These were intoxicating times. After a busy week with Laban or taking classes for Lisa, I would rush to catch the train to Ormesby, and either be met at the station by Ewan, or make my way by bus to the road leading to the drive up to the Hall where he would otherwise be waiting. He was busy working on an adaptation of Aristophanes' 'Lysistrata', renamed 'Operation Olive Branch', which was scheduled to go into rehearsal quite soon. He would always read to me what he had written during the week. I have read other adaptations of 'Lysistrata' since, but never one that matched his. It was autumn, and the evenings were crisp and clear, and after supper we would walk across the parkland while he talked about everything under the sun, from the state of international affairs to the special recipe for porridge his grandmother had taught him. (In fact I now know he probably never met her, but whether by hearsay, reading, or more probably a fertile imagination, he described it all very vividly.) Before making our way back to the Hall, we would sit on top of a gate looking down at the town of Middlesbrough in the far distance. Every now and then, great flashes of orange would light up the sky – from the iron-ore furnaces opening up, I think he said they came. It was an awesome and spectacular sight and, whatever it was, somehow matched the dramatic mood of the times – times of change, of optimism for the future for all young people, and Theatre Workshop in particular would be at the forefront. The war was now won, after all, and the Fascists defeated. The Soviet Union, our ally in the war, had suffered dreadfully, and we hoped their friendship would continue with the peace. There was nothing that could not now be achieved by the young, who would make the world a better place for all mankind. And Theatre Workshop was pledged to be part of that international struggle. Ewan MacColl did indeed seem to be a man of the moment, and I could go along with so much of what he said. I only needed to think of the many people close to me who had been directly threatened, uprooted or otherwise persecuted by the Nazi regime – Laban and Lisa, Marckwald, Sylvia and her family; Andrzej, and Willi and Herbert, under the same roof but destined to be on opposing sides; my brother Pip, almost left behind at Dunkirk and only getting away at the last moment. Our friend Paul Bouthors, who rushed to his aid, prepared to risk his own life; a schoolfriend of mine who, commissioned Lieutenant within months of leaving school, was killed by a hand grenade during a training exercise; all the brave RAF men I had met at the local dances, many of whom took off never to return, like the crew of the bomber that crashed on my school with their aerodrome in sight. And later I was to hear of a French Jewish friend whose father was dragged from his bed and shot outside in the street.

The drama courses that Joan and Ewan had arranged were proving popular. Apparently Laban invited Joan to watch a choreography he was rehearsing in which I had a solo part. Laban had always encouraged me as a performer even during the war years, advising me not to accept a teaching job in newly set-up British schools during the latter part of the war as I would become trapped in the educational system. His work with Lawrence was now attracting others, and Laban himself was already developing new ideas. He was generous and wise when his students eventually left him to flex their own wings. In my case, he knew I could teach, but also saw my potential for performing, and gave me his blessing to work with Theatre Workshop. I was, of course, on loan at first, but I think Laban realised before I did that I had found my niche. We later came to an understanding that if I ever changed my mind, he had other things for me to take on. I took both Laban and Lisa to see Theatre Workshop's productions of 'Johnny Noble' and Ewan's adaptation from Molière, 'The Flying Doctor'. Talking with us all afterwards, Laban said that this was the theatre that excited him and that – had things been different in Germany – he would have wanted to work in this way. This was praise indeed, and he gave me his blessing to go ahead.

'The Flying Doctor'
courtesy of Theatre Royal Stratford East Archive

Everyone in the company came to the business meetings that decided their collective policy. When the company returned from touring, Joan asked if I could now train them on a regular basis as the drama courses had finished. When I did take over their training, their enthusiasm was very stimulating, probably because they were all extremely talented, young, and very eager to learn. The company had no stars and all felt of equal status. However, the artistic guidance supplied by Joan and Ewan – in the history of theatre, in the choice of play, or their criticism of contemporary theatre practice – inspired and educated everyone. Something of the same spirit animated our lunchtime meals, when the company would mysteriously be swelled by a regular group of visitors who would join the queue, be handed a plate of food, and join the communal table. They sat eating quietly with the rest of us, before disappearing whence they had come. No one knew them and no one asked any questions, but we guessed, from their only slightly more impoverished appearance, that they were 'gentlemen of the road'. A rather different type of stranger stayed with us for a few weeks. Smartly dressed, as I remember, he seemed to have found a spare bedroom and always enjoyed his food. He never seemed to muck in with any of the chores, and never appeared at rehearsals or other meetings. Then one day he disappeared as quietly as he had arrived. Such was the easygoing and generous atmosphere of our vibrant group that, so it turned out, everyone had believed he had been invited by somebody else, and no one had thought to challenge him.

'Johnny Noble'
courtesy of Theatre Royal Stratford East Archive

Arriving directly from a sustained period of study and work with Laban and Lisa, it was only now that I realised how much I had missed the energetic company of people my own age. I had of course derived enormous satisfaction from the classes I took with

Lisa, but these were mostly for older people, and it was now, working with the theatre, that I began to see a larger potential for my own ambitions. It was both an inspiration and a joy to work with a group of young professionals who worked hard, day after day, to hone and practise their skills. When I was told that my own skills were in demand by the company, not only to train them with movement exercises, but also to take on the role of choreographer, and even as a dancer in several forthcoming productions, I came close to believing that my future was turning out to be, in just about every respect, perfect.

Laban recognised this exceptional opportunity, and was generous enough to ask me what I would like to do. He saw me as a performer from my years with him and knew I could teach. He also reassured me that he would always be ready to work with me whenever I was free to do so. I knew that being free to help build a wonderful theatre company meant that one was also free to starve but I had never been overly concerned with earning a lot of money. These early months with the company at least supplied me with a basic education in the economics of theatre, where magical effects can sometimes be achieved with minimal costs – and vice versa. I always believed that one day we would achieve the breakthrough of public recognition, and in any case, I was absorbed in this exciting and exhausting work.

The eccentric humour in this young and carefree company was infectious, and led to some strange events and flights of fancy. Among the first of these I encountered was the bizarre figure of 'The Admiral', to whom I was introduced during my first working weekend at Ormesby. Part presiding spirit, part company mascot, the reclusive Admiral was a wholly fictitious character dreamt up by Joan and Ewan – an old mannequin with a floridly painted face, dressed by the costume mistress Ruth Brands in an impressive jacket of Navy blue and gold braid. Everyone spoke of him with such a mixture of awe and reverence that when the time eventually came for me to meet him – Ewan opening the bedroom door to the dim light of a low-watt bulb – I was almost taken in. Indeed, some members of the company believed in him completely – unsurprisingly, perhaps, since the old boy kept to his room, preferring a solitude in which to contemplate his adventurous past. Only the chosen few waited on him – Joan, Gerry, Ewan, and Ruth – and the fantasy of his existence was sustained with utmost care. The Admiral was part of our extended family, and I became a willing and privileged accomplice to the gloriously creative deception.

So once I had been initiated into the mystery, Joan, Ewan and I planned a lively return for the rest of the company, who had been away on a short tour. A whole scenario was arranged, and we enlisted the help both of Colonel Pennyman (our host and landlord in Ormesby) and my old friend Jo from the A.T.S., who was coming for a weekend visit and was asked to bring along a nurse's uniform. In an address to the group before supper, Joan announced that due to the Admiral's continuing ill-health it had been regretfully decided that he would be better off in a nursing home for old sailors, where he would receive proper treatment. He would be leaving that night. Silence followed the announcement. A few of the more sceptical company members took the opportunity to creep up to the old boy's dimly lit bedroom, peer round the door – and hear some extremely effective heavy breathing and wheezing. (It was, of course, Ewan under the bed, invisibly putting in another fine vocal performance, while simultaneously lifting and lowering the mattress with his back.) Convinced, they returned to the refectory and reported what they had seen to the others. And it was at that moment that Jo (who had been carefully kept out of sight until now) briskly strode through the room in her spruce nurse's uniform, carrying a very professional-looking tray filled with medication. She returned some time later with a bedpan. After two or three of these sorties, fetching and carrying for her 'patient', she was at last invited to share our evening meal. A complete stranger to everyone, she was treated with the respect lesser mortals always give to anyone associated with the medical profession. She played her part well. So well, in fact, that I felt a mild envy of her success, and it was probably this – or else my memory of her own practical joking in the Pay Office – that led me to whisper to Howard that she had a glass eye.

After supper, an ambulance arrived to take the patient to the 'St Neots Home for Retired Naval Officers' in Scotland – said vehicle kindly supplied by Colonel Pennyman, in his capacity as President of the local St John's Ambulance Brigade. It was a solemn scene as, very gently, the old warrior was carried down the stairs, laid on a stretcher held by Ewan MacColl, Colonel Pennyman, Howard Goorney, and Gerry Raffles, the company standing back, respectfully and forlornly, on either side as, covered in blankets, he was carefully placed in the vehicle. The Colonel, having magnanimously offered as a fellow officer to travel with him on the long journey north, fetched up the rear in his car, and the doors of the ambulance were closed. It was all very moving as we watched them process out of the courtyard. The company returned to the refectory in sombre mood. As previously arranged, I meanwhile slipped away in the commotion of the sad departure, and hastened to the stables, from where I saw that the ambulance had come to a sudden halt. The performances now resembled a difficult, though not impossible scene change. It was an extraordinary sight: as figures roughly manhandled the stretcher, dragging it out of the back of the open vehicle, the Admiral himself appeared to stand momentarily unaided in the fading light before teetering over the edge to fall flat on his face onto the cobbles below. Unceremoniously scooped up from a fall that would have proved lethal to lesser men, he was hauled off to the harness room, Colonel Pennyman leading the way (as befitted an officer and gentleman of His Majesty's Forces). By the time I arrived at the door, all hell had broken loose. It appears that the light switch was faulty and our intrepid leader had touched a live wire, and immediately burst into furious army expletives as he nursed a painful arm.

Yet even this was not the end of the old Admiral: he kept in touch with the company, sending newsy letters on his new home's embossed notepaper (supplied by Ewan's publisher Bill MacLellan). I remember that Ruth Brands later borrowed a sheet of the same notepaper to write a sad little letter to London Zoo in the old man's name, requesting a parrot for company. He got a very sympathetic reply. Weeks later, Howard approached me nervously on another, related matter. Could I tell him, he asked, which of Jo's eyes was the glass one? There was some controversy within the company, he explained, and a few members were placing bets. Jo herself, on the other hand, impervious to all these discussions, had thoroughly enjoyed her stay with us – though I think she was rather shocked at the extent of our poverty. She sent a box of Scottish kippers to keep us going.

It must be said, for the more serious-minded among my readers, that all these activities came after long days of training and rehearsals, but we were obviously an energetic and creative team of young people, and even our spare moments were filled with discussions on theatre, plans for the future, sing-songs, and spontaneous improvisations. One of these was a memorable gun battle or shoot-out between Cowboys and Indians that erupted in the courtyard one day. The Cowboys were shooting from the hip in the best John Wayne manner, and without a prop gun or stetson hat in sight, Indians were dropping from low roofs, down steps, in doorways and around corners. The competition for the most spectacular demise was strong, until the fun was stopped by a heavy downpour of rain.

All these high spirits were probably in part a reaction against the hardship and terror of the war, the effects of which were still everywhere plain to see – particularly so in the case of one newcomer to the company, Benedict Ellis, to whom I was introduced on one of my weekend visits. I was told he had served as an army captain, but had been injured in an explosion on D-Day and been invalided out. Ben certainly seemed of a nervous disposition, although he appeared to enjoy rehearsing for his role in Operation Olive Branch. What we did not realise at the time was how unstable he was, though this was perhaps unsurprising since the army medical authorities themselves had failed to diagnose his condition. Equally unsurprisingly, our eccentric lifestyle at Ormesby confused him. As he later explained, his nerves already felt on a 'knife-edge' and, not fully understanding events or able to rationalise resulting situations, he felt reality slipping away from him. One night he got up from the supper table, and went outside into the night for a couple of hours, trying to get it all together. We were surprised but not too concerned. Later that evening, however, he was discovered in bed with his wrists slashed, a favourite bust of Beethoven smashed, and most of his notes and scripts torn up – but with no recollection of what he had done.

Gerry immediately phoned for an ambulance, and he was taken to a local psychiatric hospital and given a sedative. Next morning, he was told by a nurse that he would be kept there, against his will if necessary, for the foreseeable future. While the paperwork was being prepared, however, a young doctor in charge of the case dramatically intervened. He realised that if Ben were ever to overcome this trauma, it was of paramount importance that he be allowed to perform his role – ironically enough, as an enslaved soldier – in Operation Olive Branch. I remember the tension amongst us all as Ben left for the theatre in a taxi. Mirrors were banned in his presence because he had a fixation about glass, smashing it wherever possible, so Gerry made him up in a separate dressing-room. As a slave soldier, Ben carried a wooden dagger, which he now dug deeply into his bandaged wrist, in an effort to cling on to his sanity. The script called for him at one point to angrily hurl this dagger, and when the moment arrived on stage, he was not play-acting. One actor said later that when he was on stage, he had seen Ben looking fixedly at the lighting, and feared the worst: 'All that glass!' But with his doctor standing supportively in the wings, and a white-coated attendant in case of disaster, Ben heroically and successfully got through the night's performance. Joan always said afterwards that that young doctor had saved Ben's sanity. Our guest on this particular weekend was the M.P. Tom Driberg, who wrote in a newspaper column that his readers would not believe the weekend he had just spent with Theatre Workshop. Ben was completely cured and later married a student from Lisa's Art of Movement Studio.

'Operation Olive Branch' : Ewan MacColl,
Kristin Lind, Gerry Raffles, Rosalie Williams
courtesy of Theatre Royal Stratford East Archive

The first productions that Laban and Lisa saw were 'Johnny Noble' and 'The Flying Doctor'. The former was a ballad opera written by Ewan; the latter, his adaptation of Molière's 'Le Malade Imaginaire'. They were full of praise and enthusiasm for both the style and the production, Laban especially excited by what he saw as a confirmation of some of the ideas he had tried out himself in pre-war Germany. He thought there was definitely a role for me 'in dis company', as he put it, and I think he saw, even before I did, the gradually inevitable breaking up of our own 'family' unit. The bonds we had established were stronger than many blood-ties, and were to remain for the rest of his life. It was typical of the man, though, that he did not seek to persuade me to stay when the time eventually came for me to test my wings, but instead offered an open invitation to return to work with him whenever I was free. I was to take him up on this invitation – as well as the warmth and breadth of his friendship – in the years to come.

Chapter Thirteen

'In the Mirk'

1946–1947

The weeks were now fairly flying past. Ewan and I were now becoming more seriously involved and I was, once again, heading for an Ormesby weekend. We were both looking forward to being gloriously free, since the tour was over and the company were enjoying a well-earned break. Some had returned to Ormesby, others going their separate ways before the start of the intensive rehearsals scheduled for the following week. Ewan, a great fan of the Marx Brothers, discovered that one of their films was on at the local cinema, and when I told him I'd never seen them, insisted on improving my education, and we set off for the Saturday evening showing. I'm not sure I enjoyed the film as much as Ewan – though I loved Harpo and Chico's musicianship, and could have done with seeing more of it – but we had a great evening anyway, and it was especially nice not to be surrounded by other people on this visit, and have the time to relax in each other's company. We took our time strolling back, both of us very much in love. I was aware that life was pretty good at that moment.

Turning into the drive from the dimly lit road, we saw a couple of very bright stationary lights some distance ahead of us, which seemed rather strange to me. As we drew nearer, I could see that they came from the headlamps of two powerful motorbikes, then that the shadowy riders astride them were policemen. It looked as if they were positioned to guard the drive. At this point our conversation flagged. I don't know what Ewan was thinking, but I was beginning to feel very uneasy. A patrol car had taken up a strategic position in the courtyard, along with another motorbike.

Like lambs to the slaughter, we walked past them and made for the front door. An officer of the law now introduced himself, and asked for Ewan's identity. Was he James Miller, otherwise known as Ewan MacColl? He nodded. It was all very civilised and low key. Everyone was most polite. But the brutal fact remained that he was being arrested for desertion – an extremely serious offence.

Ewan was allowed to collect a few things and told to shave off his beard. We managed a few moments together, during which he apologised to me and I offered to tidy up after he had gone – one always makes the most banal remarks in unexpected crises. He said he'd contact me as soon as he knew where he was being sent, and begged me to wait for him. And with that we returned to the waiting officer, who led him out to the car. If I hadn't been so stunned, I might have seen the humour of Ewan being driven off at speed with out-riders and a chauffeur, for all the world like some departing general.

Joan eventually found out that the police were actually looking for someone else with the same name, though at the time we didn't know that. In fact, I knew almost nothing – except that everyone else in the company knew more. Looking back over our brief time together, I did recall that Ewan had never liked going into shops, always sending me in to make a purchase. I hadn't given it much thought, treating it as one of his foibles. I certainly wasn't prepared for quite such a brutal severance of our growing relationship, and I felt completely numb. The following morning I was back in Manchester, quietly devastated, carrying on with my work with Laban and awaiting developments.

Over the next couple of weeks, Joan alerted several influential friends to Ewan's plight, all of whom immediately rallied to his support – among them Hugh McDiarmid, Scotland's greatest poet, and Bill MacLellan, his publisher. Contacts were approached in various ministerial departments, and letters went regularly to and fro. As the wheels slowly started to turn, Joan got on with the theatre's immediate needs and started rehearsals as scheduled – though she decided not to accompany the production but instead stay behind to carry on working for Ewan's release. Although the company was not due to leave until the end of January 1947, there

'In the Mirk'

was no way of knowing how long this would take. Meanwhile, I pressed on with all my commitments to Laban and awaited Joan's phone calls. Word eventually came through that Ewan was at a camp at Oswestry, and was allowed a single prison visit: it was me he wanted to see.

A few weeks earlier I had heard from my family that my brother Pip was engaged to a Junior Commander in the A.T.S. The wedding was imminent and I was invited to be the bridesmaid. I'd also inadvertently let slip that I too had found someone special, and I believe a similar announcement was expected from me in the near future. The happy day arrived, and I wore a pink suit which at least looked more cheerful than my less than rosy mood. The celebrations went without a hitch, and I couldn't help thinking as I waved goodbye to the bride and groom that some lives were turning out to be much simpler than others. I also knew that everyone has a choice in life – which in some cases, like mine, was no choice at all, since the complicated and unconventional path I had taken always seemed the only possible one for me. All the same, it was still more than a little irksome when a stranger came up to me at the reception and enquired about my 'young man'. At least I could say, in all honesty, that I was soon going to visit him.

Lisa and Laban had of course been kept informed of the latest developments, and when the time came, at the end of a bitterly cold November, Lisa lent me her magnificent white fur coat, in which I left with their blessing – and a few goodies for Ewan. Checking in to my Oswestry hotel around lunchtime (a rather upmarket affair, with a log fire in reception), I dropped off my luggage, asked for directions to the army camp, and immediately set off. From there it was a short journey to the guard room – where my arrival caused a minor disturbance (it was probably the fur coat). The duty officer was hastily sent for.

Meanwhile I watched the behaviour of the guards with interest. They were not exactly standing at ease. In fact, one might go so far as to say that a state of nervous confusion prevailed. After an awkward period, a young Captain hurriedly arrived, who, somewhat to my surprise, immediately began to apologise profusely to me – both for keeping me waiting, it seemed, and also for keeping Ewan incarcerated there in the first place. It really wasn't his fault, this young man assured me, and 'everything possible' was being done. I can only think that all the phone calls and letters of support from various well-known people arriving at the guard room had completely rattled Ewan's 'minders'. Nothing was going according to Army regulations: where would it all end? No one seemed to know. Meanwhile, it behoved them all to be overly polite. After all, the prisoner might have 'brass hats' on his side.

A door opened and I caught sight of a large cell beyond, with several men in it. Ewan grinned as he was released by the guard. The rest of the prisoners looked at me in surprise. I noticed they addressed him as 'Prof' – he'd already made his mark! The apologetic young officer then led us to an empty Nissen hut and said he would come back in three hours. To break the ice, I gave Ewan a twirl in my white fur coat and asked Ewan what he thought of it. The answer wasn't slow in coming: 'You look like a polar bear!' I gave him the small gifts and delivered all the messages. He was bearing up pretty well and was delighted at the support he had mustered in his defence. I suspect, too, that he relished his predicament: it fed the writer in him. Then there were his avid listeners, his cell-mates, who seemed to have elected 'The Prof' as their leader and spokesman. I suspect the guards too, could not help overhearing his conversations . . . probably about everything under the sun and especially the working-class struggle. Maybe he sang to them too. Left there another six months, the camp would probably have surrendered to him. He confided in me that he could only remain optimistic because he counted on my staying with him. Again he begged me to stand by him, that we had a great future ahead of us, once this problem was out of the way. He would then be free to go anywhere with me and to write the best play he had ever written. It would be dedicated to me. Heady dreams!

All too soon, the officer returned and took us back to the guard room. When the inner door opened and Ewan was returned to his cell, a gruff voice whispered in my ear, 'Bring a hacksaw next time!' The owner of the voice coughed and melted away to the

'In the Mirk'

back of the cage. I returned to the hotel reassured that Ewan was bearing up well. If all he had said was true, that his optimism and well-being depended on my standing by him, as he and others seemed to think, then there was no problem. The past was the past and we were concerned with the future.

A little later that afternoon, there was a knock on my door and I was confronted by the manager of the hotel. 'Madam,' he began, falteringly, 'there are . . . er . . . certain . . . ahem . . . gentlemen who are asking for you. I hev placed them in the bar h'adjacent to the residents' lounge.' There was no doubt in my mind that he disapproved of my visitors. Rushing down, I saw three privates in brand-new uniforms, fluff and dull bronze much in evidence. (I was the expert here.) Ewan had arrived with two cronies. I was relieved to see 'Hacksaw' was not one of them.

The three were over the moon at being allowed their freedom for a few hours. Blessings on whoever worked this miracle . . . allowing three prisoners out unattended! As far as I can remember, one of them was a graduate and actor, and the other a younger lad from a public school. Neither had found the army to their taste. It was a very jolly party. They were like children let out of school early. It made me realise what an effect being locked up and confined to a small area without privacy can have on an individual. The strain must become unbearable at times. At ten-thirty, I watched the three giggling musketeers disappear noisily into the darkness and could not help noting that none of them were remotely aggressive types. Once back in their cell, this outing would seem like a dream but might help them to survive incarceration a little longer.

It was during this period that I was able to receive letters from Ewan, written in pencil on both sides of some squared notepaper. More often than not, they took the form of poems. He said they were not very good but conditions were difficult and it was hard to write anything at all.

In the Mirk

In a deathlike dwarm I ling i' the grey nicht
My mind jummummlit an' choked wi' faukled weeds.
Nae hunger ony mair the body kens
Only despair at a room universe o' grey wa's
Illuminit wi' the blear e'e o' an electric licht
A' syne I mind the lass that I lo'e weel
An' the hot, saut tears are prickly in my throat
Her bonny mou' on mine again I feel
Her lauch sounds in ma ear a lilting note,
An' then I ken the bluid loups hech again
An' the world's no' blindit yet
An' life is still for us for a' their whispered fears
An' promises o' tears tae come.
They canna pit us doon, luve,
For we carry the sun on oor shouthers
An' a' the starry ligt is in oor veins
An' for every staur that's blinded by a curse
A hunder mair are kindled wi' a kiss.

The Forge

It'll no be aye lik this, lass, dinna greet.
The luve that we ha'e lit will burn the mirk
Wi' sich an unca flame that folk will greet
Each ither in the street wi' news o'a new, bricht
bleezing comet i' the ligt'.
Ach, let their ghaist-like legions trauchle roond
An' roond the glowing core o' life
They canna hurt us wi' their stinking breith
For we will temper luve intil a dirk
And point it at the very hairt o' grisly deith.

'In the Mirk'

I don't remember what happened over Christmas but the New Year of 1947 brought some news, when Joan rang to say that Ewan was on his way to being demobbed but that it necessitated a transfer to Birmingham. He was in an army psychiatric hospital and was hoping I would visit him as soon as possible.

This time without Lisa's fur coat, I turned up at the hospital like Red Riding Hood with a basket of delicacies. I was asked for my name and the name of the patient I had come to visit. It was checked against a long list. A door was unlocked and I was ushered through it, having to wait for the attendant to lock up again behind us. After walking through several large, empty, sparsely furnished recreation rooms, I was handed over to another white-coated attendant carrying an enormous bunch of keys. Another door was unlocked for me and locked again behind me. The procedure happened a third time. Without a word, I was then shown into a large dormitory and Ewan's bed was pointed out to me. Most of the inmates were dressed, and wandering aimlessly around the ward. It was a paradoxical situation. This was a much worse and far more unfriendly environment for Ewan than Oswestry, but on the other hand, it indicated how much closer he hopefully was to demobilization, on account of being judged 'unsuitable material', I supposed.

He was delighted to see me and seemed to find the other inmates fascinating, as did I when he described each one in detail. One poor fellow kept walking by us and saluting with his hand at the back of his head. He said it was for 'back pay'. Some patients were obviously deranged by their experiences, though not necessarily through active service, I found out later. One middle-aged man was literally euphoric – deranged by a perpetual state of well-being. The more brutish of the male attendants, Ewan told me, enjoyed punching him hard in the stomach, to see if they could wipe the smile from his face. They never succeeded. One chap I really admired was a clever member of the awkward squad who absolutely refused to wear army uniform. Since nothing else was allowed, he refused to dress at all. This was thought to offend propriety, so he was kept in a padded cell, hidden from view, and only let out when nature called. It called while I was there. The cell door was unlocked, an army blanket thrown round him, and he marched elegantly and confidently out of the ward. Returning to his padded cell, he smiled in our direction and called out, 'Open Sesame,' while waving an authoritative arm to his minders. This didn't go down well with the guards who thought – correctly – they were being made to look foolish. He was roughly thrown into the cell minus the blanket and his door locked. Next to Ewan, I reckoned he was the sanest one there . . .

Again I reassured Ewan that nothing had changed in the way I felt about him, and indeed it hadn't. We were all waiting for his return to the company, and felt very optimistic that it must happen soon. As for me, I saw my future with him and told him so. He looked very happy when I left.

With the rest of the company in Germany, I spent more working time with Lisa, Laban, and the studio. It was during this period that Lisa decided that her dance students should enter an International Dance Competition scheduled to be held in Copenhagen later in the year. Sylvia was to be the choreographer. Any free time was now severely limited. Even so, we were given a short break over Easter and I went home.

It must be admitted that my parents wondered very much about the new man in my life whom they never saw. I think my father thought a future husband should be healthy in both body and morals, and believe in Christian values, though not necessarily a church-goer. Of course, this simplistic outlook included, amongst other things, faithfulness and honesty. My man certainly appeared to be healthy, but I couldn't as yet vouch for anything else, and felt that I couldn't admit he was at present under observation in the psychiatric ward of a prison hospital. It seemed better to overlook the imponderables. Much later, though, when I told them, I must say they took the news remarkably calmly.

A telegram arrived for me on Easter Saturday. Ewan was free! I was, of course, delighted. He rang me soon afterwards and I invited him over to meet the family. We were all excited for different reasons. Even Willi and Herbert looked forward to this stranger about to descend on us. I went to the station where Ewan arrived in a state of euphoria. I didn't say anything to dampen his spirits but privately rather hoped he would calm down before we got home since as far as my family was concerned, we had simply finished working together on the recent drama courses.

He was a polite if diffident guest. Every effort was made to make him feel welcome, and on leaving he gave Willi and Herbert a ten-shilling note each. My grandfather thought he must be a good fellow. Of necessity, though, our time in Lincoln was short: Ewan was needed for some urgent rehearsals before going on tour with the company, who had recently returned from Germany; and I was meanwhile going to Copenhagen with the students from Lisa's Art of Movement Studio, led by her and Sylvia Bodmer.

The sea was like a mill-pond as we rehearsed on the sun-drenched deck on the crossing to Esbjerg and on to Copenhagen. My memories are of a delightful city, charming people, a glorious heat-wave and the privilege of seeing some first-rate dancers perform. Geoffrey Mostyn-Lewis, the RAF pilot, and Ben Ellis, who had recovered from his psychiatric problems and was now in love with one of the dancers, came with us to help with the lighting and scene changes. Ewan was back in England, heavily involved with Theatre Workshop on tour.

Our contribution to the Dance Competition run by Rolf de Mare could be called a 'woodland fantasy'. Some of the scenes were interesting enough, but I felt that it didn't 'hang together' well enough. To add to the problem, all the other mixed dance companies seemed to be professionals. And, most importantly, our pastoral offering was also untimely. At this period, with the war only recently over, and people still suffering from its aftermath across Europe, the other competitors had far more serious problems on their agenda. 'La Cellule', a piece by Jean Weidt and his modern dance company, was a good example of this, telling the story of a man locked away in a prison cell, visited by his friends and enemies in dream sequences. Sylvia and our lighting team also had a few problems with the resident Danish backstage staff, who mistakenly brought on the 'dawn' before the 'sun' had set, leaving a number of confused wood-nymphs scampering for cover.

A Swedish modern dance company were the popular winners. Their choreographer was Birgit Cullberg, who had studied with

Jooss at Dartington. She was later to interview me in 1948 in Stockholm about my own choreography. Her leading male dancer, only about five feet six or seven inches in height, caused a great furore in the audience. The scene opened with him as Herod, enveloped in a purple cloak. He started to 'grow' very, very slowly. A pause. Then he continued to grow in height once more. A sigh rose softly from the auditorium. Another pause. Then when it was thought he could not possibly reach further in his upward climb, he continued to grow until he seemed to be a veritable giant. It was pure artistry, quite brilliantly executed and drew tremendous applause from the audience. The figure of Herod now dominated the stage. Later, when Theatre Workshop was playing at Norrköping in Sweden, I became a friend of the dancer's brother, who was an art critic and started writing about our own productions.

One other performance stands out in my memory by a very young classical ballet company led by a young Czech. I was to meet him again in Brno, Czechoslovakia. After he had seen our performance, I was invited to see his work as ballet master and choreographer. He told me that immediately after the war, he had recruited starving youngsters off the streets and had begun to train them for the new company. We shared his pleasure at the excellent results so far achieved and wished him well for all his great plans in the future. Unfortunately he did not live to see them carried out, as he tragically died as a result of his wartime experiences.

On the final evening in Copenhagen there was a great celebration and banquet. No one told us about the banquet. Having saved my meagre pennies throughout the week, I went off with a friend to a restaurant in a wood on the outskirts of the city, so we arrived at the reception quite replete. It was heart-breaking: with rationing still in force at home, to be confronted by tables groaning with great quantities of food, and unable to eat a bite!

In our spare time, we would take a short train trip to the Baltic coast where we sun-bathed and swam. Helsingør was quite near and I went to see Hamlet's castle – not as eerie as I would have wished! I also had my photo taken in my Vogue-style demob coat. Geoffrey Mostyn-Lewis and I, with a couple of friends, also

'In the Mirk'

invested in the luxury of a whole Danish Blue cheese. As we embarked for the return trip, hatches were being battened down. Despite these ominous signs, we merrily carved the cheese up into four equally large quarters on the deck. Before long, everyone was looking queasy and disappearing. I felt fine. After some time, it seemed unfair to feel so well and not offer support to my weaker colleagues. This was a great mistake. Going down to the cabin was an unhappy experience. I have only once suffered a worse trip and that was returning from Sweden in a gale with Theatre Workshop.

Ewan met me off the boat at Harwich and I went with him to Felixstowe to start the company training. They were playing at the Pier Pavilion. As usual, the finances were virtually non-existent, so my slab of Danish Blue cheese came in useful. (I have never been able to face it since.) Everyone was happy and seemed oblivious to the hardship, totally committed to the theatre's aims. I remember once walking behind 'Camel' (as we called our stage designer John Bury), and glancing down at his shoes – for my eyes to become transfixed. Although he seemed to be wearing a pair of casual plimsolls, I soon realised that there was only an 'upper' part to each plimsoll with its neatly tied laces. But the upper part was all there was: there was no sole, and he was walking on his bare feet.

From Felixstowe we travelled to Ryde on the Isle of Wight. After leaving the island, Gerry called a brief meeting just as we were getting off the ferry. He told us quite seriously that the company's finances would not stretch to cover our rail or bus journeys to Liverpool en route for the Isle of Man. I cannot remember whether this also meant the sea crossing as well. It probably did! Today was 29 June; everyone was expected to check in on 2 July; and it was understood that everyone would have to make their own way there. Meanwhile he would be driving the lorry with all the gear up to Liverpool. Considering the state of the vehicle, his trip promised to be only marginally better than ours.

I looked at the serious young faces around me. They dutifully dispersed, intent on getting to the destination on time. I watched the lorry making for the open road, then fell about laughing to see one of our much older members, Charles Turner, sitting on the tailboard with his back against some sets, ropes lashed across his chest. He gave a tired little smile and a gracious wave of the hand . . . the only part of his body he could move. I don't know whether or not Gerry knew he was there, but he certainly deserved a prize for his ingenuity. It was impossible not to feel great warmth for one's colleagues at this time. No one ever griped about conditions, they all felt so privileged.

There were many stories circulating about Charles. It was believed that the mere mention of his name would make him appear from nowhere. Ewan and I had proof of this ability years later, long after Charles had left the company. Driving through dense fog in Notting Hill with two friends, we were recounting this tale, and just as we reached the part about our friend's uncanny ability to materialise, like Hamlet's Ghost, at the mention of his name, a well-known shape loomed out of the fog, right in front of the car, and smiled in our direction. It was, of course, Charles Turner, whom we hadn't seen in years!

Chapter Fourteen

Taking Flight in the Parrot House

1947–1948

After my vagabond friends moved off, I travelled back to Manchester alone. Although I was not a full member of the company, I was increasingly committed to helping them. This meant that apart from working with them officially in my professional role, I would also join them during the breaks between terms at the Art of Movement Studio. Within a week the studio had closed for the summer and the students disappeared. I had already been invited to join the company on the Isle of Man. It was suggested that I met them in Castletown on 13 July, where I would be given transport to Ramsey, the second town and our next venue. Transport, of course meant the back of an open lorry: at least I'd had plenty of experience of that mode of transport. While I was preparing for the trip, I telephoned my mother, who told me that Dominique had just arrived from Paris and was staying with them for three weeks. Could I possibly, she asked, give her visitor a much needed break and take her with me to the Isle of Man? She thought the company of young people would do her some good.

A word of explanation is needed here. Returning from America after an abortive emigration at the age of sixteen, my mother had returned to London a year later, before embarking on a career in nursing in France and Spain, eventually settling in Paris, her favourite city, on the eve of the First World War in 1914. She soon became friendly with the Liewers, a Jewish family who lived at Neuilly, on the outskirts of the city. Devoted to babies, it did not take long for Mme Liewer to persuade her to take charge of her youngest child who was still at the pram stage. His name was

Philippe. There were older children, Marie-Louise and Bobby, aged eleven and thirteen respectively. It was hoped that Philippe would acquire a good grasp of English at an early age. Apart from that, the whole family wanted to practise their English. My brother was later called Philip (Pip) after Philippe. My father was working for American Express in Paris at this time, and studying art in his spare time. Parc Monceau was the popular meeting place for the young couple, who were celebrating their engagement at Asnieres when war broke out. Mother helped the Liewers with their flight south and eventually returned to Paris where she was married at the British Legation. Towards the end of 1915, they both returned to England. As with the Bouthors family, we had kept in touch over the years. We knew that Marie-Louise had married and was the mother of two children, Dominique and Denis. We also knew that her father had died, and that her mother, Mme Liewer, had still been alive in 1939. After the war, Mother spent a lot of time making enquiries as to their whereabouts. Eventually, the Red Cross traced them and Marie-Louise was able to come over for a visit and tell us the full story.

It seems that her little brother Philippe had been a leader in the Resistance, a secret agent who made a number of journeys between England and occupied France. His pseudonym was Major Staunton, and he features in the book 'Carve Her Name With Pride', as the boss of the agent Violette Szabo. To all intents and purposes, he had transformed himself into an Englishman – Paul Scofield played him in the film later made from the book. Marie-Louise herself had her own terrible story to tell.

Following the fall of France in 1940, she had been awakened in the early hours of the morning to the dreaded sound of the Gestapo banging on her door. They had come for her husband. Still in his pyjamas, he was dragged out to the railway sidings and shot with other Jewish victims. The family heard the shooting. Philippe managed to supply them with forged identity papers and ration cards through the underground movement. From then on, though, they were constantly on the move – 'one step ahead', as she described it. Although Marie-Louise did not look Jewish, her daughter Dominique did. The grandmother – Mme Liewer – was by now elderly and frail and found travelling difficult. Any meal taken in a restaurant was dangerous in Occupied France, since German soldiers or, worse, the SS or Gestapo, were quite likely to drop in as customers. They could arrive unexpectedly, bar the doors and check everyone's papers. For the Liewers to rent accommodation left them at the mercy of intrusive neighbours who could not be trusted. Nowhere was safe.

Then a piece of good fortune came their way. A Catholic school offered to take Dominique as a boarder. And when the other convent children were led out in crocodile-fashion for their daily walk, the nuns would say, 'Not you, Dominique, your health is still much below par. One day perhaps . . .' She vowed that if she survived the war, she would convert to Catholicism, a pledge she lived to fulfil. I never found out what happened to the grandmother.

So now that the war was over, Mother told Marie-Louise to send Dominique, and later Denis, for a holiday in England. Their beautiful home in Neuilly had been stripped by the Germans and nothing of value was left. Meanwhile she also wrote to Philippe in Casablanca, where he was now living. Delighted to hear from her, he arranged a visit. Apparently, he had tried several times to contact her but hadn't the 'foggiest idea' where to start looking. (His English seemed pretty good.) A few days before he was due, however, a letter arrived from Bobby. Philippe had been found dead in his office from a heart attack. Doctors believed it was due to the stress of his wartime experiences, which included many parachute jumps from England into occupied France. He was only in his thirties when he died.

Dominique and I got on well from the moment we met. I tried to warn her about what to expect from our visit to the Isle of Man, but soon gave up. After all, anything had to be better than what she had gone through. Her arrival did present one immediate difficulty, however. There was a tense moment when Herbert and Willi joined us for an evening meal, and were introduced to her. They had been made prisoners of war very early on in the war, and were ignorant of much that had happened since. I think my father took them aside and told them about Dominique's personal tragedy, and presumably also about the wider atrocity of which it formed part. Dad was the best person to do this – he could be very direct at times – and the outcome was that our German friends still felt welcome in our house but also tried to be very solicitous towards Dominique for the duration of her stay. Perhaps Dad hoped they would return home with good memories and more understanding. I never met Willi or Herbert again. They came to say goodbye shortly afterwards, and promised to write. Herbert did – his adored wife had left him for someone else, and he wrote in a moment of utter desolation. As for Willi . . . we never heard.

Dominique and I arrived on the Isle of Man, after a bumpy crossing, and met up with the company – just in time to see them breaking camp. Their first engagement was over, all the equipment had gone on ahead, and the lorry was now back to remove the human cargo. This surprising turn of events was not explained to me and, after a short lifetime of experience in the vagaries of the Army and now the business side of Theatre Workshop, I knew better than to ask. Instead I introduced Dom (as I was soon calling her) and we all climbed aboard. Rumour had it that Kristin had found us superb accommodation, and I was pleased for Dom's sake. As we trundled through Ramsey in the balmy evening air, old men were sitting outside their cottages smoking their pipes. I think this was all too much for Joan, who stood up and saluted them. Breaking the tranquillity of this peaceful scene, she called out in ringing tones, 'Hail to the commune of Ramsey!' The residents hardly noticed.

When we turned down the drive on arrival at our digs, we could hardly believe our eyes when a large country mansion loomed into view. Could this really be true? We all tiptoed into the beautifully furnished interior to be met by an extraordinarily eccentric character. She had cropped hair, a lorgnette dangled on a chain and a cigarette hung from the corner of her mouth. She was short and extremely stout, almost as wide as she was tall, and the corduroy trousers she wore emphasised her rotundity. Her language was mind-boggling, every other word was an expletive. (It all passed over Dom's head, I'm pleased to say.) But she was a marvellously kind and generous woman. This week was out of season and the place, usually run as a hotel, was empty. She was glad to hand it over to us, provided we cleaned our own rooms and didn't expect maid service.

The following day, as I was shaking off a touch of flu by luxuriating in bed, my rest was suddenly interrupted by a clamorous commotion below, where our hostess was venting her rage on some poor culprits in the kitchens. She was screaming and banging doors – the whole building shook with her fury. It appeared from the snatches of loud abuse I could make out that she had run out of gin for her 'snifters'. The front door slammed, and I peered from my window as she crossed the gravel yard and jumped into an open jeep. With a painful clash of gears, she hurtled down the drive at breakneck speed. Sometime later, the jeep returned and, now all sweetness and light, she was singing loudly and tunefully as she screeched to a stop. With a practised ease, she hefted the crates of drink out of the back of the jeep and carried them indoors.

Back in the theatre the following day, Joan suggested that I took on the role of Lucille, the inamorata in 'The Flying Doctor', Ewan's adaptation of Molière. For this production, we needed lots of flowers. I have no idea how it was arranged – though I think it must have been the miracle-working Kristin – but each lunchtime an open-topped Rolls-Royce would draw up outside the theatre, and the chauffeur would ask for me. His mistress, Lady R., had sent the flowers with her compliments: they filled the back of the car. They were used to adorn the set, all but cover my dress, and were plaited into my hair. But they were so profuse that they were also used to decorate the front-of-house, the aisles, and even the dressing rooms. Then every evening, after the performance, we took them back to the hotel in the certain knowledge that a fresh delivery would arrive the following day.

There were wings on either side of the stage, with steps leading down to a large basement area underneath, where we had dumped our spare sets, and costumes. During one performance, I smelt something strange. It definitely wasn't the scent of flowers, to which we had all grown accustomed, but it certainly wasn't unpleasant. In fact, it was a smell I knew from somewhere . . . I just couldn't place it. Throughout my scene I puzzled over the smell and wondered if the audience could smell it too. Then, exiting left and rushing down the steps to pass under the stage, to re-enter stage right, I was taken aback to see Joby Blanchard, who played my father Gorgibus, hunched over a bubbling cauldron and stirring busily. He looked like one of the witches from Macbeth. He didn't notice me. I saw him cock an ear to the stage and then rush upstairs for his entrance. Looking into the pot, I realised it was the strawberry season: he was busy making jam!

Our hostess came to see us on the last night, and afterwards threw a wonderful party which went on to the early hours. I remember Dom laughing happily and calling out to me, 'My muzzaire will nevaire believe it!' Even after most of us had retired to bed, the music continued. A colonel and his wife who had only just arrived on their holidays did not appreciate the noise, and he complained loudly from the top of the landing. The owner shouted back to him that he 'should be grateful to God that there was such music in the world' and promptly turned the sound up a little louder.

We were all extremely sorry to leave in the morning. As we all lined up to say our goodbyes, she told us gruffly to 'bugger off', but she was visibly moved.

The next venue on our tour was the Library Theatre in Manchester, from where Dom returned home safely, having thoroughly enjoyed her time with us. While Lisa's dance studio was still closed for the summer holidays, I was gradually being inducted into the continuing mysteries of acting. Having spent ten days as Lucille, the inamorata, I was now enlisted as a dancer-actress in Ewan's ballad-opera 'Johnny Noble'.

'Johnny Noble', *with Jean, Kristin Lind and Isla Gledhill
courtesy of Theatre Royal Stratford East Archive*

At the same time, Joan also wanted me to re-stage the opening of 'Operation Olive Branch', and I became quite carried away with ideas. The set was superb – its two central pillars, and ramps and steps set at different levels, were a gift to any choreographer, and the Library Theatre was wide enough to show it off to full advantage. My idea was for all the women to move in character – some moving through their lines, others after speaking, and occasionally everyone moving simultaneously. There was no music, but the whole effect of lighting, sets, spoken verse, and airy dance-like costumes, together with their movements, gave the appearance of a scene from a ballet. It took quite some rehearsing, but looked stunning when finished. One actress played a sort of Carmen Miranda type, with a large basket of fruit on her head, bare midriff, and long, clinging skirt.

Saturday morning dawned. With both a matinee and an evening performance scheduled, I was looking forward to sitting at the back of the auditorium and seeing my innovations premièred – until Joan approached me with a very serious expression on her face. In those days I had not yet learnt to associate that look with 'I am in a desperate trouble and am counting on you to get me out of this mess'. It seemed that 'Carmen Miranda' had had to leave for London unexpectedly, to raise money for the company – that was the story I was given, at any rate – so would I take over her role? Except there was no 'would I' about it: there was no one else to do it. It's one thing to arrange an intricate piece of choreography from the leisure and safety of the stalls. Trying to memorise the individual moves of a single element in that arrangement, while at the same time learning her lines in the minutes before curtain-up, is quite another, especially when you're a newcomer to acting. But after my tentative début at Ramsey, Joan began to consider me as a 'spare' actress.

Her optimism proved unfounded. For one thing, the basket of fruit I was supposed to carry on my head weighed a ton. As the choreographer, I had been unsympathetic to the performers' plight. Now, however – as I found myself staggering about the stage, up and down the ramps, in the quick run-through our producer had kindly allowed – I suddenly understood that I had perpetrated a grave injustice on the actress.

Sheer terror somehow got me through the matinee, and I thought the worst was over. I was wrong . . . It all began to go wrong when I missed a single cue during the evening performance, which meant that I found myself always one move behind the other actresses, all of whom were carrying out the choreographer's instructions to the letter. And since I was the choreographer, part of me admired their dedication. But then one actress darted daintily into my path when I least expected her. Knocked off balance by the weight of my fruity basket, I staggered drunkenly into the paths of others, who ricocheted off me like bullets flying in all directions. By this time, of course, my head-dress had wilted and slumped over my left ear, so in order to redress the balance, I had to bend my head over to the right; which made it look as if I had broken my neck. Turning my back to the audience, I committed the unforgivable sin of the amateur, and started to 'corpse', giggling uncontrollably at the absurdity of it all. I also saw that many of my fellow dancers were similarly affected, trying very hard not to laugh – in part perhaps at the pleasure of witnessing their choreographer's come-uppance. The movements continued as rehearsed, providing I was not in the way. All this was far too much for me: I delivered my few lines, gave a Carmen Miranda wiggle and, controlling my hysteria, made what I hoped was a graceful exit.

I learnt two valuable lessons from this experience which served me in good stead. One: always be wary of a producer who says that only you can save the company in its present crisis. Two: if you're working with Theatre Workshop, never make the dance arrangements so complicated that the choreographer can't jump in at a moment's notice.

August Bank Holiday Monday, 1947 was a washout. Literally. The heavens opened up and torrential rain fell ceaselessly, leaving the population desperate for shelter, even if it meant going into a theatre. Before we knew it, both houses were sold out. Entrepreneurial as ever, we took advantage of the situation and carried all the heavy chairs from the dressing rooms, round to the front of house and deposited them in the auditorium, thus confusing the ticket office. When these had been sold, we searched the building for spare chairs which appeared with alarming regularity in the auditorium. I noticed that the spirit of making do was catching. Some of the audience could be seen lugging their chairs to more advantageous view-points before the lights went down. Even if the majority might never have come in but for the rain, they all loved the show and gave us a great ovation. At the evening performance we proudly displayed a 'Sold Out' notice.

I returned to Laban and the studio after my time away (less of a 'break' than a process of 'breaking-in') for the autumn term and I was once again involved with all sorts of classes. The theatre company had meanwhile departed for the Rudolf Steiner Hall in London. It was during this short period that I joined the voice classes of Nelson Illingworth with the rest of the company. He lived in a bungalow alongside the Thames. I remember him as an eccentric figure, gnarled, brown as a berry in his khaki shorts, and about eight feet tall. He was an Australian and had been the voice coach at the Metropolitan Opera House in New York. I felt apologetic for every breath I took in his presence, but he was painstakingly kind. I learnt to drop my voice a couple of octaves . . . or so it seemed. Of course, it played hell with my movement classes. When I encouraged the actors to 'leap' or move 'lightly', they became totally earthbound.

The theatre finished the year in debt, but I was becoming inured to this state of affairs. It seemed to me that that was the price one paid for being so fulfilled in one's work. Nevertheless, a decision was now taken to disband the company temporarily, since the debt had, somehow, to be paid off. New premises were being sought as a base, with Manchester high on the agenda, owing to the proximity of the Art of Movement Studio and possible contact with Laban. We also had another summer booking at the Library Theatre. Ewan now returned to his mother's cottage outside Manchester to write his next play, 'The Other Animals'. He was offered some acting roles by the B.B.C. in a few Children's Hour programmes which just about kept him solvent; and I returned to help out at the Studio.

During the previous two years, I hadn't experienced a dull moment. Apart from Theatre Workshop (and its playwright), my trip to Copenhagen and my acting début, there had also been an exciting dance course in Shropshire, when Laban had taken over as choreographer. Dancing to the music from Borodin's Prince Igor, we were divided into three groups (high, medium, and low dancers), with each group having its own piece of music before coming together as a whole. The event took place in the open air, in the grounds of Moreton Hall. It was quite thrilling to see dancers leaping over the brow of the hill and rushing down the slope to the lawns below, where other dancers were performing. Laban caught all the wildness and excitement of the music and its story.

Lisa and Laban at Moreton Hall summer holiday course in Oswestry

Lisa had also mounted a dance performance at the Library Theatre in Manchester. Laban arranged a group choreography and chose me as the soloist. This was the only time he worked professionally with a dancer on a one-to-one basis in this country. He encouraged me to express my ideas and honed them until the result was a polished and highly dramatic piece – essentially themed around the idea of an individual breaking free of a hostile encircling group. Although I had enjoyed the earlier work at Moreton Hall, this was infinitely more demanding of me. He was now treating me like a professional dancer and choreographer and it was a wonderful period in my life to have Laban devote such time and effort to directing me. My parents came over to see the show and I remember my father being especially impressed with the whole programme.

From time to time, Ewan and I would meet up with Joan and Gerry Raffles, who had acquired a flat in Manchester. It seemed that Gerry was battling on, trying to find a permanent base for the company, having unfortunately just missed getting the lease on the David Lewis Theatre in Liverpool.

In the very early days of my L.L.I.R. training, Laban had once counselled me to look upon 'our work as a business'. I believe he had recognised a kindred spirit in me. But he was certainly no businessman himself, and the business side never concerned me much. This burden fell entirely on Lisa, who had to organise all that side, as well as promote and pioneer Laban's work in this country. We all owe her a great debt for the remarkable job she did.

Gerry eventually managed to pay off the debt, and found a way for the company to rent a large semi-detached house in Withington, Manchester. We were only a stone's throw from Palatine Road and throughout this summer of 1948 we were able to maintain close contact with Lisa and Laban. A short period of intense domesticity ensued. Rooms were allotted and the odd piece of furniture – often very odd – was acquired. We cooked and catered for our own small groups and designated areas were set up in the large walk-in pantries for those groups to leave their groceries. I enthusiastically pinned up a house-cleaning roster.

While I have to admit that no one seemed particularly keen to carry out their chores, it seemed to work quite well in the initial stages. But like everything else in the theatre, as one became more involved with rehearsals and worked longer and longer hours, there was simply no time for any other activities and the house began to look distinctly squalid. The stairs were in a terrible state. This was Gerry Raffles's responsibility, and at our next company meeting, I denounced him for shirking it. The following morning he was to be seen with dust-pan and brush and a hang-dog expression. Unfortunately, his lack of expertise filled the hall with such clouds of dust that the other residents voiced their complaints in no uncertain manner. Manchester grime landed on previously hygienic surfaces, and this demoralised those who had been public-spirited enough to try to keep up with the roster. It was then that I tacitly decided to retire from my self-imposed status as housekeeper. It was just as well. A few days later, in my absence I was voted costume designer and dress-maker for the European trip. I think only Joan, with completely misplaced confidence, could have bestowed this honour on me, probably brought about by her total ignorance of sewing matters.

Ewan and I shared a room overlooking the back garden. It had a minute dressing room, some four feet square, which was euphemistically considered to be his writing den, a perk for the resident playwright. There was no bed. We made do with part of the set from Operation Olive Branch, and this worked quite well until the day came when rehearsals started on Ewan's new play, 'The Other Animals', and the 'bed' was just spirited away. Denis Ford, a young actor with the company, assured me that he could replace it with 'something'. I had fears that what he had in mind was the bed from the set of Lorca's 'Don Perlimplín'. This was fixed at such an angle (for perspective reasons) that the cast continually found themselves sliding down to the foot of it. When I voiced my concern, Denis assured me he had other boxes and I would never know the difference. He was wrong.

A jumble of small rostra of different sizes and heights duly appeared, together with, inexplicably, a short stepladder, last used in Chekhov's 'The Proposal'. Denis was nowhere to be seen. However, after my Army 'biscuits', I was rather experienced in improvising beds at short notice. But this was a more challenging geometry problem. There seemed to be no way of making it both rectangular and flattish. It always came out three-cornered, which gave it a rather a jaunty air. With sheets and blankets it even looked quite good. At least, it looked more like a bed than a pile of assorted wooden boxes. I felt rather pleased with myself, and placed the stepladder at the head, more for decoration than utility. With some curtaining it could almost pass for an antique four-poster. Carried away, I climbed the steps to look down on this work of art . . . and jumped. This was a mistake. Pride coming before a fall, I landed at the point where three adjoining rostra met, which immediately burst apart, rather like the splitting of the atom, and deposited me on the floor. I abandoned the ladder.

The front room downstairs was reserved for entertaining visitors and company meetings. A flock of large colourful birds paraded their garish plumage as they swooped and dived over the brocade-type wallpaper. Others peered balefully out at us from behind swathes of brilliant green jungle, their beady eyes uncannily following us to wherever we sat in the room. In honour of their vivid presence we christened our new residence 'The Parrot House'.

I'm not sure how long we all thought we were going to stay there, but Camel (John Bury) was certainly planning ahead, since he had soon started to dig over the garden and plant vegetables. His single-mindedness was very impressive. On returning from buying my very first piece of kitchen equipment, a small omelette pan, I was horrified to see him checking the temperature of his stew on the stove by thrusting the palm of his hand, with the soil still attached, onto the contents of the saucepan. Seeing my expression, he airily explained that when the temperature reached so many degrees, any bacteria would be destroyed. I just wondered what had happened to the worms I had earlier seen him holding.

During this early period at The Parrot House we were all supporting ourselves as best we could. A few were on the dole; others took whatever work they could find, John Blanshard managing to supplement his acting career with a skilled job in an engineering factory. Ewan continued to work on and off as an actor for the B.B.C., and I had my work with Lisa and Laban to keep me going, of course. By hook or by crook, we all felt it was necessary for the company to hang together. We had a season lined up at the Library Theatre in July, but meanwhile there was no doubt that we were all as hard up as we were busy, with our evenings given over to lectures on the theatre or preparatory rehearsals. I think Gerry was away for at least part of the time trying to raise money for our survival, but it was always very difficult to get any information out of him. And meanwhile, we scrimped and saved as best we could.

One day, for example, I noticed that the local greengrocer was offering large sacks of potatoes at half-price. I invested in one of these, and persuaded him to deliver it. We'd be rehearsing all day, and it seemed to me a good, time-saving investment. On my return home, however, I found that it had already been delivered – and was already half empty. It seems that at first no one had been willing to accept delivery, but when the driver had desperately pushed the sack through the closing door, and shouted out that it had already been paid for, willing hands had dragged it in with such dedication that by lunchtime the kitchen resembled a chip shop. Another factor in my kitchen status was the fact that I had borrowed a set of cutlery from a friend, which was constantly being used by everyone else. Needing to return them eventually, I came up with the idea of identifying my pieces by tying a short thread of coloured wool around each one. This system worked very well, at least until another prominent Theatre Workshop admirer, the Labour M.P. Harold Lever (later Lord Lever), came to dinner, I think as part of a fund-raising initiative for the company. I was quite pleased with the meal I dished up, at least until I noticed a piece of wool unwinding itself from Harold's fork and dangling, like a rogue strand of spaghetti, in the gravy. He fiddled with it for some time, before asking me, in complete bewilderment, 'Jean, does this have some . . . deep significance?'

Another of our guests was the Scottish concert pianist Agnes Walker, the wife of Ewan's publisher, Bill MacLellan. She was a strict vegetarian. We had once stayed with her and it was the first time I had seen anyone steam potatoes for twenty people. It seemed to take for ever. Again, it was understood that I would prepare the visitor's food. She had a concert the next day and it was of the utmost importance, naturally, that she ate a balanced meal – a vegetarian balanced meal – the night before. In our conditions, I had to compromise. I steamed the leeks and cabbage over the boiling water containing the potatoes and carrots, improvised by throwing in a pint of milk, some butter, herbs and seasoning, and mashed half the ingredients. She was kind enough to ask for the recipe.

Word came one day from our friend Tom Driberg M.P. that the great Constant Lambert was expected in Manchester, scheduled to conduct the Hallé Orchestra in a Shostakovich symphony. Since Lambert was another early admirer of Theatre Workshop, Tom wanted to bring him over to visit us, and we arranged an impromptu party. Laban and Lisa joined us at The Parrot House, and we managed to procure some wine. The conversation was lively, with Laban regaling us with hilarious tales of his early days in the theatre and opera, and the marvellous evening culminated, as always, with a sing-song led by Ewan. An eccentric and brilliant figure, Constant Lambert was a musical prodigy who felt that the experience of classical music should not be restricted to the concert halls. In his early days he had therefore put his theories into action by loading an upright piano onto a barrow which with the help of a friend he pushed through the streets of London to the different improvised venues where he would perform. That philosophy was, of course, very close to the agit-prop, no-frills ethos of Theatre Workshop, and we were natural allies.

It was in the same spirit of making do that I returned from a weekend at home with all my old ballet costumes, which I donated to the 'wardrobe department'. Their début took place late one evening, when Howard Goorney and Ewan pranced down the stairs wearing two of these, and performed a very moving pas de deux. Overcome with their success, they broke into a lively rendition of the 'Dance of the Little Swans', until Camel, who had been asleep, complained of the noise.

We were booked at the Library Theatre from 5 to 24 July 1948, but were all wondering what the future held in store thereafter. The answer came at an important company meeting in the Parrot Room. Following an intensive period of training and rehearsal, we would be leaving England for an autumn tour of Czechoslovakia and Sweden. This was hugely exciting, but also presented some new problems of logistics. Despite my personal contribution, for example, we didn't have the material to costume the new production ('The Other Animals'), nor to refurbish 'Don Perlimplín' and 'The Flying Doctor' for the proposed tour. Kristin

Lind was accordingly dispatched to use her considerable charm and turn up with the goods.

There was general excitement as we all began to work towards a common goal. Some had managed to save a few pounds from their jobs and now tried to live off this tiny capital so that they could work for the company full-time. I think one or two lads initially tried to keep up their shift work and presented themselves for training, exhausted and saucer-eyed, in the morning. We quickly put a stop to that. Everyone had to take on extra jobs within the company – sets, props, and costumes were now a priority. For the first time, we had an immediate future planned and could look forward to performing over several weeks, taking our kind of theatre to a much wider audience.

Kristin was extraordinarily persuasive. I only remember one occasion when her charm and Swedish accent didn't work. She had just flown back from Sweden – a flight she had cleverly financed by allowing herself to be adopted as a mascot by a visiting football team who paid for her flight on condition she watched the match. This was typical. I remember once walking with her past Paulden's store in Manchester, when she saw a street-trader's barrow filled with beautiful tomatoes. She was looking extremely glamorous, wearing an apple-green needle-cord trouser suit. She asked how much they were a pound. Too dear. Could he knock the price down? No. Could she buy just one? How much would that be? He chose the largest and weighed it. Hearing the price, she gazed into his eyes meltingly: 'I am so desperately poor: do you think . . . cut it in half?' His language was explicit. I was overcome with embarrassment and disappeared halfway up the street, but Kristin followed unabashed. She had been absolutely honest. She had no money, but she always looked a million dollars.

Our day started with voice classes. Then we all went to Lisa's studio and worked out for two or three hours. (Her students were on holiday.) I remember once we worked so energetically and with such enthusiasm that we all forgot about the time until hunger pains affected our concentration. It was nearly two-thirty and we had been going since eleven without a break. Afternoons were filled with rehearsals, some of which continued into the evening. If one was not needed in rehearsals, there were always other backstage jobs needing attention. As we still had no material for costumes, my first priority was the choreography for the new play, Ewan's 'The Other Animals', in which Mahler's Second Symphony was used as a running theme. This was one of the most ambitious plays we ever attempted to stage, and it was at this time that many of us were introduced to microphone technique, reciting Ewan's verse in unison over the background music. There was also plenty of scope for group action and dance. I prepared my own 'Moon' solo in the basement of Laban's house which could double as a studio on occasion. When it was finished, I showed it to him and he liked it very much and thought it fitted well into the scene. We had both now decided that my immediate future lay with Theatre Workshop because of my increasing work within the company and my relationship with Ewan – though Laban did joke that if he had been twenty years younger, there would never have been a Ewan MacColl! Lisa was, I think, in two minds, since it would leave her in a difficult situation: she had many educational obligations, and would now have to find someone else to assist her. However, none of us wanted to break the strong ties we had already forged and, as Laban said, there was still plenty of work for us to do together whenever I could be spared. Meanwhile, there was still the summer to get through.

'The Other Animals'
courtesy of Theatre Royal Stratford East Archive

Kristin did not fail us, returning with huge bales of material. Unfortunately, it was all satin, with ornate patterns in glass blown onto it, far more appropriate for the London Palladium or the Bluebell girls in Montmartre than any of our productions. It had been decided to keep me on in my extra role of costume designer and sewing lady. My heart sank as I looked at the glass, which was obviously going to make it hard to cut. When I finally plucked up courage to cut into the satin for the Molière costumes, the scissors packed up. I managed to borrow a pair of proper shears from somewhere, and this was a great improvement, but the needles on the decrepit old sewing machine were constantly breaking and holding up work. I had had no previous patterns to go by and no previous experience, so it was with some trepidation that I asked Peter Smallwood to try on the first costume. The general verdict seemed to be that it could have been worse. Peter went round all the grand theatres in Europe playing Valère, the young lover in 'The Flying Doctor', with one trouser leg much narrower that the other. He never complained. Perhaps he was just too tired.

'The Other Animals'
courtesy of Theatre Royal Stratford East Archive

By this time, we were rehearsing and working on all manner of backstage jobs during the day until it was time to go to the Library Theatre for the evening performance (with a matinee on Saturdays). After the show we would stagger back to The Parrot House on public transport. Most of us would prepare a simple supper before carrying on working into the night. I remember giving up sewing at about four o'clock in the morning, as others still hammered away at the sets in the cellars. Two or three hours' sleep was the norm so it wasn't surprising that the company began to come down with a number of minor health problems. Two or three days before we were to set off on our grand European tour, everything was ready. Spirits were high as we packed our personal belongings. And then the bombshell fell. Ewan's cold had turned into pneumonia. His was the central role in 'The Other Animals'. He was on-stage – or, more precisely, suspended in mid-air over the stage – throughout the play. He had no understudy.

But there was nothing else for it: he had to travel with us, in our third-class railway compartment, for two days across Europe, at the outset of a five-week tour of twenty different towns. I remember that Camel and his sister, among others, shared our compartment. We lay our suitcases in the centre of the carriage so we could lie across them rather like sardines. Camel's nickname was well chosen: the Bury family are tall, and their legs seemed to get in everybody's way. Not that this worried Ewan too much – for the first twenty-four hours he was delirious with fever.

Chapter Fifteen

Given a Great Welcome, Despite Recent Horrors

Czechoslovakia, 1948

By the time our train rattled into the Czechoslovakian town of Cheb, a small distance from the German border, Ewan had made a remarkable recovery, and one doubtless assisted by the excitement generated by our arrival. Ours was the first company from the West to tour Czechoslovakia since before the war, and we were given a very warm reception – presented with flowers and subjected to lengthy speeches of welcome. We were also introduced to our two interpreters – Zoe, and Vladimir – as well as our coach-driver, Carl, who faithfully conducted us through our five-week tour of twenty towns.

Our first stop was Karlovy Vary (formerly Karlsbad), a magnificent spa-town that in its prime had once catered to the rich and famous (including Edward VII), and in one of whose luxurious hotels we were now invited to an official meal with the local dignitaries. After the stresses of our journey, I was suffering from a crashing headache, and therefore declined the meal, and instead sat outside on the verandah – where I was later asked if I fancied anything lighter than the main meal being served inside. I replied that I would rather like an omelette, which in due course came. I didn't realise at the time that there was a local shortage of fresh eggs; indeed, we none of us quite realised how very difficult it was for the Czechs to offer us such lavish hospitality, after the appalling circumstances of the war.

Given a Great Welcome, Despite Recent Horrors

After such a great welcome to their country, we continued on our way, and arrived in Prague where, once again, our hotel treated us to much more comfort than we had been used to for the week of our run there. I remember eating my breakfast, sitting on a small balcony overlooking that glorious city, and seeing the countryside in the distance. When I told Zoe that I thought her capital was very beautiful, her eyes lit up and she answered mistily, 'Oh, I think Manchester must be even more beautiful!' It seemed unkind – or perhaps in retrospect naïve – to disillusion her. Of our interpreters, if Zoe was the wide-eyed dreamer, Vladimir was the solemn cynic. Walking with him to the State Opera House, on my way to take a work-out in one of the studios there, we were almost mown down by a motorist coming to a sudden halt – though not quite suddenly enough, since the car mounted the pavement and missed us by inches. Vladimir shrugged wearily. 'Before the war,' he announced (with what authority I do not know), 'our drivers drove on the left side. Then came the Germans, and overnight we have to drive on the right-hand side. Now, well . . . now we drive on both sides.'

Our performances were received rapturously, and one evening we counted more than twenty-five curtain-calls. Joan and Ewan were in great demand for interviews as the founders of Theatre Workshop. In what little spare time we had, we explored the city and the cathedral. On our first Sunday evening, a few of us went to a park with fairy lights twinkling amid the trees, where we enjoyed listening to group of local folk musicians. At about one in the morning, after the last tram seemed to have left, we followed a guitarist, singing as we went, back through the streets to our hotel. Do I imagine, or was it the novelist Graham Greene I remember meeting one evening in an appropriately dimly lit bar?

Our evening meal was always accompanied by a single bottle of Pilsen beer for each of us. As I had not acquired the taste for beer, preferring water, I found myself very popular with the chaps, who took it in turns to sit next to me. This all changed later on when I visited the brewery at Plzen (Pilsen). The spectacle of those huge underground vats, the gutters full of foaming froth, and the workers carrying large jugs of free beer and rye bread across the yards at lunchtime, all whetted my appetite – as did the temperature, which was in the eighties as we entered the richly carved and decorated hall set aside for visitors. This time I fell on my ice-cold lager as gratefully as the others. One sip and I vowed never to share another bottle of this nectar again! Another of the visits arranged by our hosts was one to the Bata Shoe Company, interesting mainly because of an insight into the mind of a pre-war owner of the factory it afforded. We saw a small fleet of run-about cars, looking rather like miniature land-rovers, which this man had apparently introduced in order to save time in the vast factory grounds; to save still further time, he had had the doors on these vehicles removed. It could all have been a good capitalist story, but since the company had recently been nationalised by the Communist government, I wonder how long these innovations were continued.

On another visit, we went to see a factory that made hats for the British firm of Dunn's. On leaving, we were all given the opportunity of choosing a hat. I think we all felt rather embarrassed at so much generosity, surrounded as we were by pricey velours of all kinds. We opted for berets. The last factory we visited produced chocolates, which reminded me of my time with Laban at the Mars factory in Slough a few years before. By an extraordinary coincidence, I recognised one of the workers in the kitchen, who was wrapping chocolates by hand. She was a dwarf, now in her mid-forties, and the last time I had seen her was in a circus in England before the war. Unfortunately, although she spoke good English, we only had a short time to speak.

Although many goods (including eggs, coffee, and milk) were in short supply, the Czechs continued to overwhelm us with their hospitality. Each performance on our tour was preceded by welcoming speeches of friendship and a banquet – for that is indeed what these meals were. Audiences were even made to wait until we had dined; they did so uncomplainingly. Replete, we would then be driven by Carl to the theatre, to find our dressing rooms and try to make up for lost time. Afterwards, the overwhelming applause dying away, we would return to the never less than excellent hotel accommodation. On one occasion, Ewan and I were given a truly magnificent suite. The doors leading from

Given a Great Welcome, Despite Recent Horrors

the hotel corridor were oak, inlaid with scarlet leather embossed with brass studs. They led into a vestibule, with a bathroom on one side and wardrobe space on the other. Similar double doors led into huge bedroom with a large balcony overlooking the town square. We were told that Field Marshal Goering had once commandeered this particular suite for himself. It was all a far cry from The Parrot House.

When we joined the company in the dining room downstairs, we were taken aback to see a door suddenly swing open to reveal eight immaculately attired waiters bursting through with silver salvers held high over their left shoulders . . . a performance any choreographer would have appreciated. The timing, precision, and sang-froid were all spot on, like a scene from some American musical. One of the courses was universally popular: sausages and mash, as we had never tasted it before, creamed potatoes that simply melted in the mouth. We were so impressed, we gave the staff a spontaneous round of applause. The final course brought the corps of waiters pirouetting back with the most exotic cream cakes. David Scase, a founder member of the company, was sitting near the door and caught a glimpse of these delights before the rest of us, and whispered across, 'Lamp the confectionery!'.

Despite such lavish scenes of unfailing generosity, there were of course constant reminders of the terrible war the Czechs had ensured. One in particular sticks in my mind. During our stay in Prague, we were approached by a Hungarian doctor then working there, who politely asked whether a girl in the company would mind not plaiting her fair hair round her head in that particular style: apparently it reminded everyone of the German women who had come with the occupying forces. He explained that, immediately after the war, he had been in charge of a temporary medical base, treating newly freed prisoners from the camps as they tried to make their way home. Too long without food, thousands of them could no longer keep any nourishment down and passed by in a state of near-starvation, only to die on the road in the next day or two. Liberation had come too late for them. Nor was it rare among our generous hosts to encounter individuals with a camp number tattooed on their arm. After such horrors, it is perhaps unsurprising that this was a period of great hope, and widespread belief – at least among the Communists – in the new and prosperous Czechoslovakia they could build. 'Peace and Friendship' was the ubiquitous slogan, which isn't a bad one as slogans go, and few could have anticipated the later Soviet invasion.

We often travelled long distances by coach and one of the features of the countryside I noticed at that time was the enormous amount of rusted railway rolling-stock lying idle in the middle of nowhere, the line overgrown and half hidden from the road. It was at the end of one such journey that we had our only embarrassing moment of the tour. Having travelled for most of the day with only a small packed lunch, we were looking forward to the usual gargantuan spread – one quickly becomes conditioned! – and we were not disappointed. After all the bouquets, and the toasts, and the speeches of welcome, we were all invited to sit down and enjoy a meal specially prepared in our honour. This was to be a particular treat – the national dish of Czechoslovakia, dumplings and venison. But the latter, to our simple palates, was rather high; in fact, to be honest, very high. And the best that could be said of the dumplings was that they were . . . heavy. So despite our hunger, none of us – with the honourable exception of that later stalwart of TV sitcom George A. Cooper, who tucked in heartily – could bring themselves to force the food down. After an uncomfortable few minutes, Joan graciously lied through her teeth by saying that we had already eaten, and apologised on behalf of us all. We saw the food being returned to the kitchen and felt unhappy for our hosts – but not as unhappy as some of the lads in the company, for whom Joan's white lie meant a long wait until the next morning's breakfast for any more sustenance.

Following our performance at Brno, the next venue on our itinerary, I met up with the ballet-master I had previously seen in Copenhagen, who took me to see his state-run ballet school. From there we travelled to Bratislava, some twenty miles across the border from Vienna, and the birthplace of Laban. It was there that I saw my first ever opera. As honoured guests, we were ushered to the Royal Box. I can't pretend to have been particularly impressed.

Given a Great Welcome, Despite Recent Horrors

Laban had related some of the horrors of opera in his young days, and I was able to report back that things hadn't changed much since his day. As far as I could see, ladies with long tresses were dashing about the stage in their nightgowns, crying out loudly and passionately in a state of the utmost panic as simulated flames burnt their off-stage houses, while rape and pillage went on in the background. And in the middle of this bedlam, a young actor dressed in Shakespearean costume and sporting a blond page-boy wig, sidled to the front of the stage. Stroking his hair, after precisely achieving the correct profile for us to catch, he announced, just loud enough for us to hear over the orchestra, 'Good afternoon. How do you do. I am very well, thank you.' After which he disappeared into the pandemonium going on behind him. The evening did not significantly improve, since after returning to our hotel that night, armed militia-men burst into our bedrooms asking for passports, apparently investigating a smuggling racket around the nearby border.

Towards the end of our eventually extended tour, we were given a three-day break at a youth hostel high up in the Tatra Mountains. By now our repertoire included a few Czech folk songs, including one tune we all knew as 'You can't put your muck in our dustbin' (a rough transliteration of its Czech original). We sang in the coach, foraged for ripe berries after picnicking under a hot sun and blue skies, and eventually arrived, tired and relaxed in the early evening. A few locals had gathered at the sight of our coach going up to the hostel beyond the village. From its open windows, overlooking the forests, we could hear trees being felled. A few of us took a short walk during that evening, and met up with the local woodsmen, all of whom were very friendly. They probably looked older than they were – their skin was wrinkled and weather-beaten to a deep tan, and when they smiled, they showed an extraordinary amount of silver. Now without an interpreter, we managed to explain that we were actors from England and had come to the Tatras for a short break. The upshot was that they invited us to a party in the village hall the following night.

We duly arrived in our party gear and were greeted by our new friends, who were also spruced up and carrying a number of musical instruments. The only drink I remember on the trestle table was something called 'slivovitz' – made from 'wood alcohol', someone told me later, but which to my taste was very raw and unpleasant, and I naively wondered if it might have been home-brewed. The accordionist struck up a tune, and the woodsmen made a beeline for the girls. The first surprise of the evening, at least to this particular choreographer, was that they really could dance! They stamped and they twirled and they jumped, swinging their partners and putting our own company quite to shame. In the breaks between songs, they would knock back the slivovitz, encouraging our men to drink with them. David Scase showed willing but soon sank to the floor, where he remained for the rest of the evening. Our hosts were by now warming up, aided by their favourite tipple. Not one of them appeared to be drunk, and not one of them stopped dancing. As one girl after another – including yours truly – laughingly refused the next dance in order to get her breath back, they would ask another with more stamina, or else gave dazzling solo performances of their own.

The final performance of our Czechoslovakian tour took place in the mining town of Ostrava, after which the company attended a packed question-and-answer session. This time, however, the questions were not about theatre but about the atom bomb, on safe-guarding 'Peace for future generations', and the potential dangers of a divided Germany. Amidst much hand-shaking, we left the hall to board our coach waiting to take us to the station. Carl was wearing his best suit and looking downcast. As we boarded the packed train, Zoe cried, and expressed the hope to see us in Manchester one day. We travelled through the long night, via East Berlin to the Polish port of Szczecin (formerly the German port of Stettin) at the mouth of the Oder. The port was an amazing sight, a graveyard of stricken ships, their skeletal frames and super-structures like rigid angular arms, reaching pathetically upwards to a darkly threatening sky. Two years after the end of the war, one can only guess at the horrors endured here. From this bleak spot, we embarked on a ferry across the Baltic to Trelleborg in the far south of Sweden.

Given a Great Welcome, Despite Recent Horrors

Most of the company found a place to catch up on some much-needed sleep once they were aboard, including Howard Goorney, who described the crossing in his memoirs as 'a pleasant ferry journey'. Well, they do say ignorance is bliss. Enjoying boats, I sat alone on the deck looking across the water at the receding port, its spectral shapes silhouetted against the evening sky. Lulled by the engines and half asleep, it took me some time to realise that there was a large object bobbing about in the sea close to the boat. A recognizable shape. I came to, quite suddenly, with the appalled realization that this spherical piece of flotsam, with its jutting metal fingers, was a mine! I watched, mesmerised, my heart in my throat, as it eventually bobbed gently past the side of the boat. Needless to say, the rest of my time was spent rather urgently scanning the darkening waters, and then crossing my fingers in the darkness.

Chapter Sixteen

The War Had Not Touched Sweden

Sweden, 1948

Once safely disembarked at Trelleborg, we took another train and continued travelling through the second night to Norrköping. The Swedes' neutrality in the war showed in their up-to-date and extremely comfortable railway carriages – no rusting Czech rolling-stock or broken-down Polish trains here. Even so, it would have been more comfortable for me had not Ewan and David Scase fallen asleep, lying full-length on both of the facing benches of our compartment. At least I didn't have to worry about the danger of passing mines as I gazed out of the window.

Our welcoming dinner in Sweden was very different from those we had so recently experienced in Czechoslovakia. It had been organised by a group of businessmen, apparently at a loss to understand why we had toured a 'Communist state'. They sat on either side of us around the table, one businessman to one company member, and the evening turned out to be a rather stiff and formal affair. No wives or other Swedish females had been invited – certainly, no one felt like singing. Halfway through the dinner, someone came round collecting the dues from our hosts (the manager or treasurer of their society, I assume), and there was an embarrassing moment when a certain Count H— either couldn't or wouldn't pay up. It was all in rather bad taste, as far as I was concerned. When the coffee arrived, we were asked by the waiters what we would like to drink. The gentleman on my left turned to me and translated the message adding, 'But of course, you don't drink.' I was most put out. I was a very moderate drinker, but I was not going to be told what I should or should not drink. 'Yes, a brandy, please,' I said to the waiter, with a beaming smile.

In the days to come, the acting and dancing fraternity received us rather more warmly, and we made a number of good friends. Sweden, at that time, however, was a disappointment to me. My initial impression was of a nation obsessed with sex and cleanliness. One of their greatest achievements was apparently to provide many different and novel ways of flushing a lavatory, while the young women, all comfortably off, who chatted up our men, appeared extremely repressed. Perhaps it had something to do with their treatment by the Swedish male. (Of course, things have changed since 1948.)

Word came through one Sunday morning that Baron Mannerheim wanted Ewan to visit him urgently. He returned later that evening with a bizarre account of their meeting. He had had a very warm reception, he said, and had been shown round a vast mansion. On reaching the first floor, he was led to a door. The door had a newly engraved plaque with the name 'Ewan MacColl'. This was the Baron's way of saying that he wanted him to stay on as a writer in residence. The door opened into a study-bedroom, furnished with a substantial desk, supplied with all the writing materials one could imagine, and overlooking a large lake. The Baron explained that a well-known writer had lived here for some time. When Ewan asked what had become of him, the Baron gave an offhand shrug and explained that he had drowned himself in the lake. Ewan was always a great spinner of yarns, but even still . . .

While Ewan was visiting – and ultimately fleeing – the Baron, I was having an adventure of my own. I had taken a bus into Norrköping from the suburbs where we had our digs, and gone to see The Red Shoes, the Powell and Pressburger ballet-film with Moira Shearer playing the lead. It was dusk when I came out of the cinema, and I thought it sensible to return directly home. I thought I remembered the number of the bus, but an attempt to confirm this at the bus stop with some young locals merely resulted in their giggling, so I climbed aboard and hoped for the best. Vainly peering out into the darkness for some familiar landmark, I watched everybody leave the bus till it eventually came to its destination. The conductor looked at me with some surprise, motioning to me that he and his driver were about to start the journey back. Not seeing any lights anywhere I decided to buy a return ticket and see if I could recognise any bus stop on the way back. By this time it was completely dark, and I took a chance and got off midway back to the town.

The fading lights from the bus briefly illuminated a group of youths, some on bicycles and all very interested in my appearance. When I set off along the deserted country road, I was none too happy to hear them all following me. Not usually of a nervous disposition, I felt at a distinct disadvantage in not knowing the language or where I was. Almost before I knew it, though, I came across four small terraced houses set back from the road, with little garden paths leading to the front doors, and one of those houses had a light in the front window. Without a moment's hesitation I walked to the front door and rang the bell. Nobody came so I rang again. I could hear a murmur of voices and the door was at last opened by a middle-aged man. I explained that I was English and lost. He understood what I said and invited me in, noticing that the boys had gathered by the gate. Once inside the house, I was introduced to his wife. By this time, though, I had completely forgotten the address of where I was staying. So I asked them if they could ring Baron Mannerheim. This caused a bit of a stir, and I had to repeat that prestigious name a couple of times. My kind rescuer found the Baron's number in the book, made the phone call, and explained that I was the wife of his visitor, a Mr Ewan MacColl. The Baron was able to tell us the correct address, which turned out to be a twenty-minute walk away. I thanked the couple for their hospitality, and the man insisted on escorting me to the door.

It is strange to think that the only time in all my travels that I had ever felt so nervous was in bland, neutral Sweden. Constantly travelling on our Swedish tour as we were, there was little time to select our postcards carefully. We tended to pick half a dozen at random, before jumping on the next train. The cards usually pictured large, mansion-type buildings, which we fondly imagined to be museums or palaces. Towards the end of the tour, however, someone explained to us that most of these buildings were actually mental asylums.

Our run at Norrköping was overwhelmingly successful – so successful, in fact, that Kristin, who was directly responsible for this part of the tour, was able to book the Royal Opera House in Stockholm for a special performance. This was a first for all foreign companies, and a most prestigious affair. The Swedish and Belgian royal families were present, as well as the Swedish Prime Minister and leading artists of stage and screen. With only twenty-four hours notice, the entire theatre was sold out. It seemed that everyone wanted to see Joan's production of Ewan's play 'The Other Animals', performed by the 'incomparable Theatre Workshop players'. Although our tour had by now lasted many weeks, and we were all beginning to need a break, we were determined to give a memorable performance.

'The Other Animals' was a remarkable and highly complex play. With its unique blend of dance, song, mime, acting, Expressionist staging, and superb lighting, and heightened by Mahler's glorious music, the production was, to my mind, the perfect synthesis and masterpiece of Theatre Workshop's talents. Artistically, we aspired to perfection, and while, of course, we never achieved that, there were occasional moments when it felt as though we had. In the sixty years since then, I have seen many, many plays, but not even the best of those productions has inspired me as much as 'The Other Animals'. That the opportunity to choreograph something this special came so early in my theatrical career was a special privilege – though of course in hindsight and with more experience I would, perhaps, have altered a few things. Nevertheless, it stood up well, and Laban himself was very pleased with my own dance performance as the Moon. The women in the play were conceived as figments of the fevered and tortured imagination of the main character, Hanau, a political prisoner, played by Ewan. Suspended in an elliptical cage in mid-air – which apart from the interval, he could not leave until the final curtain-call – his character drifted in and out of delirium, conversing with his alter ego, played by David Scase.

I had had no part in designing my 'Moon' costume. The costume department had always managed to dress poor and needy characters, like the seedy Lomov in Chekhov's Proposal, but by the time I arrived on the scene they were hard put to find sumptuous-looking material for Shakespeare's kings and queens, or in fact any other prosperous character of 'substance'. Kristin's brilliantly scavenged glass-blown satins had, at least at first, depressed me, but beggars can't be choosers, and we gratefully acknowledged all our benefactors in the programme notes. In the event, though, the designs worked rather well. It was clear to me from the start that the actresses needed to be able to move well and freely, and so a long, simple, flowing 'Princess'-style was required in the costumes. By a happy accident, the sheer weight of the satin-and-glass fabric enhanced the wearers' dance movements, while the lighting gave a subtle glow to the sheen of the material, to quite magical effect. I don't actually remember finishing the sewing on these particular costumes – though Freud would probably think I had repressed the trauma of their production deep into my subconscious. I think the real answer is rather more mundane: I was much more likely to have been urgently called away to get on with the choreography!

Apart from playing the Moon in 'The Other Animals' (personifying Hanau's dream of unobtainable womanhood, chaste virginity, and purity), I also played the part of an old lady suffering from 'euphoria', in a home for the mentally disturbed. (Ewan had clearly been taking notes during his incarceration in Birmingham.) I had researched the part quite thoroughly since at the time of rehearsals I frequently accompanied Lisa on her visits to her mother, then in a convalescent home. Although, as far as I knew, no one there was suffering from this particular mental illness, these very old patients had some marvellous mannerisms which helped me tremendously in preparing the role in Ewan's play. I think all the actors playing mentally disturbed characters loved exploring their roles, Howard Goorney in particular being quite brilliant as a catatonic patient, remaining quite still for hours on end. As for me, I blacked out my teeth and greyed my hair, adopted some of the tics and mannerisms I had observed, and retreated into a private world that encouraged me to smile constantly.

My parents had attended the Manchester première of 'The Other Animals', the first time that they had ever seen me in an acting role. I'm not sure my poor mother ever got over the disappointment of seeing her only daughter's début with missing teeth, hag-ridden, and completely out of her mind. She preferred the Moon's dance. My father was, as always, quietly supportive. Whether it was Laban's work or Theatre Workshop's productions, he had a keen awareness of what we were trying to do, and I always found his acute observations very helpful.

John Bury's lighting was superb, and throughout the Moon sequence I don't remember a single murmur from any of the audiences who witnessed it, rapt as they were in the atmosphere. That silence was a great help to me, giving a sense of infinite space and timelessness to the dance movement. Even such ethereal presences as Ewan's Hanau imagined in his fevered imagination, however, required practical costumes to achieve their effect, and a prosaic and heated debate about seams, hems, zips, and press-studs constantly haunted the production. Joan had tried everything – except, of course, making the garment herself. We had gone through leotards and tights and skin-tight dresses, with various arrangements of slits and veiling. It seemed to me that wherever we played, I had to acquaint myself with a different costume. I certainly remember Joan's voice crying out from the back of the auditorium during a run-through on our Czechoslovakian tour, 'That bloody costume's ruining her performance. You can see the seams. I can see where the sleeve ends and her hand begins.' On that occasion I even tried using make-up to hide the join, but nothing worked. I knew what effect Joan was after, though: the impossible.

And so now here we were, arriving at the Royal Opera House in Stockholm in mid-afternoon, for yet another performance of 'The Other Animals', and once again the general view (i.e. Joan's) was that the Moon's costume was 'totally wrong'. It therefore seemed to us all a good omen when, trooping backstage, we came across a veritable army of dressers, cutters, and seamstresses. These conditions were a far cry from the basement of The Parrot House back home, and Joan wasn't going to let the opportunity go by –

especially when she saw a bolt of steel-blue metallic material appear from somewhere. Seizing the initiative, Joan conveyed to these astonished and unsuspecting ladies that I had to wear a costume, made from that material, for my performance that evening. She may even have produced a rough sketch of what was wanted. Then, after a pantomime of gestures by which she gave them to understand that all seams and zips on the costume were forbidden, she smiled sweetly. And left.

There I stood, all but naked, as samples of this marvellous material were draped over me, first one way then the other. Gradually faces began to grow longer, and more dismissively pessimistic. I sighed in sympathy – there was no need to speak the language to understand the mood. No one from the company came near me. I hadn't even yet seen my dressing room, let alone unpacked my make-up or sorted out my other costume as the mad Old Lady (though I was beginning to feel I could play that role perfectly). By now, most people would be ironing their costumes, or doing warm-up exercises, I thought; getting the feel of the stage; walking through the acting, lighting, and music cues. Talking of which, I felt I should really go through my dance solo – but I could hardly leave with what still amounted to barely a loincloth to hide my modesty. It was very important to get the following spot just right, I explained to these ladies, and the stage really had seemed enormous; I really needed some time on it – not to mention the essential need to limber up in advance of performance . . . But no, the ladies would not hear of it.

As they had elsewhere argued in other languages, so the same familiar and interminable discussions went on, and over the very same subject. It seemed to me as I stood there, that one or two ladies left to do other work, to be replaced by new people being called in. I began to get the distinct impression that I was swiftly becoming a lost cause. The clock was now on the hour call – count-down to curtain-up! My agitation was obvious to all. One motherly type patted my arm reassuringly, and sighed, as she took the momentous decision to make the first incision into the material. Each new piece was now put against me, and moulded to my body. Raw edges were treated with glue and left unsewn.

The half-hour call came and went – I suppose it must have, though I never heard it. Meanwhile, though, despite Joan's formidable instructions, it was actually impossible not to use the odd stitch; and before these essential stitches were made, the material was carefully pressed before and after the hand sewing. It was a very slow and a very laborious process. Somebody opened the door and I heard music. – My God! The play had already begun, and here was I, still in a state of nudity. I told them that this time, I really had to go. A few larger pieces were now assigned to strategic points of my anatomy, and tentatively attached with fine thread-like pins. I fled.

But where on earth was the stage? I could hear the play well enough from the Tannoy system, and immediately realised that my cue was coming up. But as I dashed from one identical corridor to another, there wasn't a single soul around to direct me. Then, suddenly, an enormous vacant area opened up in front of me. There were long gaps in the floor, several inches wide, carrying the sound up to me. Peering through one of these gaps, I was amazed to see David far, far below me . . . and quite obviously on stage. Somehow I had arrived in the flies!

I suddenly realised that I should have paid more attention to the Marx Brothers films Ewan had taken me to see – that would have been the easiest way, descending swiftly on-stage by clinging to a curtain. But from where I was standing, high above, David looked like an ant – as he now exited beyond my line of vision. Nearing panic, now, I looked around for a staircase and suddenly came across a lift. I had missed it earlier because the door looked identical to all the dressing-room doors. I pushed a button at random and glided silently down. When it stopped, I got out only to find out that I was still too high for the stage. In again, and down again, another couple of floors.

Breathless, I flew across the back-stage void to where Chuck Fowler was casually waiting in the wings, the apparatus of the Moon's 'aura' in his hands. This was an enormous piece of lightweight metal, circular in shape and attached to my neck by the finest of wires, four in all, which were still strong enough to take the metal's weight. Chuck's job was to attach the wires round my neck in the semi-darkness and undo them when I came off-stage for a quick change. The aura was a very impressive piece of kit. At the end of my dance, when I started to spin, its weight made it precede my body and take me round with it, though I had to be careful not to let the momentum carry me away. It was very easy to lose control. However, the illusion it created was marvellous, as the silver glowed in the spot-light and the wires remained invisible. On this occasion, though, probably because I arrived in a state of barely controlled panic at the very last moment, Chuck tied a slip knot by mistake.

I climbed into the archway at the top of the ramp and started my descent just as the music and lighting came up. The 'tranquil' Moon began her journey across the heavens. My worries over my new costume's ability to stay with me through the dance had now been superseded by my frantic efforts to find the stage and to arrive on time. All was well. The stage was huge and had the most beautifully smooth wooden floor for my bare feet. The spot followed accurately and all problems were forgotten. I danced to the music and, finally began to spin, slowly at first, and then gathering momentum. As always, the aura increased the speed and I had to hold back slightly as I moved across stage to go up the ramp, still spinning. It was then that I felt the wires tightening around my neck. As I continued to turn, so they got tighter and tighter . . . Spinning off-stage, my face now more like a fiery sunset than a pale moon, I desperately pointed out the slip knot to Chuck, who with great difficulty at last managed to loosen the wires which were now almost embedded in my neck.

The 'Euphoric Old Lady' had to force a smile that evening, and her neck showed the distinct marks of a ligature. But the show went very well. In fact, we received a standing ovation, receiving in this beautiful theatre the recognition which had long been denied us in our own country. It was heady stuff. Howard Goorney, who had himself been part of the cast, recorded some of the adulatory reviews in his Theatre Workshop Story, Ewan being described as 'a brilliant new star in the dramatic firmament', and Joan's work compared to that of Reinhardt and Piscator. My work was also singled out for praise.

Birgit Cullberg, Sweden's foremost choreographer and dancer, wanted to interview me for an article due to appear in the next morning's paper. I had read all about her work while still at school, and I knew that she had once had links with Dartington Hall and the Ballet Jooss. We had also met briefly in Copenhagen when her group had won the competition. I was surprised and flattered that she wanted to interview me. She was full of praise for the performance that evening, and especially appreciative of the movement skills of the actors. A choreographer who works only with trained dancers can generally expect recognition from the press, since his or her dance composition is the central premise of the spectacle. But the job a choreographer does with actors, within a theatrical production, and often without a predominantly musical context, is far less obvious – indeed, is really only successful when the work is unobtrusive, discreetly contributing to the production as a whole (though in this play there were opportunities also for dance). Birgit recognised this truth. Having seen some of our productions in London, she was already a great fan. She wrote as follows:

'It is not dance, it is movement,' says the choreographer of Theatre Workshop, who is of course a very important person in this artistic collective. Her name is Jean Newlove, and she looks like a quiet and nice bourgeois girl but has tremendous energy to train and keep this group together. Where in Sweden have we a group of actors that can use their bodies and voices on the stage? At least to my knowledge, I have never seen a theatre here where movement itself takes the place of props and scenery. The movement can describe a gun-fight, the storm, the sea, the tension between characters, everything, in combination with sound and light. The quickness and suppleness that the actors possess are not restricted to their well-trained bodies – but derive also from their dynamic movement technique. And it's in this that the greatness of the Theatre Workshop choreography lies. It is the system of Rudolf Laban. He went back to the natural movement of mankind, but developed it, and found its quality and its dynamics. Press, glide, float, flick, etc. – an endless scale of expressions that is technically trained. It was such a revelation to see the Theatre Workshop actors because they feel the floor under their feet. They did not use one single muscle in vain and could therefore invest tremendous strength when necessary. To have the body under control also helps the mind to concentrate. It must be that in Theatre Workshop there exists a perfect co-operation between the producer and choreographer: in this collective group, it is impossible to say where the work of one ends and that of the other begins. The work of the choreographer is not isolated, but forms an important part of the rhythmic expressiveness in the production as a whole.'

'Revolution at the Opera House!' read the headline in the Svenska Dagbladett, writing that 'The storm of applause for Theatre Workshop yesterday was fully justified. It was an exciting experience. It is not very often that we see such high standards in Sweden . . .'

The cast party was in full swing when we finally arrived at the restaurant. Ewan was singing, and everybody joined in the choruses. We now had quite a few Czech and Swedish songs in our repertoire. I recognised actors from the theatres in Norrköping and Linköping, where we had played to full houses and where I had given movement classes to the resident companies. I was also amazed to see in the group a young English girl, now a chiropodist, whom, I had last met on a P.E. course at South Wigston in our A.T.S. days. It also turned out that the brother of one of the Swedish journalists was a well-known modern dancer with Cullberg's ballet company, whom I had seen brilliantly dance the role of Herod in 'Salomé'.

Gradually, members of the party drifted away, exhaustion finally catching up with them. We were on the road again tomorrow – or rather, later that morning – and the technical crew had to load up. But that term was something of a euphemism, since most of Theatre Workshop's so-called 'technical crew' were also members of the cast. So it was very late indeed when Ewan and I waved our final goodbyes from a taxi, which then took us to the outskirts of Stockholm where we had our digs. This particular suburb was in the process of development, which meant that there were no roads as such, only muddy tracks, scattered with builders' rubble and the occasional huge pot-hole filled with water. These led to a depressing network of identical, grey prison-like blocks several storeys high and in various stages of completion. We squelched across this no-man's land towards the few completed blocks. Then we looked at each other. It was immediately obvious that neither of us could remember the number of our address. Was it Block 16, Flat 25, Floor 6? Or, perhaps, Block 25, Flat 16, Floor 4? The permutations seemed endless. There was only the odd working light outside each of the finished buildings, and a short-time switch inside. We had no torch. Attempting to reconstruct our departure that morning, we agreed that it must be a sixth-floor flat, and possibly Number 25. But which Building?

We tried the nearest block, climbed the stairs (there were no lifts), but the key didn't fit the lock. Down the steps we went, and out into the cold night air – just as the heavens opened. We ran to the second block. No luck. Outside once more, we silently made our precarious way through a torrential downpour which threatened to turn the entire site into one huge muddy lake. Halfway to the third block, all the lights abruptly went off. We couldn't see a thing. I felt hysteria threaten to get the better of me, but controlled the temptation to give way to mirth since Ewan did not find the situation remotely funny. We scaled the staircase of the next monstrosity in total darkness, and much to our amazement . . . the door opened. We fell in gratefully.

The last leg of our tour took in Gävle, Linköping, and the university town of Uppsala, among other venues, and we were shown over the wonderfully restored eighteenth-century theatre at the royal palace of Drottningholm, with its tiny dressing rooms, candles for lighting – and the metal rollers used to great effect to simulate the sound of thunder. I just wished – and still wish – we could have performed a commedia dell'arte play there.

We returned home by boat in November, democratically sharing the boat with the King and Queen of Sweden, and a group of Irish labourers, who had earned a considerable amount of money and couldn't wait to get home to spend it. By evening, they were all well and truly drunk. One of their number had bought twenty wristwatches, 'all guaranteed waterproof,' as he loudly and repeatedly boasted to anyone who would listen. I watched, fascinated, as he proceeded to prove this assertion by dropping each one by its strap into a full pint of beer. There were few other distractions for me, since this crossing was even worse than the one he had endured on the way back from Denmark the previous year, and most of the other passengers had disappeared to suffer privately down below. With my proven sea-legs, I sat up through the night, watching the heavy seas swell and rock our boat, and by morning, as we neared harbour, the worst seemed to be over.

I noticed quite a few injuries among the first-class passengers from my observation post that morning – someone had a broken leg, another a broken arm, and there were a handful of bandaged heads. I also saw the Irishman violently shaking a wristwatch, then holding it forlornly against his ear, before retrieving another – then another – then another – from an apparently inexhaustible stock.

Chapter Seventeen

Back to Poverty: From Parrot House to Dilapidated Schloss

1948–1949

Returning to home shores from what can only be described as our triumphant tour of Czechoslovakia and Sweden in the autumn of 1948, we were all rather disappointed to be met by the same total indifference that had accompanied our departure. Despite the profile we had established abroad, the battle at home for official recognition – and financial support – had to go on. The home we found ourselves inhabiting that cold winter of 1948–9 was much worse than the Parrot House which aspired to a certain middle-class ambience. Dilapidated, old, and unloved, the house was unearthed by Gerry Raffles on Bury Old Road, North Manchester. We rented it from a certain Dr Schlossberg – and therefore of course immediately nicknamed it 'The Schloss'.

There was a large back garden, including a couple of old stables where we were able to stow all our gear. The kitchen had a walk-in larder where the more trusting of us left our few groceries. I made no attempt to draw up a cleaning rota, restricting my domestic urges to the large bed-sitting room I shared with Ewan and to keeping my few kitchen utensils spotless. Someone must have tended the boiler because I do remember the water was always very hot. A rehearsal room was rented from a local Polish club, where classes in movement, voice, and Stanislavsky were held each morning; in the afternoons, rehearsals for 'Twelfth Night' were in full swing. Howard Goorney was selected to approach all the schools within a thirty-mile radius, and generally had a good response; the company enjoyed playing Shakespeare to the schools, since in addition to a fee, they were also given a substantial school lunch, which they greatly appreciated.

It seems that the draughty old Schloss had once been a branch office of the Inland Revenue – or so Ewan discovered one morning. Sleeping in after a long night's writing, and with the rest of the company busy rehearsing at the nearby studio, he was awoken by a tentative tap on the door to our first-floor room, followed by the appearance of a bewildered stranger apparently expecting to settle his tax bill. Startled by this apparition, Ewan jumped up stark naked from his bed, thrust a pointing finger towards the window and shouted 'Begone, varlet!' in his best Shakespearean manner. The poor man was so terrified he flew down the stairs, out of the front door, and continued running all the way down the drive into the road until out of sight. In retrospect, since the Schloss had been left unoccupied for years, the money the hapless stranger was trying to pay might have subsidised Theatre Workshop productions for years to come!

Since everyone else was engaged with 'Twelfth Night' rehearsals, I took myself off on a short trip to London. I had read as a girl about Kurt Jooss, and his Ballet Jooss company, in which the German choreographer Sigurd Leeder had been a partner. They had come to Dartington together in 1934, but Sigurd was now running his own classes in St John's Wood in London. I wanted to observe how he worked and catch a taste of the Jooss Ballet's method. Knowing my background, and my friendship with Laban, he gave me a warm welcome, always addressing me as 'luv from Manchester'. I worked with Sigurd Leeder's class for the best part of a week, and was fascinated to see him recreate dances from the various Jooss ballets he had worked on with a wide variety of students – some of them professional dancers and choreographers, others teachers of modern dance.

On my return to the Schloss, I discovered that Joan and Ewan's divorce had finally come through. During my early years with the company, no one – not even Joan or Ewan themselves – had mentioned to me that they had once been married (at a youthful nineteen years). Had I known at the time, I suppose, it is possible I might have immediately fled the scene – though by the time I arrived it was completely obvious to everyone that Joan and Gerry were a couple, and that her relationship with Ewan was now strictly a professional one between close friends. The only reason the official divorce had taken so long was – as always – the sheer cost of the procedure at a time when money was short, and we were all struggling to keep the theatre afloat. Ewan and I were eventually married at a Manchester Registry Office on 13 April 1949. Lisa and Laban signed as witnesses, and Lisa provided a special lunch afterwards. My parents were very disappointed that I didn't have the full church wedding and celebration but this was of course impossible given Ewan's status as a divorcee. Knowing his views, such a ceremony would in any case have been unacceptable to him. As for me, I think I would have liked the traditional day. In any event, I was tempting fate enough since the 13th of April was a Friday.

The next few months brought a lively variety of 'happenings' to the Schloss, beginning with a company meeting to discuss, yet again, our precarious financial state. I arrived a little late, having paid a fleeting visit home, where my parents had given me a beautiful silver-plated tea service. This I had carefully wrapped up in cotton wool, before putting it into a paper carrier-bag for the journey. On sitting down, I heard someone ask if there was anything any of us might be able to sell to raise some funds. To my consternation I saw Camel eyeing the carrier bag, where the cotton wool had slipped down, exposing my tea pot. Over my dead body! This was a gift of great sentimental value and I would sell almost anything else before it . . . at least, that is, if I had anything else to sell. At the end of the meeting, I looked for a safe hiding place. The only possible one seemed to be under the mattress at the bottom of the bed. And there it remained during the rest of our time at the Schloss. I came to find the occasional feel of the slight bump very reassuring.

Jean Newlove - Yum Di Dee Dah

'Don Perlimplin'
courtesy of Theatre Royal Stratford East Archive

'Don Perlimplin'
courtesy of Theatre Royal Stratford East Archive

Back to Poverty: From Parrot House to Dilapidated Schloss

It was around this time that Trudi, a young actress, first arrived among us. She was Austrian, and had been granted a temporary work permit; her English was moderately good. We now had another company meeting, where it was proposed that one of the boys would have to marry her – not for any indiscretion, I hasten to add, but simply a marriage of convenience, in name only, in order to secure a more permanent place for her in the company. Joan worked her way down the list of eligible bachelors, finally arriving at Edmond Bennett's name. Benny (as we called him) reluctantly agreed, on condition that it was done quietly and then forgotten. But he had reckoned without Trudi's womanly pride, for the next thing we heard was that her elder sister was coming to visit in order to inspect 'her young man'. There was general consternation all round, but we were, after all, a theatre company, and the opportunity presented itself for a spot of improvisation. We cleared up the Schloss, and furnished Trudi's bare room with pieces of the set from the current production, Lorca's play 'The Love of Don Perlimplín'. I was charged with the task of supplying a few biscuits and sandwiches for the occasion.

Trudi's sister looked as severe as only an Austrian elder sister can. The two of them spent some time alone chatting in their native tongue, then Benny knocked at the door – surreptitiously observed by the rest of us – looking for all the world like the the anxious suitor he was playing, and as if this was the most difficult part he had ever attempted (which it probably was).

After observing a decent interval, it was time for my cue. I knocked and entered with a tea-tray (from the props department) and an 'English tea'. It immediately seemed to have been a welcome diversion. Trudi was sitting nervously on the edge of her small makeshift bed, Benny bolt upright on a white-painted wrought-iron chair, with a set smile and glazed eyes. As for the elder sister, she had been given the place of honour, on Don Perlimplín's wrought-iron garden bench, with its sharply angled plywood seat, high at the back, low at the front. For a stage, the perspective was perfect. For Trudi's sister, though, it was less convenient, and she was having difficulty bracing herself against the back as she stolidly pushed against the floor with her sensible lace-up shoes. It was all she could do not to slide onto the floor entirely. By now an 'experienced' actress, I was like a maid in a Noël Coward play – though thankfully without the costume – dispensing tea and sandwiches, and retiring when the job was done. Trudi eventually disappeared without putting Benny through the ordeal of a marriage ceremony – though not before falling through the kitchen skylight, almost into Toby Blanshard's soup. She was lucky not to have been seriously hurt, suffering only a few minor abrasions. She had thought it was a good place to sunbathe.

Meanwhile, our tour of local schools had come to an end, along with the free lunches that went with them, and we underwent another financial crisis. Odd jobs were taken on to keep us in food. One member of the company gave private Latin lessons, another worked as a carpenter, a third manufactured engineering parts, and so on. They would leave early and come back late, and only be able to get down to proper theatre business after a frugal meal. But it was obvious that this state of affairs couldn't go on for much longer. It was decided that Ewan and Howard would have to hitch a lift to Scotland and rally our Scottish friends for financial support. I made them a packed lunch of sandwiches from an entire loaf of bread, and waved them off at seven in the morning. But at six o'clock that evening they were back: no one had picked them up. The following day we shared out the dry, curling sandwiches, and the day after that they set off once again, this time successfully reaching their destination.

On their return, the company had a few weeks' grace in which to await developments, and some of us decided to take a break while we could. The weather was excellent that summer, and camping was the obvious solution. This was a new experience for me, but Ewan was an old hand; it was the only sort of holiday he knew.

We hitched lifts on various lorries until we reached Fort William, arriving there long after dark. Walking through the town, footsore in my new boots and weighed down with a full rucksack, I felt a momentary pang of apprehension as we climbed a rocky outcrop, and I stood looking out over the twinkling lights – and comfortable beds – of the town below. The fine mist chilled me through on that first night, but morning broke with the promise of another fine day, and though a wash in the stream before the sun had struggled up was not quite as idyllic as it sounds, a breakfast of porridge and tea made a great difference to morale.

We had expected Howard to join us there after some 'theatre business' but as there was no sign of him, we decided to carry on to Mallaig, our final destination on the west coast of Scotland. He had details of our itinerary so we knew that it was only a matter of time before he caught up with us. We broke camp, hoisted our heavy rucksacks aloft and made a difficult descent to the road below. It was that morning that I learned something very useful: never to bend too far forward when you have a mammoth load on your back. It has a habit of suddenly propelling you forward at alarming speed into a somersault.

We walked for most of the morning as there was very little traffic and lifts were few and far between. Walking along a very minor road leading to the coast, we were overcome by the heat at midday, and the afternoon saw us frying gently by the side of the road with the sun scorching the baked earth. There was very little shade and not a cloud in sight. After eventually resuming our trek, we came across a little run-down cottage, where it was my job to ask for water. A brown, wizened face answered my knock and the old lady kindly filled our bottles from her well. Saved from dehydration, we staggered on, ever westward. Mallaig nestles by the sea and its only road, leading from much higher ground, has a steep gradient. Young people would gather together to watch the cars of the tourists collide at weekends, there being no other equally exciting sport. We camped on the high ground leading out north of the town. It was a good vantage point, with the additional benefit that Howard would be able to see our tents. There was more than a touch of self-interest here, since he was carrying the rest of our basic supplies, such as the oats that formed our staple diet.

The following morning, looking across the hill, I was delighted to see a well-known figure stagger over the horizon. It didn't need an expert in movement observation to realise that here was a fellow in the final stages of utter demoralization. Dwarfed by his enormous rucksack, he staggered from side to side, drunkenly undermined by the weight he was carrying and wearing an expression of total despair. Cruelly, my first instinct was to laugh. 'Howard's here!' I managed to announce, before falling about at this extraordinary transformation of my usually well-organised friend.

As Howard told his story, after dramatically collapsing in front of our tent, it was easy to feel great sympathy but equally hard not to burst out laughing, so we did our best to assume expressions of compassion. It appears he had only just missed us at Fort William, and had camped where we did, after seeing the ashes of our fire. Throughout the night, however, mosquitoes had dive-bombed him and by morning he was a mass of weals and woe, and exhausted from lack of sleep. He and the sleeping bag were bloody from continual scratching. Then, in his hurry to pack up and leave this terrible place, the bags of oats and rice had rolled downhill and ended up in the stream. Knowing they were vital supplies he had managed to salvage them and continued on his way. But his troubles still weren't over. It seems the mosquitoes had an efficient bush-telegraph service and frequent attacks were kept up by their relatives all along the route until just outside Mallaig. And as if that wasn't enough, the oats and rice had now swollen to astronomical proportions after their soaking, making an already heavy rucksack a ton-weight. Unable to jettison the lot for fear of meeting a cool reception, like Stanley (though without his native bearers) he had soldiered on.

We showed our appreciation both for the supplies and the story by washing his sleeping bag and tending his bites. A few days' rest and he was looking much better – at least until we learned from Joan, whom we telephoned from the town, that Gerry had given us more time. The two of them were going off for a break together, and it was arranged to meet up at the Schloss in three weeks. Faced with this unexpected extra time, Ewan suggested going further north, up to Gruinard Island. Perhaps unsurprisingly, Howard decided to set off for England there and then.

*

We spent a couple of nights camping on the Isle of Skye, where Ewan took me climbing in the Cuillins. The map said they were 'hills'. As far as I was concerned, they were mountains. It was here that I saw the fantastic sight of an albino goat and her kid acting as decoys for the rest of the wild herd, when we inadvertently disturbed them. They were pure white, and both stood motionless while the others flew down the steep slope and up the other side, where on reaching safety, they stopped as one, and waited. A moment's delay, and then the two decoys were off to join the others.

The next surprise was to see Ewan suddenly leap into the air with a cry and run sure-footed down the shale, which slipped and slithered and followed his progress as he gathered speed. He jumped from side to side like a skier while constantly making small running steps with his feet. In no time at all he was a small figure at the bottom of the 'hill'. If he could have run up as fast he would have equalled the performance of the wild goats. Having no experience of climbing or shale-running, I pushed off sitting on my heels – not very elegant, but I travelled at a fair pace. Returning to the mainland site, we decided to pitch our tent on the machair (the low grassland) opposite a few cottages. This was almost civilization as far as we were concerned. Chatting to the curious children who soon gathered brought an invitation from their mother to visit the cottage 'later'. The hours passed and I thought that perhaps they had forgotten all about us. It was dark when eventually a slightly older child was sent over to escort us to our hostess. The room was small and crowded, with family and neighbours sitting well back against two walls. The fire gave out most of the available light, although there were a couple of lighted candles on the table. Two children slept in a small curtained area by the wall containing the fireplace.

We had managed to buy a bottle of whisky earlier from the local shop and it was accepted with great dignity and pleasure. With true Highland hospitality, our hostess plied us with scones and bannocks and jam and currant buns of all descriptions. Invitations had been sent to all the neighbours and they in their turn had not arrived empty-handed. It suddenly became obvious that all this baking had accounted for the earlier delay. A few drams later and we were shyly asked if, since we were in the theatre, we might 'do something'. Ewan's singing was a great success. I felt rather more apprehensive, thinking that they would do Highland dancing much better than I could. This proved not to be true, and it occurred to me later on that it was only the wealthier communities further south that could afford to indulge in Highland dancing and costumes. I danced to their sung accompaniment – first the Highland Fling and then the Sword Dance; an improvised Strathspey and reel; and that was about my lot. Then they started to sing in Gaelic. Dawn was beginning to break as we said our goodbyes. I had seen, and been hugely struck by, their great dignity amidst what many would call extreme poverty; their hospitality had been overwhelming.

Lifts became fewer the further north we went, and we covered a good many miles on foot before finally arriving at a beautiful bay near Little Gruinard, within rowing distance of Gruinard Island. We pitched our tent on the machair overlooking the sea, protected by its gentle breeze against the clegs, or horse flies, inhabiting the bracken. It was an idyllic spot – though appearances can be deceptive. The Island of Gruinard may have been close, but it was out of bounds to visitors since being used as the site of an experimental germ-warfare programme during the war. The whole of 'Anthrax Island' was contaminated, and would remain so – we were told – for twenty-five years. (In fact it was not until the early 1990s that the area was declared safe.)

Unlike the poor sheep on Anthrax Island, the wildlife on the mainland were in energetic good health. Rabbits would frisk around us early every morning and evening, and seemed to regard us as friends. The same could not be said for the poor chap who arrived in the area one morning, a gun slung over his shoulder. After spending an entire day hiding in a copse, his patience was rewarded with not a single rabbit crossing his sights. Despondently, he made off as the evening grew darker; within minutes, all our many and sensible friends were back.

On another day, during a climbing expedition, I pulled myself up with my fingertips to find myself face to face with a Merlin.

Only a couple of feet separated us as he looked at me ferociously with huge beady eyes and a hooked beak. In no position to argue with him, I said a polite 'Good morning' and eased myself down. Continuing our climb, we came across a small loch, its water dark blue and icily cold, extremely high up, where I was amazed also to see a boat – the fishing must have been very good to warrant the haulage of a boat all that way up. On the way down, we came across the carcass of a stag that had fallen over a cliff-face.

I was inside the tent one glorious sunny morning, tidying up while Ewan went to the village for groceries, when my attention was caught by a strange noise, which I can only liken to the brakes of a bicycle being applied at frequent intervals. Then the whole tent was briefly thrown into shadow, despite the cloudless sky. I quietly stepped outside – to see two enormous golden eagles soaring overhead. Magnificent creatures; I couldn't take my eyes off them as they flew out over the sea and circled once again, returning past me to disappear over the hills. Over time, I learned to associate the eagles' presence with deafening silence – no birds singing, no rabbits appearing. There was also much night hunting, especially by wildcats, inevitably accompanied by the heart-rending screams of their victims. One evening I carried a terrified Cairn terrier home to a farm about a mile away. It was very dark, with only a little light spilling down from a hazy moon. We were stalked by a wildcat all the way, occasionally running across in front of me to wait in the ditch at the side of the road.

We supplemented our provisions with fresh milk, which we bought from two brothers who lived in a small local croft by a swift flowing river. Both Highlanders, they had served in Burma during the war and had gladly returned to resume their simple life-style. There were plenty of salmon in the river, but they were not allowed to fish there since it all belonged to the absent laird. They told me there was a 'big fellow' in the river that, so far, had eluded the laird and his friends.

Leaving the milk-can in a cold pool, I sat for a moment in my shorts, feet dangling, at the edge of the water. Traffic was so infrequent here that the sound of any engine was a novelty. The fish lorry would pass by every morning at seven o'clock on its way to the town of Ullapool, but that was all we had come to expect. Now, though, at mid-morning, a van stopped on the bridge above me and four Tam o'Shanters appeared over the parapet. Within moments fishing tackle was being assembled and three of the men joined me on the bank, the fourth staying with the van. As they spread out, I was asked, in a very friendly fashion, if I might help them net their catch since in my shorts I was more suitably dressed for the water. They pointed to a large rock somewhere in the middle of the river, and handed me quite a large net. It was a beautiful day, and I didn't have any immediate plans, so of course I immediately agreed. Over the next hour or two, I was heaped with praise as I successfully netted the fish without damaging them. One man said we made a good team and wished they'd had me on earlier trips.

At that moment, the noise of another vehicle caught our attention. It pulled up behind theirs on the bridge. Before I could see who it was, the three fishermen had dismantled their equipment and were up the bank, and everything was disappearing into the back of their van. The fourth one suddenly seemed to be busy photographing the countryside. Now I could see that the new arrival was a large touring coach, full of Americans, who got out and smiled at me. My photograph was taken from all angles as I smiled at them. 'Isn't she just darling! Do you think she speaks English?' No wonder I was laughing as they disappeared back into their coach again, waved on their way by us all. I suppose they were doing the Highlands in a day.

My new fishermen friends now decided it was time to go. They had lost their concentration to fish any more, they said, and they had a few calls to make. But they insisted on giving me a share of the booty – three or four grilse (young salmon). After returning with the milk to our campsite, I gutted and cleaned them, and within twenty minutes they were in a pan with butter over an open fire. When Ewan arrived, supper was ready – and I discovered that I had unwittingly been part of a poaching team who were quite notorious in the district. Sadly, they came back later and got the 'big fellow' without my help.

Back to Poverty: From Parrot House to Dilapidated Schloss

These were idyllic days and nights, but the time eventually came to strike camp and make for home. Unfortunately, we missed the fish lorry, and had to re-erect the tents for another day, but we got our lift the following morning, and travelled for a good hour before being dropped off. It was a good start, but the next few hours saw us on an extremely lonely road stretching as far as the eye could see, with nothing else in sight at all: no animals, no people, and certainly no traffic. These occasions never worried me; I always remained optimistic that something would turn up eventually. Ewan, on the other hand, grew more and more disheartened, until we heard and then saw the welcome approach of a small, red postal van! We were almost prepared to lay down in the road in front of it, but this was thankfully unnecessary. We bundled gratefully into the back, and apart from a couple of brief stops, travelled hour after long hour towards Glasgow and civilization. We arrived at around three in the morning, utterly exhausted. After thanking the driver, we climbed over the nearest, very low railing into what we assumed was a field in the city's outskirts, where with practised ease we pitched our tents in complete darkness, too tired even to find the torch. We immediately dropped into deep sleep.

I was the first to wake up, disturbed by the unaccustomed sounds of early morning traffic. Peering sleepily out of the tent flap, I was dumbfounded to see people hurrying by on their way to work; buses, lorries and cars went past us in a never-ending stream. Looking around me, I realised that far from being a suburban field, our final campsite was a well-kept municipal park, in the city centre, on a beautiful lawn surrounded by flower-beds. I wonder if that van-driver had a greater sense of humour than he let on.

It took us another twelve hours to reach Manchester. As we queued for the bus back to the Schloss, our fellow passengers gave us some strange looks. We were deeply tanned by now, after weeks under glorious Scottish summer sun, and so used to carrying heavy loads that the rucksacks no longer presented any problems. Despite occasional trimming, Ewan's beard had also grown apace, obviously intriguing a small child sitting on its mother's knee in the bus. 'Mam,' the small voice piped up, 'what's that man got on his face?'

Our Scottish excursion had marvellously cemented our relationship, but had also rested and inspired our minds, and improved our physical fitness. It turned out to be the perfect training for the months – and years – to come. We returned to the Schloss ready to take on the world – or at least the next production.

Chapter Eighteen

The Knights Save 'Alice' in Barnsley

Summer 1949 – New Year 1950

It was announced in the Manchester newspapers that Theatre Workshop were looking for a dog to appear in a forthcoming production of one of their plays at the Library Theatre; auditions would be held the following week. A publicity stunt of Gerry's, it excited great interest, and a variety of canine wannabes duly arrived with their doting owners. The play in question was 'Rogues' Gallery', a satirical modern comedy by Ewan. On this occasion, however, the play it was that died, with the critics deciding that naturalism was not our métier – though whether the playwright or the producer were to blame was left unclear. What they missed was the blend of music, dancing, and singing that soon became known as our signature style.

While rehearsing 'Rogues' Gallery' in the morning, we were also daily performing Ewan's Molière adaptation, 'The Flying Doctor', on an open-air stage at Boggart Hole Clough, a park near the Schloss. Howard played the leading role of Sganarelle, and had been rehearsed to hoist up his female co-star at the climax of a scene. Cast against him in this production, however, was a certain well-built young woman whose weight now proved too much for the altogether more slender Howard. Three times he tried to lift her high, three times he failed – before the actress herself angrily turned the tables by grabbing Howard round the waist, throwing him up on high, and abruptly exiting. Then, as Howard returned to earth, and readied himself for his soliloquy, a child's whining voice cut through the tense silence: 'Mam, when is the dogs comin' on?' She had obviously been brought to the wrong play.

But then, at that very moment, her wish was granted, as a stray dog slowly and deliberately wandered up from the audience, mounted the steps onto the stage, cocked its leg on the set, and just as casually strolled off, stage right. Of course, the dog got the laugh that should have been Sganarelle's; doubly upstaged, Howard was furious. It was all a far cry from the Stockholm Opera House.

Our next production was a season of short plays, which we called collectively 'Summer Fare', comprising Lorca's 'Don Perlimplín', 'The Flying Doctor' (in both of which I acted), and a new version of Chekhov's 'Proposal'. During its run we decided to take the production to Edinburgh, where we joined an exclusive and small fringe of the Festival. Once again we were fêted on all sides, and 'Summer Fare' was named the Highlight of the Festival. My concerns were more immediate, and more basic. I played one of two 'sprites' in the Lorca production, Denis Ford playing the other one, each of us wielding an enormous fan, and each of us covered top-to-toe in green make-up. However, there was only the briefest of intervals before the Molière adaptation, in which I was playing the roses-and-cream inamorata, Lucille. I had always therefore dreaded appearing insufficiently cleansed of the vivid green body-paint for my first scene. In the second scene I had to run up a small backstage ramp, and throw a rose through the delicate window-frame attached to one side of the ramp. My lover, Valère, played by David Scase, was to pick it up as it dropped at his feet. It was a simple enough manoeuvre. Or at least, it should have been.

Unfortunately, on the first night someone had white-washed the ramp so zealously that the rough surface my ballet shoes needed for gripping was completely obliterated, so when I ran up the slope, I barely reached halfway before sliding down backwards. Realizing what had happened, I tried again, this time running a little more energetically and eventually reaching the top. But before I could lean out of the window and fling my rose at David, my momentum faltered, and with nothing to cling on to but the flimsy plywood of the stage window-frame, I couldn't prevent my unceremonious backward retreat out of sight. By now, of course, I was corpsing, though this mattered less than my sustained invisibility – and the failure of my third attempt, after a really Olympic run-up, to deliver the rose to poor David, who remained alone on stage looking rather bewildered unable to proceed with his lines. In some desperation, I bowled an over-arm delivery from the dark recesses of the theatre, and the rose, jet-propelled like a rocket, flew over the window and flopped at his feet.

The last week of the Festival saw us playing Ewan's 'The Other Animals'. An international audience was, once again, enthusiastic, and the press gave us excellent reviews. We celebrated with a marvellous party at Dr Boyd-Orr's house, where Ewan and I had our digs. The good doctor lived alone in an enormous granite-built house on several floors. The first-floor lounge swallowed up three large sofas and several armchairs, apart from various occasional tables, footstools, and other pieces of furniture. All the company came, along with our many local friends – the poets, the writers, and the folk-singers – many, perhaps most, of whom were dedicated Scottish nationalists. The poets Hugh MacDiarmid, Hamish Henderson, Sydney Goodsir Smith and Norman MacCaig were there; so was the publisher, Bill MacLellan. This was an evening of 'cultural exchanges'. MacDiarmid, Scotland's foremost poet, sought to broaden my education by explaining the finer whiskies to me in great detail. For my part, I introduced an inebriated Sydney Goodsir Smith to Laban's theory of 'efforts'. He gallantly endeavoured to follow my mini-lecture, then – less successfully – tried to summarise it to his 'minder', the serious and kindly Norman MacCaig. Sydney always carried a piece of paper with his address on it, and a list of the phone numbers of taxi drivers who would be willing to take him home if Norman couldn't manage to do so.

After our success at the Edinburgh Festival, we returned in October 1949 to the Library Theatre in Manchester, with a production of 'The Gentle People', by the American playwright Irwin Shaw, set along Brooklyn's waterfront. The notices generally praised the production's sense of atmosphere. One particular scene was so beautifully staged, I watched it every night from the wings. Standing at the rear of a small rowing-boat, a light attached to its prow, with stage smoke suggesting the mist shrouding the waves,

Howard Goorney delivered his lines while, invisibly to the audience, bending and straightening his knees. The effect was designed to give the impression of a gently bobbing boat. It was thrilling. A tour round the schools of 'As You like It' followed until the end of November, Later we took 'The Gentle People' to Kidderminster.

Meanwhile, with Christmas season approaching, it had been decided to make an adaptation of the two Lewis Carroll books, 'Alice in Wonderland' and 'Alice Through the Looking-Glass', selecting and combining the most lively and interesting parts for a single production. Nearly ten years after playing Alice in a drama competition as a schoolgirl, here I was unexpectedly rehearsing the role of the White Queen in a professional touring company. The production was a typically eclectic Theatre Workshop mixture of styles and personalities. I was able to bring two professional dancers over from Sweden – Sonja (who had been in the Herod ballet we had seen in Copenhagen) and Rita – and Stella Maude, a former student at the Art of Movement Studio, was cast as my opposite number, the Red Queen.

The music for the production was composed by an old friend of Joan and Ewan called Jack Evans. Jack had been visiting the Soviet Union when war broke out. Unable to return, he became a journalist, spending much of his time reporting from Stalingrad, where he had married and started a family with a local girl. After a visit to England at the end of the war, however, the Russians had refused to allow him back, and his family were forbidden to join him. These terrible experiences must have scarred him deeply. Unable to find an outlet for his true talents, he had only managed to find a job as a railway porter by the time we came briefly into his life. To me he seemed a kindly, if understandably quiet, individual, and was always very professional in regard to his music – music that was challenging and complex, testing for the musicians who had to play it, but quite brilliant for the 'Chess Ballet' I was devising.

For the first time that I can remember, a 'professional' agent had been called in to book our pantomime season, and this gave us more time to rehearse and to work on the rather exotic sets. The chequered board for the 'Chess Ballet', for example, was enormous, with one corner pointing towards the audience, lying flat against the ramp of the stage, but the opposite triangle rose in tiers – truly a striking setting for the dancers playing out their game of chess upon it. All the 'pieces' moved according to the game, so that while the pawns entered to lively music, advancing one step at a time, the knights leapt in an appropriately jerky action of their own. Their intricate leaps and turns (each always landing on the correct square, but never even touching the other as they fought and struggled to the death) bringing the ballet to a formal and exciting close.

It may be that I remember these rehearsals so vividly because it was while they were going on that I discovered that I needed to plan for another future production of my own: I was pregnant. I was overjoyed, though Ewan, given the perilous nature of our financial circumstances, was understandably more cautious. I reckoned that pregnancy would never be 'convenient' in the life we led, but still felt sure that I could cope, confident and happy to be a mother whilst I had never saw my future role as a full-time housewife – a point of view rather more unusual in 1949 than it is today. As the production went on, 'Benny' Bennett's Red King continued to hold his White Queen above his head in the moment of triumph; fortunately for all concerned, our tour finished when I was four months pregnant.

Meanwhile, though, in the early stages of our production, the company now decided to sub-let the Schloss while we were on tour, which would at least cover our rent, and an advert was placed in the evening paper. Looking out of the front window the following morning, we were astonished to see a queue winding down the drive and along the street, as far as the eye could see. I don't know how well our tenants were vetted, but the lucky ones were shown various rooms and amenities. To safeguard the costumes and props kept in the cellar, we graciously allowed a Manchester University undergraduate to live rent free in a spare room, in return for acting as unofficial caretaker. Unfortunately, just before leaving, we discovered there was in fact no spare room for him, so he gamely agreed to 'bed down on the slats' in the cellar itself – and from then on he was known simply as 'Slats'.

We arrived in Barnsley at lunchtime on Christmas Day 1949, in good time for our matinee performance on Boxing Day. As four of us waited in the hall of our digs for the landlady to appear, and the smell of the traditional turkey dinner enveloped us, we silently congratulated ourselves on our good luck. Then a sharp-featured woman arrived, and told us to go into the dining room for lunch, since our rooms were not yet ready. We sat at card tables in a room only slightly less bare than those at the Schloss, and waited hopefully. A moment later, she bustled in, a roast-dinner aroma wafting in her wake, and presented each of us with a small plate of . . . Spam salad.

Barnsley was a tough old town, and it was quite clear that the Yorkshire miners and their families were a tough breed. A traditional pantomime would barely have survived at their Theatre Royal; playing 'Alice in Wonderland' was certainly asking for trouble. Even Wilfred Pickles had reportedly been 'given the bird' when he had a go, and the Young Vic had failed dismally, only recovering after interesting the local schools. To be confronted by roses and water-lilies, a Gryphon, a Caterpillar, a Mad Hatter's tea-party, Tweedledum and Tweedledee – not to mention their conversations with the rather prissy, self-contained adolescent Alice we had cast – must have seemed something of a mockery (of the non-Turtle variety), and the audience voiced their dislike in no uncertain terms.

Our poor Gryphon began the run by enthusiastically seeking to get the audience to join in with his song, 'Beautiful Soup', above the uproar. By the end of the third day he had lost his voice – no doubt a psychosomatic result of his thrice-daily ordeals. Howard Goorney, beautifully attired as the (non-dancing) Red Queen, was pelted with copper coins. During the first performances he ignored them. Then he started to pick them up and throw them back. By the end of the run he had hit on a far better idea, scooping them up and stuffing them into the prop purse he carried. For such a hard bitten audience 'Alice' was a disaster – though other audiences admired the imaginative props and costumes. Joan as usual had carried on sitting in the 'gods', taking notes, at every show. I had noticed that the boos and heckles had always subsided during our 'Chess Ballet', and the knights' fight had even drawn the rare sound of applause afterwards. Joan told me that some of the local retired miners sat up there daily, just to watch the ballet, perhaps most especially the knights' final combat. She overheard one old ex-miner whisper to his friend, 'Now, this part's good.'

Returning to our digs between shows one afternoon, I heard a terrible argument going on in the kitchen. It appears that our landlady had been buying her eggs from her husband, who kept chickens, but who had been systematically overcharging her for some time, and she had only just found out. Whatever else we didn't get, I guessed eggs would now be added to the list. Despite the majority of our audiences expressing their vociferous disapproval of Alice, there were also a few letters of appreciation. The quality of the show was not in dispute, but we were slow to realise that, if not quite a dodo, Lewis Carroll's surreal fantasy was at least too rarefied a bird for those brought up on a more earthy, pantomime diet of stock characters, broad innuendo, and ribald audience participation (though I suppose we could be said to have achieved the latter). Gerry did his best to cheer us up by announcing that we had made a small profit, but since he never usually bothered to mention such things, he must have realised that morale was low. On the other hand, profits were so rare a feature of Theatre Company's accounts that he may simply have been unable to contain his excitement. Perhaps those coppers Howard collected had tipped the balance.

The clock of Barnsley Town Hall showed midnight, heralding another New Year: 1950. Howard and I had not quite caught up with the rest of the company, who were now loading the gear into an empty truck in the deserted railway yard. As midnight chimed out, we stopped running for a moment, and wished each other a Happy New Year. Then we realised that we were standing outside the public toilets. It seemed a fitting end to a truly disastrous week.

By the following day we had arrived in Llandudno, in North Wales, and were being welcomed by the local Dramatic Society. High tea was set out in the Green Room of the theatre, and hospitality offered to the entire company. Because Ewan was not directly involved with Alice, he had returned to Manchester to get on with his writing. Left to my own devices, I took an evening walk and sniffed the sea appreciatively. This theatre life was certainly not dull, I thought. One moment we were in an industrial town, stricken by unemployment, where husband and wife warred over the price of eggs, and where the only part of Alice not to be barracked was a ballet sequence. Now here I was in Llandudno, being treated with the greatest kindness, and enjoying the finest home comforts. We were also to find appreciative audiences throughout the week. It seemed almost like a holiday. I went out the next day, and bought some baby-wool and a knitting-pattern.

A week later, on the following Sunday, we set off for a stint at the Theatre Royal, Stratford East – a venue we would soon all come to know much better. In fact in many ways, our short run there anticipated our later residence. The local population weren't particularly enamoured of Alice, it is true, but there was as much curiosity as hostility in our reception. Crucially, though, we also attracted many people from further-flung areas of London who, already aware of our work, had come to see 'something different'. They nearly saw something very different during the 'Chess Ballet' one night. I recall Benny spinning round, holding me high above his head. And then, slipping slightly in his arms, I hovered momentarily above the pit far below me. Benny swore under his breath as he regained his balance, while the pale face of Jack Evans, conducting his own music, peered nervously up at us. Poor, dear Jack. I felt tremendous sympathy for this brilliantly accomplished musician and composer, whose tragic personal circumstances (as I later learned) eventually led to alcoholism and suicide, and I still wish we could have done more to help him.

The next leg of our tour was bleak: the coastal resorts of Hastings in Sussex, then Weymouth in Dorset – neither of them ideal venues for a freezing late January. Weymouth seemed little more than a ghost town, and the entertainments hall we were booked into, on the promenade next to the sea, was really designed for the summer. There was no heating, and the gusts of wind blew into the dressing rooms through every conceivable crack. The audience fared little better, but at least they had come prepared – and I watched these stalwarts arrive with blankets, thermos flasks, and hot-water bottles, with envy. We might just as well have been playing in the open air.

None of these deprivations, however, could have prepared us for the miseries of the final week of our tour, at Leigh, back in Lancashire, in early February 1950. Our digs were unpleasant; the theatre was squalid; and the necessary rehearsals for the ballet sequence, in our new surroundings, were an unmitigated disaster. It didn't help that the local 'orchestra' was manifestly incapable of playing Jack's music. He tried hard with them, but they seemed ignorant even of following the score. Even worse, to my mind, was that they were apparently completely content with the atrocious standard of their playing. Rehearsals stretched out interminably, and with little discernible improvement, throughout our first morning. Then the arguments began, with one or two musicians suggesting ideas of their own, compressing the intricate rhythms of Jack's original score into simpler ones, and making nonsense of the whole piece. The pianist in particular, I remember, kept insisting on finishing his part with a staccato flourish of notes – thereby killing the dramatic intensity that had previously riveted the attention of Yorkshire miners.

By lunchtime we had succeeded in getting precisely nowhere, and having downed their instruments, we were now told that the musicians had refused to rehearse in the afternoon, on the grounds that it went against Union rules. I can't remember exactly how we lured them back – perhaps they were paid overtime out of our own straitened finances – but something quite interesting happened that afternoon. While one or two of the musicians blithely played on regardless, a few more began to listen to what Jack was saying, and then a few more still, and so by the end of the rehearsal, we had made enough progress to get through the piece once – and make a success of it. But this was a rare exception. Most of the time, the dancers never knew what tempo to expect, and there were angry frustrations on all sides. One night I came close to publicly denouncing the orchestra from the stage. I still believe that if this production had been put on at the Library Theatre in Manchester, or on a London stage, with a professional and well-rehearsed orchestra, the story of Theatre Workshop's rise to fame might have been a very different one. Unfortunately, our 'Chess Ballet' was never seen at a major venue. While all our productions used movement and dance as an integral element, only 'Alice', 'The Other Animals' and 'Uranium 235' could be described as incorporating modern ballets. And only for Alice did we hire trained dancers. But we were all by now exhausted, and could hardly wait to travel the few short miles to Manchester, the Schloss, and home.

I remember one evening, in particular, of that dreadful stay in Leigh, which shows just how exhausted we all were. Sonja and I had returned to our shared digs after a full day's rehearsal and an evening's performance, depressed by the reception we'd encountered. Sonja had a long-standing knee injury and I watched from my own bed as she sleepily followed her nightly ritual: dipping a wad of Thermogene wool into a little warm water, she squeezed it gently, and applied it to her knee, before starting the lengthy process of bandaging it in place. After seeing the careful wrapping pinned snugly into place, and after saying goodnight, I turned off the light, and we both settled into our beds. There was a moment's silence – then a terrible scream from Sonja. Fearing the worst, I sat up quickly, but it was soon obvious that she was laughing. From her bed in the far corner, she exclaimed that it had all been for nothing . . .

She had bandaged the wrong knee.

Chapter Nineteen

A Special 'Production'

February 1950 – September 1951

We were all glad to get back to the Schloss for a welcome break, after the rigours of a difficult tour, in early February 1950. Since Ewan had not been with us, apart from the occasional visits, the room we shared had not been sub-let. The other, temporary tenants had been warned of our imminent return, and most of them had gone on their way. As I walked into the kitchen, the door leading down to the cellar opened slowly, and a pale face emerged, tousle-haired and blinking in the light . . . It was Slats! We had all but forgotten about our faithful caretaker. Living in darkness for the previous seven weeks, he looked as if he had become an urban troglodyte. How he had coped with University life from his subterranean basement digs I never did learn. Perhaps he had given up: he was certainly one of the poorest individuals I ever met, and we gladly shared our food with him. A few characters were still lingering on, he told us, while they found alternative accommodation. These included two little old ladies, in Trudi's old room, who were constantly reading their tea-leaves, and seeing omens in the most commonplace events. He also revealed that there had been a few early difficulties with the first-come-first-served tenants we had installed. There was a nice young couple, for example, who had paid their rent and were just settling in when the girl's irate parents arrived: she had eloped, it seems. And then there was an older couple – inevitably nicknamed Mr and Mrs Fagin – who kept their seven-year-old daughter away from school in order to spend the days teaching her how to steal things, and instructing her in the art of crime. The education authorities were apparently on her case, and had also come knocking at the door. So much for our beautiful post-war world!

My pregnancy was going very well, but I was glad of the relaxation of our schedule. The company returned to Hastings with 'The Gentle People'. I was not involved in this production, but joined them at the Adelphi theatre in London a week later, for a Sunday charity performance of our 'Summer Fare' programme. This was later repeated at the Alexandra Theatre, Stoke Newington, and the King's Theatre, Hammersmith. Then, after a few more charity shows in London, we had no alternative but to disband through lack of funds, so I now had time to prepare for my own very important production.

Going home to Lincoln for a short break, I was able to reassure my mother that I was 'looking after myself', despite not yet having a home to call my own. She had been busy sewing and knitting small garments, and proudly showed me her preparations for her second grandchild. (Pip and his wife had had their first child, a daughter, two years before.) My father, as always, drove me to the station and saw me off, quietly offering me his kindly, supportive advice before the train left. Back in Manchester with my parcel of baby things, I had time to consider my own future and try to sort out my priorities.

The Schloss had now been vacated by the company, and Ewan and I were staying with his mother Betsy at a cottage outside Hyde, some six miles from Manchester. There was plenty of room, but it was not an ideal arrangement. Ewan was Betsy's only surviving child, and she doted on him, and it would have been difficult for anyone to come up to the wifely standards she expected for her son. We were both grateful, though, since flats were in short supply in those early post-war years, even if one could pay the going rate for one. We had no capital and would certainly never ask for help – I don't think it entered our heads. After all, we were both doing what we wanted to do.

At this time, Ewan was busy with freelance acting work at the B.B.C. and preparing ideas for a new play. From time to time there would also be meetings with Joan and Gerry about the company.

Laban asked me if I might assist an old student of his from before the war, Albrecht Knust.

Knust had made Laban's notation his life's study, and continued to develop it secretly throughout the war in Hitler's Germany. He was now staying with Lisa and Laban, who had moved to a small house not far from their old flat. I was delighted at this opportunity and worked with him three or four times a week – Laban would tease me by saying, 'Your boyfriend is waiting,' whenever I arrived, and laugh when I made a face.

It is true that, as my pregnancy neared full term, and the summer developed into a heat-wave, Knust expressed increasingly edgy concern for my welfare. He was primarily worried about the long bus journey – I didn't tell him I had to make my way up a one-in-five gradient to the cottage. Another assistant joined me, Joan Russell, from a teacher training college around this time. She was interested in furthering the teaching of Modern Dance in schools and hoped to learn more about notation. We were both soon engrossed in the work of interpreting the symbols that Laban and Knust had developed to replace conventional descriptions of individual physical movements. We would experiment with 'reading' a page of notation, which meant performing the movements expressed by the written symbols.

That was the summer that Lisa asked me to go with her to the nursing home where her mother now lived – the old lady had said she would like to see me again. I remember this because I was by now very pregnant, and Lisa happily introduced me to the other old ladies in residence as 'Miss' Newlove – before realizing her mistake and hurrying to correct herself. In those days such things mattered. It was so nice to see her again, looking very well, and during our long chat about my activities in the theatre since we'd last met, I got the distinct impression that she had missed me, at least a little bit, from her Laban 'family'. Some time later, I learnt that she had opted to rejoin her old housekeeper in Berlin, still then suffering severe conditions, and she died not long afterwards – hopefully unaware that her son, long since missing in action on the Eastern Front, had in fact been shot by the Russians.

I rang for the ambulance from the telephone kiosk across the way from Betsy's cottage in Hyde, at around seven-thirty in the evening of 13 July 1950, and I was duly ferried off to St Mary's Hospital in Manchester. Along with my small prepared suitcase of clothes and toiletries, I held on to the book I had read and re-read throughout my pregnancy. Written by the pioneering obstetrician Grantly Dick-Read (regarded by many at the time as unconventional), this handbook on 'Natural Childbirth' had offered an inspiring alternative to all the horror stories one heard. From St Mary's – after five hours of sitting around waiting for a full quota of pregnant ladies to be assembled – we continued our journey to the maternity annexe at Prestwich, arriving in the early hours of the morning of the 14th. Gratefully sinking into a bed, and by now very tired, sleep still did not come easily: the crèche was next door, and the babies' caterwauling kept me awake most of the night.

Friday and Saturday were long days of intermittent labour, during which I continued to read my book, following the exercises it recommended as best I could. At about six o'clock on Saturday evening I was taken to the delivery room, where I was left on my own. Since I had taken my book with me, I suppose they could be forgiven for thinking this was a D.I.Y. job! But my bed was eventually surrounded by a team of white-coated medical staff – and just before the final stages of labour began, a particularly surreal exchange took place with a woman doctor. I had recently played a 'euphoric patient' in Ewan's 'The Other Animals', and now, looking up from my bed, I was struck by the resemblance to my stage-role – surrounded by white coats.

'It's just like 'The Other Animals',' I said. 'It most certainly is not,' she replied.

At around seven o'clock that evening I had given birth to a beautiful baby son.

I felt inordinately clever and proud – as well as ravenously hungry, since I had eaten almost nothing in the previous thirty hours. A nurse kindly found a half-pound packet of biscuits, and I demolished the lot. That night, I listened to the babies next door again, but I didn't hear any caterwauling now – Was that my baby crying? Why didn't they do something! Clearly, my maternal instinct was already strong.

The next morning, after the preliminaries, my baby was brought in to me. He had a serious expression; thick jet-black hair which was beginning to curl; and he looked about twelve years old. I named him Hamish – a name I had always loved, and appropriately Scottish for our new surname. All the nurses were delighted with him, and with me – and with Grantly Dick-Read's 'Natural Childbirth'. To my utter surprise and rather awkward embarrassment, I now found myself being held up as a perfect example of motherhood – and the book was suddenly in great demand, being passed around (rather belatedly) from bed to bed. To escape this scene, I took a chair and walked into the gardens, easing myself back into a few gentle barre exercises. Looking up a little later, I was amazed to see a row of white coats watching me attentively from the hospital balcony. Finding my bed empty, the doctors had gone in search of me – and were (or so the nurses told me) deeply impressed with my recovery.

An enormous bouquet of flowers arrived at the ward in the afternoon, leaving us all to wonder briefly who the lucky recipient was. Knowing Theatre Workshop's parlous financial state, I had already declared 'It won't be for me' when it was laid on my bed. Howard had sent it on behalf of the company! Ewan came a little later that day, and was wreathed in smiles at the very first sight of his baby son who, he said, vividly resembled his father.

Eventually returning to the cottage by ambulance with my sleeping baby, I found Ewan and his mother eagerly awaiting us. Before long the baby started to cry: all eyes turned to me and I realised with something of a jolt that I was in sole charge of a small new life. In those first few days and weeks, the baby never seemed to sleep, and Ewan and I began to dream of the times when we could give him a plate of sandwiches and a good book. Ewan came up with a promising idea one day. Tying a crystal stopper onto a cotton thread, he swung it slowly to and fro above Hamish's cot – but while the baby's dark, alert eyes watched the diminishing trajectory with great interest, it was Ewan who was lulled to sleep.

But sleep was always fitful for both of us, and during one particularly busy week, when Ewan was trying to learn a part for the B.B.C., he packed up his script, and a tent, to spend a night on the nearby countryside at Bleaklow, just outside Hyde. He reckoned a few hours' unbroken sleep would make a new man of him. He arrived back at six in the morning, soaked through and shivering with cold – the tent had sprung a leak. I don't remember if I had the heart to tell him that this had been the first time that Hamish had slept undisturbed all night.

The next three months saw me getting to grips with being a full-time mother. Laban, Lisa, and Joan were the proud godparents, and my parents (as most grandparents are) were delighted, my mother declaring Hamish to be 'perfect' – and so he was. But this wasn't the only new production to which we now had to attend. For at the beginning of November 1950, Theatre Workshop was once again miraculously solvent, and preparing for a new tour, this time to South Wales, it was decided to mount a revival of Ewan's 'Uranium 235'.

First performed in 1946, in the wake of the Hiroshima and Nagasaki bombings, Uranium 235 had gained increasing relevance as the years wore on. 'The Bomb' was on everyone's mind, and Ewan's play presented a brilliant and extraordinary account of the science that lay behind it. He had somewhere met up with a group of scientists whose explanation to him of the relevant technology, in lay-man's terms, Ewan transformed into an apocalyptic pantomime circus: part history lesson (Pierre and Marie Curie), part physics lecture (protons, neutrons, Energy – this last played by Gerry Raffles), and part morality play (Death – inevitably – features among the dramatis personae). My part had been 'Lola, the Smasher' who had 'crossed the line' and triggered off the explosion. By now I was almost a 'seasoned' mother – Hamish was about four months old – and I was asked to take over the movement classes and to re-work the choreography. My part was taken over by someone else and I had to get the company back into shape as well as re-rehearse the Atom Ballet. This work with the company only involved me in the mornings (accompanied, of course, by Hamish), and it was helpful that a Theatre Workshop meeting from around this time decided that members with children should be kept on the company payroll when they played an important and ongoing role. I watched as the company departed on tour – including Ewan, reprising the part of the 'Puppet-master'. My feelings were mixed. It seemed strange not to be travelling with them, but my regrets were assuaged by my baby son, who needed attention and a settled existence. And I knew it would soon become easier . . . especially if I could just get him to sleep at night.

Meanwhile I looked forward to my regular telephone chats with Ewan at the local kiosk. He was always a brilliantly funny raconteur, especially when describing problems the cast faced at each new venue, and I fully understood that as the company's main playwright and actor, he needed the stimulating atmosphere of both the tour and the company. In any case I made good use of the time, enjoying the glorious new experience of motherhood, and getting to know my son. I would proudly push his pram up the lane and back, occasionally venturing down (and up) the steep hill where the few local shops were situated. But I was still uncertain in my new role. So when my eye caught a smart pair of grey shorts displayed in the window of a mother-and-baby shop, I parked Hamish in his pram outside, and walked in, trying for all the world to look like the experienced, even blasé mother I didn't feel I was. We were short of money, as always, but I wanted to buy something for my baby, and those shorts were really something.

'He's perhaps a bit young for them yet,' I told the sales assistant, 'but I don't want him to grow out of them too quickly.'

He immediately agreed. 'And how old is your child now?' he asked.

I wasn't ready for that. 'Oh,' I blustered, 'getting on for a year . . .'

'Oh, they'll fit a two-year-old' he laughed.

I put down my money, and fled with the purchase before he could ask to see my three-month-old in the pram outside.

With the arrival of December 1950, I bought and decorated a small Christmas tree, and Mish (as Hamish had soon become known to friends and family) would watch the shiny baubles for hours on end, gurgling happily as I chatted away to him. A few days later, though, he became very ill, unable to keep the milk down, and the doctor muttered something about 'projectile vomiting' and called the ambulance. I wrapped him up and, accompanied by Ewan's mother Betsy, travelled to the hospital several miles away. It awakened very unhappy memories for her, she said: we were going to the very hospital where her own sick baby, a brother of Ewan's, had been taken – over thirty years before, And when we entered the ward, she told me this was the very same one in which her own sick baby had died . . . in the corner bed. I did feel compassion for her, of course, but was unable to offer any words of sympathy just then. To put it mildly, she had done nothing to allay my own urgent fears.

The hospital never did find out the exact nature of Hamish's illness – a 'virus' apparently – but he was eventually discharged, barely recovered from the illness, due to the nursing staff's fear that very young babies might succumb to other ward infections brought in by older children. I had certainly been very unhappy during one of my visits to see how the nurse handled the teats on the babies' milk bottles. I had been far more hygienic at home. With Mish now restored to my arms, I looked outside the window – to see snow starting to fall. No transport had been mentioned, but I had absolutely no intention of carrying Mish all the way back, risking his health in the cold, changing buses, and then walking up the steep hill. So I opted for the ambulance-bus again, even if it meant we were last to be dropped off – which in the event we were. Our transport managed to climb the steep hill home despite the worsening snowfall. By morning the roads were blocked and we were cut off for the next forty-eight hours.

Since the company tour was scheduled to continue through Christmas into the New Year, I arranged for a family friend, who would be passing through Manchester, to pick me up and take me back home to Lincoln for the festive season. Ewan managed a very fleeting return visit before we left. Although my parents had visited us, this would be my first visit home since the baby's birth.

When we arrived back in the New Year of 1951, following a phone-call from Ewan to say he had thirty-six hours off, he felt unable to meet this family friend who brought me back and made tiredness an excuse. I was beginning to understand that this seemingly anti-social behaviour covered a deep-rooted insecurity in Ewan. A frugal character herself, Betsy was always delighted to present a 'lavish' spread before her son. Certain foods were still rationed and the local butcher was in great demand by housewives trying to eke out family meals. Betsy would come back very pleased to have acquired some delicacy like two small chops or some liver. But the 'Fatted Calf' atmosphere abruptly disappeared when Ewan left, and the dour, often oppressive atmosphere returned. I reminded myself that, from what I could gather, her life had been a difficult one, and that her obsessive devotion to her only surviving child was therefore to a certain extent understandable. I didn't mention these difficulties to anyone, not even to Ewan – though Joan later told me that after experiencing similar problems, with Betsy in the past, she had always been more forthright and confrontational with her. But that was Joan.

In February and March, Theatre Workshop revisited Scandinavia, taking 'Uranium 235'. Ewan did not go with them on this trip, but rejoined the company for their tour of the North-East of England in the spring, which once again featured 'Uranium 235' (with Ewan reprising his original role as the Puppet-master), and the revival of his 1949 ballad-opera 'Landscape with Chimneys'. During this time I had not been idle. During one of the many company meetings concerning the perennial subject of our lack of finance, I had suggested running summer schools as a means of raising some cash. The idea was not greeted with the greatest enthusiasm by Joan, but the idea gradually took root . . . especially when I offered to organise the venture myself. By mid-July, it was all fixed, and two venues had been booked. The basic idea was to extend the premise of our 'Theatre Workshop' to include courses for (and contributions from) a constituency of students paying for the privilege.

The first of these summer schools was at Appleby in Westmorland. The weather was fantastically good and the company enjoyed the break amidst beautiful scenery. Ewan, Joan, and I were the tutors. (Of course, Hamish came along too. He was just over one year old, and there were lots of willing minders on hand while I was working.) The evenings were filled with discussions, often ending with a sing-song. Ewan talked about the new play he was writing, 'The Travellers' (a dark and theatrically ambitious reflection on the Nazi Holocaust, the full, horrifying details of which were then becoming clear), analysing his methods and illustrating his points with short excerpts. Gratifyingly, the students, who had come from all over the country and from abroad, were full of enthusiasm. One of these, the Durham collier and folk singer Jack Elliott, joined up with us at the end of the week. It was around this time, in the early summer of 1951, that Ewan was first approached to perform on one or two folk-song programmes for the B.B.C., leading directly to his meeting the great American folk-collector Alan Lomax, and the musicologist and broadcaster A.L. 'Bert' Lloyd – both of whom became longstanding friends.

From Appleby we travelled up to Newbattle Abbey College on the outskirts of Edinburgh, where we were again delighted by the response of our students. The summer school also usefully solved the problem of our digs. Staying at the College, the company were also playing Uranium 235 at the Edinburgh Festival during the first week of the course. This was a tremendous hit. We played to packed houses, receiving excellent notices. Later, while the company went on three one-night stands, Mish and I stayed with a Glasgow family who were great supporters of Theatre Workshop. The company returned to Oddfellows Hall, Edinburgh, on 3 September 1951, with revivals of both 'Johnny Noble' and 'The Flying Doctor'. This programme was then repeated for one night at the Jewish Institute in Glasgow, before embarking on a tour of South Wales. Then, after six weeks, two new plays took over: 'Hymn to the Rising Sun' by the American playwright Paul Green, and 'The Long Shift' by Joan and Gerry. For the latter, a great deal of time was spent simulating the hardships of miners working underground in confined spaces: their bodily exertions as they attacked the coal seam gave an authentic feeling, and in doing so

A Special 'Production'

the actors actually sweated as much as the men they were playing. Once these productions were set up and running, however, neither Ewan nor I were involved in them, and we returned to the cottage, where Ewan continued to put the finishing touches to 'The Travellers'.

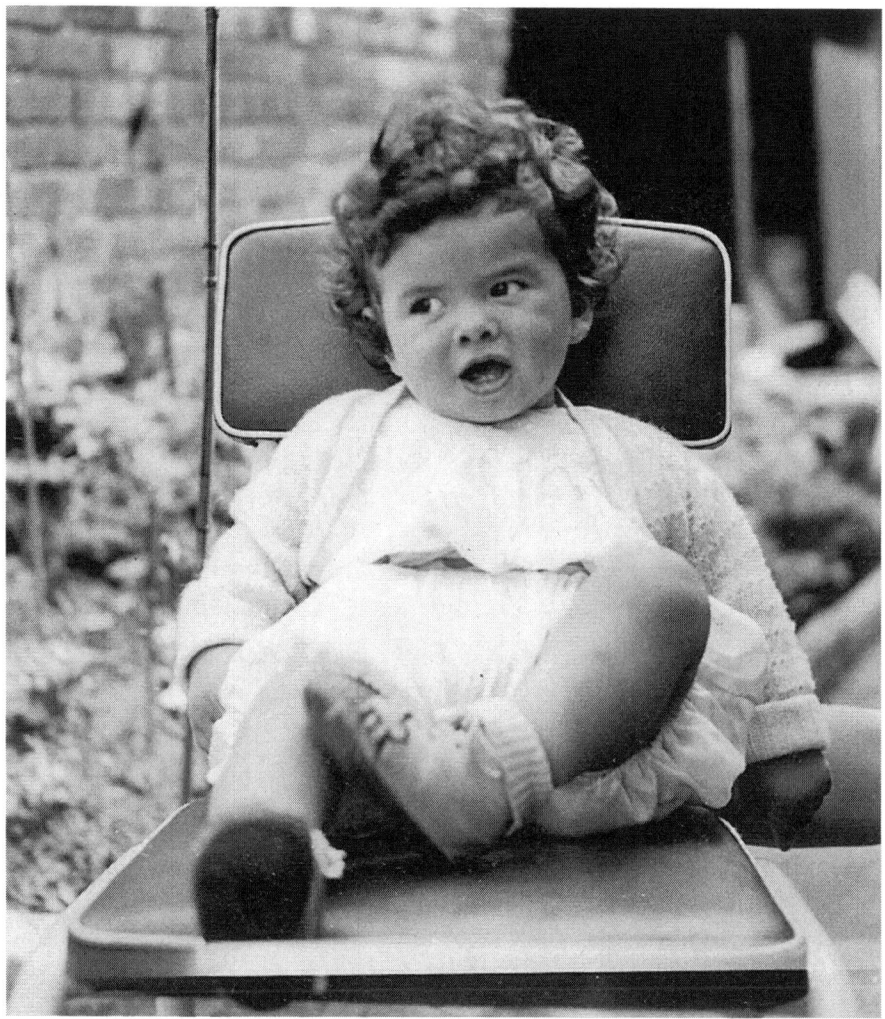

My son Hamish

Chapter Twenty

The Edinburgh Festival

1952

Another spring, another production of 'Uranium 235'. The company was now back in Manchester, and this time I was again directly involved in rehearsals. I was reworking the choreography of the Atom Ballet which was the highlight of the production. The cast of performers made their entrance on stage as a circus, to the sound of Sousa's 'March of the Gladiators': there were handstands, cart-wheels, Gerry Raffles as 'Energy supporting a three-tier balancing act, and one member of the cast performed a dazzling set of back-somersaults (without a mat). I know of no other theatre company who could even have attempted our 'Atom Ballet' as we closely followed the scientific formulae, enhanced by music, subtle lighting and performed by actor–dancers colour-coded to represent the protons and neutrons of atomic fission. When they leapt high into the air as 'Energy' burst his bonds and exploded to a crescendo in the music, followed by a blackout and silence, it created a stunning effect – the actors' stamina and split-second timing resulting in an exciting coup de théâtre. My own role had been that of Lola, 'the smasher', who finally crossed the line and upset the delicate balance. Sigurd Leeder, co-founder of the Jooss Ballets, whom I had visited some two years earlier, came backstage at the Embassy Theatre in London to congratulate me. He told me he thought my actors moved 'beautifully, like trained dancers', which was high praise indeed. Ewan also had many supporters, including scientists impressed at his ability to explain such difficult matters in simple language to a layman. They were full of praise at our interpretation.

Our run at the Embassy was made possible by two distinguished visitors to our rehearsals: the great actor Michael Redgrave and the American co-star of his present production, Sam Wanamaker – whose pilgrimage to the site of Shakespeare's Globe on Bankside at this time inspired his lifelong project to reconstruct it. These were influential friends to have, and their generous support of the production, both financially and in terms of influential publicity, was invaluable. Michael Redgrave, in particular, was generous in his praise, writing that the rehearsal had held him spellbound: 'Others have attempted to compound drama and ballet, verse and mime, burlesque, review, satire, and song, but this seems to me to achieve a synthesis . . . (Theatre Workshop) have rigorously trained themselves for over seven years . . the result is unique in this country, and I think without parallel elsewhere.'

The critics once again highly praised us and the usual interviews followed. The acclaim, of course, was not for the producer alone. It was also (as Michael Redgrave had recognised) for the actors, whose rigorous training paid off so brilliantly. It was at this point that notice was taken not only of the choreography but the choreographer, unusual in a cast of actors but their intensive training and dedication over the years had paid off. Laban's movement theory, for the first time, was being recognised on the professional British stage. And I felt very proud to have been instrumental in its success. (It was some ten years since Laban and I had first met at Dartington). Not least, it was for Ewan, whose plays were emblematic of the type of theatre he and Joan pioneered. As founders of Theatre Workshop, they made a formidable team. At meetings, when Joan's flights of fancy became too impossible to realise, it was Ewan alone who could bring her back to the more realistic and attainable goals. And without Joan, I believe, Ewan's plays would never have been so brilliantly brought to life.

However, it always seemed rather strange to me that our repertoire, predominantly aimed at working-class audiences, excited most comment from an international and largely intellectual theatregoing public. The long, grinding tours had gained us many friends, and perhaps in time critical esteem would translate into box-office success. But how long does a company have to live on the bread-line without any kind of subsidy? I had been with them for just over six of their seven years, and during all that time, the financial situation had remained dire. After our stint at the Embassy Theatre, we went to Brighton for two weeks and came back to play at the Comedy Theatre in the West End. Once again, despite good notices, the end of the run saw us struggling to balance the books. Scheduled to rehearse Ewan's new play, 'The Travellers', for the Edinburgh Festival in August, the coffers were empty.

Hamish had been with us in London and Brighton. A sociable chap, he seemed to enjoy our wandering existence, staying with friends, and liked mixing with the company. He and I now took a short break, returning to Lincoln, while the rest, including Ewan, sought another temporary solution to our money worries. I heard from phone-calls that Tom Driberg had let the company camp out in the grounds of his house in Essex. It was one way of keeping everyone together for the rehearsal period, and saved paying rent. Unfortunately, however, the actors still needed to eat. I heard later that Harry Corbett was put in charge of 'labour', hiring members of the company out to local farmers for 'stooking duties'. With his highly trained entrepreneurial skills, Harry ensured that everyone earned enough for our immediate needs – but no one, not even a member of Theatre Workshop, could be in two places at the same time, and when Joan called an actor for rehearsal, only to find Harry had already purloined him now for tomato picking, 'stooking duties' being finished, she was distinctly unimpressed. The 'real work' was in rehearsal, she said, and everyone was supposed to come to it fresh. I'm told it led to tempestuous arguments.

There were no dances in this production, which was just as well, but Joan did ring to say that she could do with my help once the set was up in Edinburgh. In the meantime, Hamish enjoyed being taken out by his great-grandfather. At two, he was able to carry on a conversation, which delighted his proud grandparents. It was quite hard for them all when the time again came for us to say goodbye, and set off for Scotland and the Festival.

The Edinburgh Festival

When we arrived, the set for 'The Travellers' at the Oddfellows Hall, Edinburgh, was almost finished – and already quite extraordinary. Ewan's play was entirely set aboard a train, and an adjacent station platform. The concept for the design, by Harry Greene, was to extend the 'carriages' throughout the length of the hall, cutting the auditorium in two. Harry had been a carpentry teacher in a technical college in his native South Wales – until the arrival there, one day in late 1950, of our Theatre Workshop touring production of 'Uranium 235'. In the best theatrical tradition, Harry threw in his job, upped sticks, and joined the company as its chippie-cum- backstage technician, and eventually married one of its actresses. His set for 'The Travellers', apparently achieved with just a hammer, a bag of nails, and four pounds in cash, was truly miraculous – so detailed that even the seats in the 'first-class compartment' were covered in an authentically plush material. My job was to devise and rehearse the movement, by which the actors simulated the motion of the train as it slowed down or increased in speed. It was fairly easy for them when they remained seated, but much harder when they had to stand up and then synchronise their movements with the rest of the seated passengers on the train. Once this was achieved, though, it had an astonishing effect on the audience who felt like fellow passengers travelling through the night to oblivion.

Hamish and I had joined Ewan in a nearby flat. Although it was up several flights of stone steps, it was roomy, with marvellous views over the city. The Scottish poets, writers, reporters, and other Festival visitors habitually congregated outside Oddfellows Hall after rehearsals. They were proud of Theatre Workshop and, most of all, of the company's Scottish playwright. Ewan was in his element at these gatherings and was very much at the centre of the group, many of whom were Scottish nationalists and literary intellectuals who admired his writing tremendously as a playwright. Taking a lead in many of his plays was the 'icing on the cake'. Of course, he also enjoyed linking up with his Scottish background. The meetings usually ended with Ewan or Hamish Henderson, poet and folk singer, leading the singing.

While I was proud of Ewan's popularity I was also trying to do my job in the theatre and needed a little support with Hamish. The rest of the company was involved in getting the set ready and the costumes organised. This left Ewan free to meet his Scottish friends when I felt he should occasionally volunteer to babysit. After finishing rehearsals, my job was done. The play was about to have its première and I saw little point in hanging around. I decided instead to accept a longstanding invitation from mutual friends in Glasgow. Telling Ewan of my decision to take a holiday and leaving my phone number with the company I looked forward to the break.

'Phone call for you.' I could not imagine why anyone was ringing me so soon after my departure, and picked up the receiver with misgivings.

'Hello?

'Jeanie?'

'Joan! What is it?' Her voice sounded grave, almost sepulchral.

'Jeanie, we have a crisis. The actress playing Kari Nielsen has suddenly had to leave the company. There is no one to take her part . . . unless you come back. If you don't, we'll have to close.'

I couldn't believe my ears. I thought of Harry Greene's work on the set, of the company's efforts to get to the Festival. Of the endless rehearsals I had conducted on the train sequences. And now all this hard work and sacrifice were in jeopardy! It didn't seem possible.

'But Joan, what's wrong with her? Why can't she go on?'

'The part's too big, it's too much for her.'

'Can't you do it?' I felt that I couldn't possibly learn the part in so short a time.

'Look, bird, I can't. It calls for a young girl, and you are my only hope. We're all relying on you. You can do it, I know you can. You'll be beautiful in the part.'

The Edinburgh Festival

Clutching the telephone to my ear, it didn't seem that I had much choice. If I didn't go back, the theatre would close; the production would lose what little money it had raised; and we'd all be worse than broke, yet again. It seemed I had no alternative. I'd never be able to face them all if . . . But if I took over the part, and turned out to be a disaster, it would be even worse. I felt sick. In spite of being a thorn in the flesh of the Establishment, we were beginning to make a name for ourselves and creating a great deal of interest.

'Is there any other way?' I asked.

'No!'

'But – but what about Mish?'

'I'll look after him.'

'Well, if you think I can do it . . . but I'm still not at all sure . . .'

'That's marvellous, doll! I'll let the cast know. I'll come over tomorrow and we'll start rehearsing. I cancelled the matinee. Give my love to Mish.'

I was left in a state of shock.

My friends accepted my precipitate departure reluctantly – but not nearly as reluctantly as I did.

The following morning I was back in Edinburgh and rehearsing with Joan in the flat I had so recently vacated. Ewan was nowhere to be seen. I imagined he was at one of his many meetings. We worked through the part quietly, making almost leisurely progress, while Hamish played happily in the room. It was a race against time, to get me on the stage in less than twenty four hours.

We stopped while I gave Hamish his tea and played with him before his bath, while Joan went to check up on the set. When he was tucked up in bed, I studied the lines and went over the moves. I went to bed, eventually falling asleep with the lines going round in my head and disturbed at Ewan's continued absence – I could have done with some support.

I was up early in the morning. While I was in another room collecting a bag of baby necessities, my landlady poured me out a cup of tea – without telling me. As I walked into the kitchen, I saw Hamish suddenly reach up to touch the saucer, just visible to him from the table. His fingers tilted it towards him, and the scalding tea cascaded all over his arm and chest. There had been no time to shout or take the three small steps that could have prevented the accident. His screams filled the small kitchen and echoed and re-echoed in my head. Picking him up, I dashed into the bedroom where Ewan was sleeping. (He had apparently come back very late.) I was trying to remember some first aid. I found a clean terry-towelling napkin and carefully lifted Hamish's steaming jersey to place it next to the angry red skin, not realizing that his arm was affected too. Ewan made no attempt to get up or help in any way: he later told me that he hadn't realised this was a real emergency. I rushed to the phone and tried dialling 999. There was no reply. The screams were unbearable.

Wrapping Mish in a blanket (because I remembered from somewhere in my unconscious that shock could bring on pneumonia), I carried him down the five flights of steps into the street, where I tried flagging down passing taxis. They all ignored me. I must have looked a wild thing, hugging my screaming child, but the passers-by only gave me an indifferent glance as they window-shopped or sauntered on. I found a public phone-box and with great difficulty got us both inside it and tried phoning 999 again. Again, nothing. Minutes – that seemed hours – had passed, and still the screaming continued. I returned to the flat in desperation. Putting Hamish down gently, I tried dialling 999 again without success. In a frenzy I shook the receiver up and down, and somehow managed to cut in on another conversation. The operator asked me to clear the line. I refused and told her of my predicament. I begged her to get me a taxi or an ambulance. She was sympathetic but explained it was quite impossible: this was Festival month, she told me, and the place was teeming with visitors. Everybody wanted a taxi. No, she couldn't put me through to 999. And no, she didn't know why they didn't answer.

The Edinburgh Festival

Once again I went down to the street, Hamish by now exhausted, flushed, and sobbing. The only thing to do, I now decided, was to take my life in my hands and stand in the middle of the road and force someone to stop. As luck would have it, an empty taxi appeared just as I stepped into the road. The driver rushed me to the children's hospital, which as things turned out providentially happened to have a burns unit.

The bureaucratic formalities seemed endless – name, age, sex, religion . . . Hamish was still crying when, without warning, he was suddenly spirited away from me. A doctor explained that it was hospital policy to leave the burns uncovered and open to air. For this reason visitors were not allowed because of the danger of infection. However, I could ring up and make enquiries . . . And he, too, was gone.

Left alone, completely numb, I stood in the stone corridor, with its tiled walls and the all-pervading smell of antiseptic, consumed with guilt for causing my beautiful child such pain. And now we were separated and I hadn't been able to kiss him or tell him how much I loved him. I wanted to reassure him that the pain would go. I couldn't even visit him. Barely two years old, he was left in a frightening world with complete strangers.

A nurse returned, busy and matter-of-fact. No, they couldn't let me know how he was – but I could ring for news tonight. She handed me Hamish's neatly folded clothes, baby shorts, T-shirt, socks, and sandals. It was such a little bundle. I remember noticing that the wet jersey and the napkin I'd used for protection were missing. So was the blanket. I held the clothes very carefully to me, afraid that I would disturb or crumple them. It was all I had of Hamish. I walked out of the hospital into the brilliant sunshine of an Edinburgh morning, and made my way along the bustling streets of this festive city.

I don't recall whether or not I was late arriving at Oddfellows Hall. I blankly noticed a few people making last-minute adjustments on the set as I walked into the backstage area, still carrying the baby clothes carefully in front of me.

'What's that you've got?' someone said.

'Hamish is in hospital.'

'Oh my God, what happened?'

'He was burned by a cup of tea.'

I felt the guilt wash over me afresh. Someone took me to my dressing room, and I sensed the message being relayed around the building in the unaccustomed hush. One crisis had followed another – but this was by far the worst.

I didn't witness Joan's immediate reaction. But this woman who could scream, rave, shout, and swear at a missed cue or a fluffed line, was now softly spoken, deeply caring, and calmly unhurried. She, who could be so impatient at times, was able in moments of extreme stress, to show tremendous compassion and understanding. We just sat together, with me still holding Hamish's clothes. I heard someone calling for the actors to go on stage for their lighting cues. I got up but found it hard to put the little parcel down. It was like being parted from him all over again, and I didn't want anyone else to touch it. We found a costume of sorts, and I made my way to the stage for the scheduled dress-rehearsal in a daze. The actors looked stricken. We rehearsed through the afternoon. They patiently ignored my slip-ups. To save time, the lighting run-through was attempted simultaneously. My character, Kari Nielsen, was supposed to be a young girl. I felt as old as the hills.

At around teatime we stopped, and someone gave me a cup of tea. I couldn't eat the sandwich. I went into the street to find a phone-box. It seemed to take an eternity to get any news – Hamish was a new patient and no one seemed to know which ward he was on. Eventually a crisp female voice announced that he was – that dreadfully inappropriate word – 'comfortable'. I didn't believe her. It seemed a stock answer. By the time I returned to the theatre, the hour call was being given. Everyone was quiet and awkwardly kind towards me; I remember that Harry's assistant-technician Karl Wood gave me some flowers. But we all had a job to do. The audience was already coming in, excited and surprised at the sight of what seemed to be part of a train taking up a large part of the hall.

The Edinburgh Festival

The girl I was playing had been repeatedly abused in a concentration camp by a sadistic S.S. guard. Travelling to meet her boyfriend after the war, she encounters the guard on the train. She expresses her contempt for him; he rapes her again. Somehow, I got through the scene, and the play finished. The audience was very enthusiastic, applauding for some time – but my thoughts were elsewhere. The cast had given everything they had, and I'm sure this had carried me through.

Returning to the dressing room, I wiped off my make-up, changed, and, collecting up my wilting flowers and Hamish's small bundle, walked home to the confusion I'd left that morning – was it only that morning? Was it only yesterday that I had started rehearsing the part with Joan, and panicked over learning the lines? I flopped onto a chair in the dark and looked out at the night sky. Was Hamish missing me? We'd never been parted before. Would he blame me? Was he frightened? Did he think I'd deserted him? I felt very cold, and suddenly very, very tired. I remember thinking that it was odd: I hadn't cried all day. Not once.

Ewan's character in the play had no contact with mine on stage, and I didn't even see him after the show. I still have no idea why he appeared to be so unsympathetic, nor why he behaved so uncharacteristically over the accident, but it seems that he and Joan had had a terrific argument about the last-minute change of casting. He was concerned that this last minute change in the cast could damage Theatre Workshop's reputation and the premiere of the play. He was not normally unkind, and I knew he loved Hamish. Locked into his own concerns, it was somehow as if he had no emotional reserves to spare for anyone else, not even for his own son. I visited the hospital regularly, taking Hamish a new present each time – but I never knew if he received them since I was never allowed in to see him. I always went alone. Ewan told me later that he had also been to the hospital, with gifts of his own – but it would surely have been kinder to tell me this at the time.

I now knew that, under the present circumstances, I was on my own.

Chapter Twenty-One

Even the Swings were Chained Up on the Sabbath

Glasgow, 1952

'I'm going on a very long journey,' announced my two-year-old son, by now the very model of a seasoned traveller, to the rest of the railway carriage – a real one this time, and not one of Harry Greene's miraculous sets. But the audience was just as soon won over. 'I've got my sandwiches in my case,' he solemnly continued. 'I think perhaps I'd better eat them now.' Everyone began to chuckle as he scoffed the lot – polishing off the last crumb just as the train started to move off, on its long journey from Lincoln to Glasgow.

Hamish had been discharged from hospital shortly after 'The Travellers' closed that August. His burns were healed, and I was assured the scars would fade completely in time, which they did: my prompt application of the napkin had helped. I sensed that the mental scars would take longer to heal, however. For a week or two after leaving hospital, he saw my absence as desertion, reproaching me for not visiting him, and it had been very difficult to explain the details of hospital regulations to my confused toddler. Even the toys I had brought him had gone to other children in the ward who were already convalescent. And there was no way he could have known of my regular phone-calls and visits, or of my desperate attempts to wave to him through a distant window. When Joan later took him out for a walk in the local park, she returned visibly upset at the change in him. I had therefore decided to make another temporary visit to my family home in Lincoln: it would provide Hamish with a happy and secure environment with my parents while the company had a break.

Ewan had meanwhile gone south, commuting from his mother's cottage in Manchester, to London, to join Humphrey Lyttelton, Alan Lomax, and others to work on the 'Ballads and Blues' programmes for the B.B.C. Since the company was now looking for a permanent base in Glasgow, it must have seemed a good opportunity for him to pursue his other work and other interests – if only in order to earn a living for the three of us – and also to begin work on his next play. It must also be said, however, that his departure had been precipitated by recent events. I was aware at the time that he and Joan had had an explosive difference of opinion, and that a cooling-off period between them was now required. It also eventually became clear that the reason Joan had asked me to replace the young actress in 'The Travellers' at such short notice had less to do with the level of her theatrical talent, and everything to do with her extra-curricular penchant for seducing most of the men in the company. When news of this reached Joan, she had hit the roof – and the said actress found herself on a train south before she could adjust her make-up.

Before I left Edinburgh Ewan and I had had a long talk and we decided that we would try and find our own place as soon as the theatre was settled. At that time we anticipated the company finding a permanent home in Scotland. Meanwhile Hamish and I returned to Lincoln while Ewan went down to London to work. Joan had written to say that there was a room waiting for us in the house in Glasgow's Belmont Street that she and Gerry had secured as our temporary base. I was delighted at the recovery Hamish had made, and we were both looking forward to meeting up with the company again. Ewan would apparently be joining us later, but until the company sorted out its new home it was important that he continued to earn a living for the three of us.

The house at No. 12 Belmont Street, Glasgow, dated from the late Victorian period. Empty for some time, its most immediately noticeable feature was the thick layer of grime coating every surface. Of the three houses Gerry found for the company, Belmont Street was by far the worst. The Parrot House was rather superior in its middle-class aura, with its expensive hand-printed wall paper, sofas and carpets. The 'Schloss' was definitely several rungs lower down the ladder, but was clean if austere. At Belmont Street we met our nadir despite having received tremendous international acclaim for 'The Other Animals'. It seems that however much success we had artistically, there was still no financial help from the Arts Council; or anyone else.

As we were welcomed into the hall, I recognised the figure of Avis Bunnage, one of Theatre Workshop's most experienced actresses, scrubbing her way down the stairs. Instead of a bucket, she was using a large aluminium bowl to rinse her brushes and cloths, and it was obvious from the disgusting colour of its contents that the stairs had been in a particularly bad way – as I couldn't help noticing on my way up them, to the first-floor room to which Hamish and I were now welcomed as privileged guests. The sound of human voices – in song, recital, chatter and argument – resonated from behind every door. Our allocated room, with its bare floorboards and a bay-window overlooking the street, was empty, save for Hamish's cot and a bed for me made up from rostra.

The welcome may have been warm, but after the full guided tour, the premises themselves made my heart sink – especially the sight of the large basement kitchen. I thought it was probably the most squalid place I had ever seen. It was infinitely worse than the Schloss, certainly. There was a large refectory table in the kitchen at Belmont Street, and an old-fashioned grate of the kind that had once been black-leaded, now red-brown with rust. The gas stove was unmentionable, and the larder not much better. The owner of the house was apparently an eccentric millionaire (or so Gerry said), and one might have been excused for imagining that his ghost – or corpse – lurked somewhere in its hidden depths. Hamish loved it, of course, especially when George Cooper warned us about the cockroaches, promising to show him the next one he caught. When I took him to the park one Sunday afternoon a few weeks later (the swings were chained up for the Sabbath), he invited another disappointed little boy, in his newly acquired Scottish accent, to 'come and play at my house'. Then turning to

Even the Swings were Chained Up on the Sabbath

the boy's mother, he boasted, 'We have cockroaches in our kitchen.'

First things first, I swept and scrubbed our room, adding a strong dash of disinfectant to the water. I made up the cot with its own sheets and blankets. It looked like a little oasis of luxury in the middle of a desert. Even so, I was grateful to the company for giving us such a nice room. With one of my parents' rugs, Hamish had a pleasant home, if slightly bare of any adult furnishings, like a table or easy chair. More importantly, after all, there was plenty of space for his toys.

Having seen the state of the kitchen, I was certainly not going to keep any of Hamish's food downstairs, so I commandeered the 'butler's pantry' off the first-floor hall. Cleaning and covering the shelves, I made sure that all perishables were properly covered, and bought a couple of small saucepans for his use only. I also made sure that we had our own tea-towels, and Hamish had his own mug and cutlery. After he saw George Cooper and Joby (John Blanshard) making a breakfast fry-up of the previous night's leftovers, Mish was keen to sample the 'grown-up' food, but I was secretly relieved when they proved reluctant to share their meal. I later explained to him that on no account must he eat anything that I had not prepared!

I rebuilt my bed from the wooden rostra from the Schloss. Although I had brought my own sheets, my blankets were following in a separate parcel, and Joby kindly donated some long curtains of green velvet – green now, that is, but I fancy they had originally been black: ancient residents of Glasgow, they seemed to be held together by grime. I reasoned that if my large cotton sheets covered me completely, from head to toe, it wouldn't matter too much, in the time before my own blankets arrived. Pernickety about hygiene as I had always been, I was learning to adapt, and make compromises, for myself – if not for my child. In this respect I was not alone – as Avis demonstrated later that night at the dinner table. Meanwhile, after tea and a bath, Mish was comfortably installed in his cot, on his rug, with his toys and books. He had enjoyed his time at Lincoln and was now all set to enjoy the return to Theatre Workshop. I felt pleased to have made our room homely, and the butler's pantry hygienic, as I left him sleeping peacefully to make my way downstairs to my first communal supper, looking forward hugely to meeting everyone again. The meal had been organised by our lighting-man Camel – and the conversation must have flowed, because I don't remember anything about the main course – except noticing, midway through it, that in the centre of the table stood a large fruit trifle (prepared by Camel) . . . in an aluminium bowl . . . last seen that afternoon next to Avis on the stairs. Neither she nor I could touch it – but what the eye doesn't see, the heart doesn't grieve over, and the others, in their sublime ignorance, polished it off with relish.

Avis and I came to develop a mutual early-warning signal for each other if the preparation of the evening meal left too much to be desired, but it was always a case of pot luck, and the quality varied tremendously from day to day. The company was budgeted to spend one pound a week each on provisions (around twenty in today's money), a sum the rest of us never saw since it went straight to the kitchen for the week's provisions. This was meant to cover a daily breakfast, and a larger main meal at the end of the day; I don't remember anyone ever sitting down to a midday snack.

What I should have mentioned earlier was that our total wages were £1 per week!

Some chefs were more resourceful than others. Not only was George Cooper, for example, content to buy fruit-and-veg well past their prime, but in my presence he actually asked the greengrocer to give him 'everything you're going to throw out'. Some of the produce he came back with was, basically, rotting – so his proud announcement that he actually had some money left over was met by shocked disbelief. In fact, he was nearly lynched – even the poor have their pride, after all!

Of course, Hamish was still provided with a normal healthy diet, helped by the money Ewan intermittently sent up to cover his needs. Two weeks into my residence at Belmont Street, Ewan sent me enough money to repay the removal expenses – with a little bit left over to spare: I felt like a Rockefeller. Unable to face the grisly breakfast preparations, I treated us both to toast, jam, and scones, with a pot of tea for me, and a glass of milk for Hamish, at a local restaurant, beautifully served, in very comfortable surroundings, opposite a real log fire. The cost for all this high living was about one-and-six – so I repeated the treat a few days later.

Movement classes meanwhile went ahead on a daily basis, in the largest room of the house – the kitchen. The large table would be dragged against a wall, and work would begin at 9.15 a.m. Everyone was expected to take part, whether or not they had sat down to breakfast. Harry Corbett was one of those who usually did not. I can still see him arriving, half asleep from upstairs, in a pair of unflattering, orange-coloured cotton tights from wardrobe, trying to limber up for these sessions, as if already dressed for a Shakespearean production.

Company meetings were also regularly held around the kitchen table, but the news was as meagre as the food we ate there. We had pitched our camp in Scotland, in this dreadful Glasgow tenement, because our numerous friends and advisers had felt sure that a more appropriate venue would sooner or later prove suitable for our needs – but as the months wore on, that miracle never quite seemed to happen. When Joan arrived home from a fund-raising trip one evening, barely able to walk on a severely strained ankle, she told us she had thrown herself off the train as it slowed down in the dark when she realised she didn't have the money for the fare. Well, it was a good story – and at least made an enjoyable drama out of a very real financial crisis. (It was expected that 'the movement lady' would repair the damage, but I could only offer cold compresses and rest, and hope it wasn't a fracture.) Kind friends would occasionally drop in for a chat, sometimes bringing a bottle of wine. A few members of the company had saved a little money, but those funds gradually disappeared. It was a hard time for the company's smokers.

Another schools tour, this time of Twelfth Night, was arranged, and this eased the financial situation temporarily. But even with the tours, our straitened economic circumstances never seemed to change. We were just tinkering at the edges, struggling to keep going – just as Gerry struggled to maintain the ancient lorry we toured in. For some reason, that lorry was Joan's pride and joy –

probably because it had all the places we had visited in Czechoslovakia and Sweden painted on its side, a reminder of the days when we were admired and fêted as the new face of British theatre.

Amidst all this poverty, however, our suppers were suddenly transformed. The food remained as dreadful as always, but Gerry suddenly announced one day that he had become a wine importer! To prove it, he had a couple of cases of Lacryma Christi stacked by the kitchen door. He would sit at a table with a little note-book: those of us who wanted a glass of this famous Italian wine would raise our hands, and he would put a mark against the names. The cost was threepence: some glasses were bigger than others, but that was the luck of the draw. I was never too sure how Gerry expected some of us to pay for this treat. I can only speak for myself, but I thought this innovation was a real luxury: in fact, to order two glasses of wine in a week seemed riotous living. And at least it made the more awful meals – like George's dumplings – slightly more palatable. Ever since our Czechoslovakian tour, he had developed a passion for them. I very much doubt whether Gerry ever recouped his outlay on the wine, but it cheered us all up at perhaps the bleakest time Theatre Workshop had known.

In order to pay our expenses, but particularly Hamish's, Ewan had meanwhile been able to take on work as an actor with the B.B.C. in Manchester. In those days before mobile phones, it wasn't easy keeping in regular touch. There wasn't even a telephone in the house, only a phone kiosk at a corner of the main road where a queue usually formed. Being cut off in mid-conversation was a regular occurrence. We depended mostly on letters. Ewan was now in great demand as a singer for Communist Party events, but was also still busily involved with Alan Lomax and Humphrey Lyttelton's rehearsals for their radio Ballads and Blues programmes in London. Travelling between the two venues was expensive. He could always stay with his mother in Manchester, but had to rely on friends' hospitality in London. While there, he did his best to promote Theatre Workshop's repertoire among his new contacts, and report its international success, while at the same time 'working like a galley slave' (as one of his letters put it) in an 'orgy' of various demands on his time. He had also written a number of programmes of his own for B.B.C. Radio's Third Programme. These had been accepted, and he was waiting to record them, suggesting Joan and Harry Corbett (for 'The Scouse') as possible narrators. He quoted his fee for each of the programmes – a moderate sum that in our present circumstances seemed astronomical. I sensed a sort of desperation in him, trying to make amends to us for not sharing our sordid conditions – but that of course would have been absurd. He was doing important work; Hamish was well looked after, and enjoyed mixing with the company; and like everyone else, it was only ever my own choice to stay with the group, through thick and thin. No one was prepared to give up. We all believed that we had something special to offer the theatre-going public. All we needed was a permanent home for the company, but none of us knew where that home would be. One thing was certain, however: on current form, we would not be able to survive much longer.

As winter drew near, the weather worsened. Although I was able to keep a small blaze going in the fireplace during the day, the area round the window was decidedly draughty. On closer inspection, I saw the reason for it. The house, built on a hill, was slowly subsiding – I could have sworn it had shifted a couple of inches since my arrival. Hamish hugely enjoyed this period in his young life, oblivious to the grown-up poverty around him. He never lacked for anything, and there was never any shortage of people willing to play with him or talk to him, entertain him or soothe him. When the snow came, Joan was the first out with Mish to play in it; and when Ewan briefly came up to the local B.B.C. studio for a concert of folk-songs, George took Hamish with him to the rehearsals, playing 'bears' with him during the sessions.

With Christmas approaching, I spent some of the money Ewan had sent on a small lamp, and a rosy glow settled over the room in the winter evenings. Ewan begged me in his letter not to be upset at his continued absence, assuring me that he loved me dearly. He knew, he said, that if we were not bowed down by economic worries, and could spend time alone with Hamish, we'd be very happy together: 'I swear to you that I look to our future together with the greatest hope and optimism. I know that being together is my only hope of salvation . . .' The letter continued with news of his plans for concerts and venues for the company, and ended, 'Darling, we are going through a difficult time, but I know we will survive it.' I tried to believe it, with all my heart.

Chapter Twenty-Two

Conditions Force a Final Decision

1952–1953

It was obvious that our hopes of finding a suitable theatre building in Scotland were fading fast. Even with the good will of our loyal supporters, it was proving impossible to raise enough capital to invest in our theatre project. Just as things seemed to have reached a final impasse, however, towards the end of 1952, a meeting was called, and Gerry announced that he had just found out that the Theatre Royal at Stratford, in East London, was available at a peppercorn rent.

It had always been our avowed intention to take theatre to the working-class population of Britain's industrial areas. This meant constant touring, and despite the many friends we made on these trips, it remained a relatively hand-to-mouth existence. The sheer hard slog of constant touring and poor conditions were beginning to tell on the company. I think most of us would have opted to stay in Scotland (or at the very least in the north of England), had we succeeded in finding suitable premises there. Ewan was certainly against the move south. His argument was that if we took a play about mining to miners, and even they didn't care enough to turn up, we should ask ourselves why and try to overcome the problem. For him, the previous, invaluable experience of touring was now being thrown away for the sake of courting the critics – always a dangerous game to play. Many of the cast agreed with him.

Looking back, though, I don't think we could have continued much longer living as we did. I remember one occasion when Tom Driberg visited the company in Glasgow. Sitting in the miserable kitchen at Belmont Street, Joan and Gerry shared a rather grand supper with him while the rest of the company managed on the usual spartan fare. George Cooper, ever the wag, sat up and begged at their end of the table. Such occasions of inequality happened infrequently. Tom was an important friend to have, after all, and Joan and Gerry can be forgiven for 'feasting' an honoured guest who had tried to help the company out. Many of us resented the special treatment, however. I saw it as a simple error of judgement, though I was surprised that such a good friend felt unable to share the 'set' meal. Maybe Tom should have taken them out for a meal but Joan probably wanted him to see how dire our position was. Then again, perhaps word had reached him of Camel's trifle!

Some of the founder members, agreeing with Ewan, had already flown the nest. Among the actors, Rosalie Williams and David Scase, whose daughter was one year older than Hamish, had returned to Rosalie's home in Manchester; Kristin Lind was back in Sweden; and Denis Ford and Bill Davidson had also left. Our 'costume lady', Ruth Brandes, was another face we missed. It was Camel's view that our present conditions often dictated immediate future policy. Offered a theatre in a working-class area of London, some company members hoped we could build up a local audience, and in due course attract a wider theatre-going public. Poverty-stricken we may well have been, but we were not, after all, entirely unknown. Productions at the Comedy and Embassy Theatres in London, and at the Edinburgh Festivals, had been favourably reported in the national press. Others argued that having our very own theatre would give us time to train and rehearse on a regular basis and enable the company to establish its long-term policy on more business-like terms.

Gerry Raffles and Harry Greene were dispatched to view the Theatre Royal in Stratford East as a possible home, and returned with a contract to rent the place from the New Year of 1953. We said our farewells to friends and one by one departed for the Christmas break. Joan and Gerry were the last to leave. On their last night in the now all but empty house on Belmont Street, a couple arrived with the gift of a large turkey, for the company to share in the festive season A few days earlier and we would all have enjoyed such a wonderful gift.

My own views about the move to London were mixed. I wanted to go wherever there was an opportunity to work, to experiment with ideas, and develop as an artist. Even after six years of it, I don't think I minded the poverty. The thrill of working at what one loved, and had some talent for, was satisfaction enough. It was the culmination of a preparation started in childhood and I was not prepared to give it up easily. Travel overseas and international acclaim – including recognition for my own work – was an unexpected and welcome bonus. Maybe the time I'd spent in the A.T.S. had toughened me up for the present difficulties. One thing I could be sure of: Ewan and I would both see Hamish's needs were met, and we both somehow expected to find a place suitable for him to grow up in.

While Ewan's sharp focus both on theatre policy and world events was appreciated by all, I began to realise he was a traditional romantic at heart. He found it difficult, sometimes impossible, to deal with the emotional problems he himself had brought about and later regretted. I did not doubt his constantly expressed belief that he loved me and saw our future together. He was so full of optimism at this time, both for the theatre's future and for us as a family, that it would have been churlish to do otherwise. We would build our future together with Hamish, and achieve better conditions for us all. Laban's idealist may have suffered a momentary hiccup along the bumpy road of life but I remained optimistic, believing that, with commitment, most of our difficulties would disappear.

It was around this time that I began to notice the changes going on within the company. It had always been my private belief that Gerry Raffles was never cut out to be a business manager. He would sit in at company meetings, smoking his pipe and hardly saying a word. This reticence on his part resulted in a lot of frustration among the cast, which would from time to time boil over into vociferous argument when we felt particularly confused. Ewan never interfered with financial matters apart from putting them in a context of wider theatre artistic policy. At such times Ewan was able to speak for the rest of us.

When Ewan eventually left Theatre Workshop, his role as company spokesman was never filled. The older members of the company realised he was the only one able to curb Joan's flights of fancy when they became too extreme. Joan had little understanding of the company's lack of finances, and Gerry gained support from Camel. There was a distinct feeling that the balance had shifted, with some members of the company suspecting that any meeting would present us with a fait accompli, the collective decision having already been made without us.

Offset against this was the fact that no one else wanted Gerry's job and, more than likely, no one else could have done it as well as he did. Even if we didn't expect a living wage, we still had to eat, and Gerry was expected to find the money, as well as having to pay for sets, costumes, transport, and accommodation. It was always a battle for him to raise the cash, and uneasy compromises were reached. When one knows what could be achieved, it is hard to settle for less. But we had a galaxy of talent willing to carry out and develop Joan's ideas on staging and costuming, (the Moon's costume in the overseas tour of 'The Other Animals' comes to mind), and while the technical experts grumbled momentarily at seeing their dreams fade, magnificently ingenious results were produced out of nowhere and on next to nothing. Gerry certainly had the loneliest job in Theatre Workshop – though on the other hand, of course, he was Joan's partner!

While the older members of the company resented not being consulted on policy, the newcomers never expected to be. The regular talks, the group discussions on the political role and/or artistic policy of our theatre, with close reference to past theatrical history – all this disappeared once we settled in our own 'home'. Most of the new actors joining the company simply recognised an opportunity to take part in great plays and to play a variety of roles. I doubt if our 'Manifesto' would have interested many of them. There were, however, three outstanding newcomers who were enthusiastic about our aims: Brian Murphy, Murray Melvin and Victor Spinetti. They understood what our theatre was all about.

As a result they appeared in several plays that transferred to the West End from Stratford East.

With Ewan's final departure around 1957, a radical change took place. Before that and after the move to London, he had been free to take on other work when he was not acting in his own plays or adaptations. Without his presence, the company's artistic direction was left entirely in Joan's hands. Howard Goorney and I both agreed that the original Theatre Workshop Company ceased to exist from that moment. In later years the press were to credit Joan with the founding of Theatre Workshop, and associate her alone with its successes. Having spent half a lifetime reading misleading articles about my family in newspapers, this doesn't surprise me. I do not recall Joan or Gerry ever seeking to put the record straight, and Ewan was, I think, justifiably upset – though not enough to do anything about it himself. The truth remains, however, that Joan and Ewan were the joint founders of Theatre Workshop. It was the product of their collective inspiration, and they made a formidable team. And it was that sense of an inspired and improvised teamwork that always characterised the company's best work, as shown in the career of John 'Camel' Bury (becoming a brilliant set designer and lighting-man after an unprepossessing start as an actor), or that of the academic lecturer turned backstage 'chippie' Harry Greene.

All these talented craftsmen were committed to our ideals and saw an opportunity to further their skills and were prepared to forgo a living wage for that privilege. In due course we had achieved great success abroad and at the Edinburgh Festivals. Ewan's plays were acclaimed, as was Joan's production of them – including much high praise for the movement training of the company. Later successes, once we had settled in at the Theatre Royal, though, had very little to do with the earlier company and its ideals. In fact, 'Theatre Workshop' should perhaps have changed its name at this point, but to do so would have been professional suicide since the name had already established a critical reputation. But what was also becoming clear to many of us was our general failure to attract the working-class audiences we sought. We had tried to fulfil the aims of our company by taking theatre to 'the masses' – on our tours of Wales, Scotland, and the North East of England – but it is equally true to say that, though they never took to us in hordes, we always retained a small band of extremely loyal supporters wherever we went. That situation did not improve in the wake of our move to Stratford; the 'Theatre Royal' was certainly an ironic destination for a company conceived as a Marxist collective.

Hamish

Leaving Hamish with my parents in Lincoln until I found a flat in London, I set off in January 1953 to join the rest of the company at the Theatre Royal. Walking onto its stage brought back vivid memories of being twirled around by Benny and almost dropped into the orchestra pit during the 'Chess Ballet' of our Alice on its pantomime tour a few years before. The place was still dirty, cold, and smelling of decay. Those of us who had nowhere to sleep immediately took over the dressing rooms. Mine was next to the 'green room', near the steps leading down to the stage – which was useful, since rehearsals and training had to start as soon as possible.

The movement training I led was one aspect of our former existence that did survive, at least temporarily, our move from Glasgow to London. Another was the pittance we earned at the end of each week, which was too little to qualify for Equity's minimum wage. I remember that on one occasion, when there was no money at all to pay the actors, Howard was dispatched to the local Social Security Office to enquire about the dole. When advised that we would each have to go and sign on individually, he gently explained to the clerk that no one could spare the time, since they were all working an unpaid twelve-hour day.

In another attempt to save money in those early days, we opened up the upper bar, and turned it into a soup kitchen for the poor – the poor in this case being the company. One view of its condition, however, encrusted with years of grease and dirt, its gas rings broken, was enough to lose one's appetite, and the facility was as soon abandoned by mutual consent. On our tiny wage, we would rather buy our own food down Angel Lane, where May and Bert, the proprietors of the wonderfully named Café L'Ange, soon became great friends of the company. Their ham and chips, or egg and chips, always served with a steaming mug of tea, sustained many of us over the years to come.

A group of cleaners was employed briefly to clean the theatre, successfully giving it a temporary facelift. But there was nothing much we could do about the more basic amenities. The ancient boiler, for example, situated almost directly under the stage, gave out acrid-smelling fumes to everyone in the immediate vicinity. The men in the company took it in turns to stoke it, but it was so expensive to run we could only afford to use it in the hours running up to the audience's arrival. Nor were the local Fire Brigade particularly happy about our social arrangements, suspecting –

quite rightly – that some of us were sleeping in the theatre, contrary to regulations. They took to visiting us at odd hours, without notice, but we eventually managed to overcome the problem. When the Tannoy message announced, 'Is Walter Plinge in the building' or 'Would Walter Plinge come on stage please?', the coded warning gave us the time required to dismantle the beds and remove the stoves before the imminent inspection of the Fire Officer. Harry Corbett would balance his bed upright against a wall, covering it with costumes, and was terrified one day that it would topple over onto his officious visitor, who seemed to want to stay for a chat. Another actor, who had raced to his dressing room from rehearsing on stage, found he had left it too late. He collapsed gratefully onto the offending bed with his script. When the officer arrived, he explained that this was his 'day bed' – a necessary perk for those with leading and exhausting roles.

Ewan was now commuting between the cottage in Manchester (where he found it easier to write) and visiting our new theatre premises in London. Fortunately we had a number of friends willing to put us up on these visits. He came back to oversee and lend a hand with the productions of one or two of his plays, but by now he was very much caught up with Alan Lomax and the folk scene. They had come along at the right time, filling what otherwise could have been a difficult time with the theatre trying to re-establish itself in a local community.

While the company was getting organised, it was my full-time job to find an affordable flat. We eventually moved into a flat in Rodenhurst Road, across the river in Clapham, in 1953, where we were soon joined by Hamish. It was good to be living as a family once again, with our own space and garden. Necessarily, I spent much of my time with Hamish and took him with me whenever I went to the theatre – he used to enjoy these half-day visits. However, this arrangement also meant that if Ewan had a singing engagement in the evenings, I couldn't go along, since we couldn't afford a baby-sitter. A request from Ewan's mother to join us there came as a surprise. He left me to make the decision, and I eventually agreed, though with some misgivings. After all, I told myself, she was a widow, and Ewan was her only child. After finally settling permanently in London, it would have seemed churlish to refuse, especially since we now had a spare bed-sitting room.

We had left the old touring problems behind us when we moved to the Theatre Royal, but we were soon to find ourselves facing other difficulties. In order to build up a local audience it was necessary to mount a new production every two weeks – effectively transforming us, as Camel complained at the time, into a repertory company. This wasn't so difficult for actors experienced in 'rep', like Avis, but it was a harder lesson for others. At the same time, however, the plays we put on were not at all typical of the ordinary rep system, and many of the cast were used to much longer rehearsal periods, preceded by sessions of movement training. With the drive to get the shows on, this regular training was at first haphazard, and then tended to disappear as rehearsals for the next week's show increasingly ate up the available time.

'Lysistrata' 1947
courtesy of Theatre Royal Stratford East Archive

'Lysistrata'
courtesy of Theatre Royal Stratford East Archive

Another tradition of repertory theatre with which we battled was the question of the set. The demands of rep required a constant minimal set that could serve for each successive production. This was in complete contrast to Theatre Workshop's established practice, by which any play's meaning was in part determined by the audience's physical relationship with its set. For instance, the bare rostra representing Ancient Greece in 'Lysistrata', which enhanced the space and added to the effect of the movement, was very different from the elliptical shape of the barred cell in 'The Other Animals', suspended over the stage, from which Ewan (as the prisoner) surveyed the characters of his imagination on the stage below him. It was this close integration of the plays to the sets they had inspired that had in part made our company unique, and it was precisely that careful attention to detail that was gradually abandoned as our policy had to change with our new circumstances.

Another central feature of Theatre Workshop's original practice jeopardised by our move south was my own intensive class-work on Movement. At first, these went on regularly enough, and Ewan's 'Paradise Street' – among the first plays produced at Stratford's Theatre Royal in 1953 – was a perfect example of what Theatre Workshop was all about. Yes, it was a bare set, but the simple positioning of the cast across the empty stage transformed the space into a street, by their simple arrangement along a diagonal line, as if seated outside their terraced houses. They looked into the distance as the yellow sun of a filtered spotlight blazed down on them. Their voice and movement drained of energy, the heat-wave of Ewan's play was experienced by the entire audience.

'Paradise Street' 1953
courtesy of Theatre Royal Stratford East Archive

This production – along with revivals of 'Twelfth Night', Ewan's 'Travellers', his versions of Molière's 'Malade Imaginaire' and Aristophanes' 'Lysistrata', and a new production of Jonson's 'Alchemist' – made a brilliantly exciting first year's work at our new London home. But these weren't very easy times for me. In particular, the shake-up in the company's personnel suddenly meant that the Laban terminology I had exchanged with the 'old' members of the company was now met with blank stares among its handful of newcomers, while the urgent schedule of our repertory timetable gradually supplanted the regular training that could have put this matter right. With my movement work slipping down the list of the company's priorities, I would soon have to reappraise my position within it. But I had learnt a great deal about myself in the last few months, and – even if I didn't quite know it at the time – I was beginning to understand where my own future career beckoned.

Chapter Twenty-Three

Stratford East and Bucharest

Summer 1953–Christmas 1954

In July 1953, while the rest of the company were settling into their new home in Stratford, Ewan and I were preparing for an unexpected overseas trip. Ewan had been invited to perform at the world Youth Festival in Romania, as far as I remember by members of the Communist Party. I arranged for Hamish and Betsy to stay with my parents; Ewan convened a few hasty rehearsals with Geoff, his guitarist, and Bruce Turner (the clarinettist with Humphrey Lyttelton's band); and we all flew into Copenhagen to join the so-called 'Festival Train', bound for Bucharest. By the time it set off, it was packed with happy and excited young people, all of whom were eager to participate in the Festival. Staggering down the swaying corridors, it seemed to me that every town and city in Britain was represented. There were choirs, dancers, and musicians from England, Ireland, Scotland, and Wales. Some belonged to the Young Communist League, but many were there without any political affiliations and belonged to a variety of youth groups. There were also some Canadians, Australians, and even a few Israelis.

I can't remember the precise location of our West–East crossing point, where we all alighted and waited for the next train to take us to Bucharest, but our excitement rose as it steamed into view and the cheering started. A huge red flag with a hammer and sickle was spread over the engine, which was everywhere decorated with wild flowers, its beaming driver waving to us. What a welcome! We climbed aboard and assembled once again into our voluntary travelling groups. So much goodwill and fellowship is a very heady experience.

The journey south across the wide plains of Hungary was slow; the earth shimmered under the heat of a blazing sun as we passed 'kerchiefed girls minding gaggles of geese, reminiscent of old Hungarian folk tales. In the far distance, sleek galloping horses were rounded up by skilled, intrepid riders. As the long magical journey continued, Bruce Turner leant against an open window trying to catch a breath of air. He looked into the far distance with a preoccupied expression. 'Jean,' he said, 'I never knew Bucharest was so far!' I saw that his small clarinet case comprised his entire luggage, with barely enough room in it for a clean nylon shirt, a little soap powder and a toothbrush. The septuagenarian Communist MP Willie Gallagher was also on the train: a 'youth' at least in spirit, he was lively and popular; when he admitted to longing for a cup of tea, willing hands immediately set up a tiny primus stove in the corridor and boiled up a kettle for him.

As the train pulled into a crowded wayside station, the first of many such stops along the route, the assembled young people welcomed us with flowers and food packages. Some of us got out to exchange badges, addresses and photographs. Then the whistle blew and we resumed our stately journey to the next stop. At the larger stations, in the towns and cities, we were met with brass bands and choirs – and once with a gypsy-style orchestra, followed by yet more flowers and parcels and gifts. By the time night fell, we were exhausted, and word went on ahead that the welcoming crowds should make no noise, allowing us to sleep. They were asked only to wave as the train passed slowly through their station. I was one of the few to stay awake most of the night. I wanted to witness as much of this extraordinary experience as I could. I remember seeing hundreds of young people crowding the platform and waving silently to us whilst the bandsmen, their instruments at their sides, watched silently. I felt so sorry: what did a couple of sleepless nights matter at such a time?

We crossed into Romania at day-break. Conical-shaped mountains were silhouetted against the rising sun, and this view looked for all the world like a child's drawing. At our first stop we were greeted by smiling workers from the Ploesti oil fields, who gathered along the entire length of the train. They were deeply tanned but when we came to exchange badges and cards, I noticed their hands were surprisingly white and soft-skinned, the result I suppose of working with oil. In the background, a darkly handsome young shepherd, in national costume, stood aloof, gazing at these strange creatures from another world.

Bucharest in 1953 was a beautiful city, now bursting at the seams with this influx of foreigners. I was woken each morning by the sound of hundreds of cicadas. Looking out of the window, I saw women already hosing down the streets, and others walking barefoot, newly arrived from the surrounding countryside with their farm produce. They would bathe their feet in the puddles before putting on the shoes they carried round their necks. Old European cities have always held a tremendous charm for me. I find the architecture quite beautiful in its ancient and weathered appearance, and Bucharest was no exception. Wooden shutters, half open or, perhaps, half closed against the heat, gave access to tiny balconies with delicate wrought-iron tracery overlooking hidden, shaded squares. The restaurant food was plentiful and of a high standard. Desserts usually consisted of huge platters of fresh fruit, glistening after being washed.

The city was surrounded by (I seem to remember) five lakes, one of which the British contingent was granted permission to use. Set amidst parkland that had formerly belonged to the aristocracy (its vast acres out of bounds to the public), it now belonged to the Railway Workers Union. We travelled there on several occasions to cool off in the clear water, which was deep enough for a number of small sailing vessels to have their moorings there.

Concerts were taking place in theatres, halls, and on open-air stages throughout the day and into the early hours of the morning. Visitors not performing officially found spaces in the streets to show off their country dances and national costumes before admiring crowds. By now, the British contingent was only a small part of the whole. Most of the European countries were represented, but others came from much further afield. I saw a brilliant ethnic dance by men and women from a small fishing community in Mongolia. It represented their daily life: hunting, fishing, and the cleaning and preparing of their catch. The movement and musical accompaniment were stunning and made a lasting impression on me as did their unique facial features.

Ewan's contribution went off well. He walked out on to a vast, brightly lit, open-air stage, and sat astride the chair placed with its back to the audience. Geoff and Bruce positioned themselves near the microphones. They all looked out onto a sea of faces peering up at them from the semi-darkness. He sang a mixture of Scottish folk songs, Child Ballads (those Medieval songs collected by the nineteenth-century antiquarian Francis James Child), and some of his own recent compositions. Walking arm in arm afterwards, we joined the late-night revellers, stopping to watch impromptu performances and to marvel again at other ethnic dancers wearing strange masks and enacting primitive hunting rites.

Over the next few days, I was to see English country dancers competing for space in the streets and was interested to watch the reactions of the international crowds. They did not watch for long, moving on to the next 'show' up the street. I couldn't blame them. I thought that, for the most part, there was something amateurishly untidy about their work, lacking in any kind of technique. No matter that it is 'social' dancing, designed for group participation: I still believe if you are 'showing' something to an audience, it has to be of an acceptable standard. It could all have been done so much better. Not that I blamed the dancers themselves; it was just all rather typical of our lack of interest as a nation, where country or 'folk' dance was something for 'oldies' or 'eccentrics'. When I heard there would be another Youth Festival in two years' time in Poland, I decided to try and do something to change this attitude at home.

Almost as soon as we were back in London, in the late summer of 1953, Theatre Workshop went to Scotland again for the Edinburgh Festival, taking Ewan's adaptation of Molière's 'The Imaginary Invalid' and Chekhov's 'Uncle Vanya'. Though neither Ewan nor I were acting in them, we agreed he should stay for the whole period, meeting up with Hugh McDiarmid and his other Scottish writer friends, while I should take advantage of a lift south since my movement work was now finished. In a holiday spirit, Hamish and I descended on Ventnor on the Isle of Wight for a week of paddling and building sand-castles.

'Uncle Vanya' 1953
courtesy of Theatre Royal Stratford East Archive

Returning to the theatre to work on the forthcoming seasonal production of 'A Christmas Carol' with Joan was a delight. Most of the old company were back, and Howard was playing Scrooge, whose cameo scenes with Stella Riley, the young actress he would later marry, added to the happiness. For me, movement training took over on a daily basis, and I was able to choreograph an ambitious skating scene that would take up most of the stage. There were couples skating sedately around the 'ice', holding hands and moving in unison; and 'children' pulling each other, some sitting on their haunches; beginners wobbled, making unexpected pathways before collapsing in a heap; and there were a few 'star skaters' who took to the ice with pirouettes and arabesques like veterans – and all this achieved in sheer movement, on a roughly surfaced raked stage. The simulated effect of moving on ice was magical, and I was overjoyed to read that the dance critic A.V. Coton – a friend of Kurt Jooss – praised the scene for its brilliantly simple realism. A choreographer working in dance will always get recognition, whereas a choreographer working in drama really needs to be as unobtrusive as possible – their work fitting in with, and growing out from, the dramatic action as part of the production. Such work is only occasionally taken further into dance, and I was extremely fortunate that Ewan's plays always allowed for that to happen, and that Joan encouraged me to compose such set-pieces as the 'Chess Ballet' in 'Alice' and the 'Atom Ballet' in 'Uranium 235', both of which formed an integral part of the whole.

'The Devil's Disciple'
courtesy of Theatre Royal Stratford East Archive

'The Government Inspector'
courtesy of Theatre Royal Stratford East Archive

At the same time, however, I always found myself having to balance my professional ambitions with domestic concerns. As well as continuing my movement training, I was now also free to take on the role of the virtuous Beatrice in 'The Dutch Courtesan' (by Shakespeare's junior contemporary John Marston) in its first modern production. According to Joan, I 'looked virginal – just right for the part'. As Harry Corbett serenaded me on stage one evening during its run, in February 1954, Ewan stood in the wings grinning and waving a piece of paper – apparently a cheque. 'Three hundred pounds,' he mouthed. 'A fortune!' One of his plays had been running successfully in Germany and with their usual efficiency, the first (and I think only) royalty had promptly arrived. This windfall meant we could now move out of our temporary flat in Clapham and settle in a larger one in a leafy part of Croydon, near our friends the Rapoport family. Before that happened, however, Ewan was invited to go to Hungary, again with Bert Lloyd, on a folk-song trip. When we eventually moved from

Clapham to Croydon, friends kindly offered to take Hamish and Betsy while we were installing ourselves in the new flat.

Having a regular baby-sitter for the evenings very soon proved an absolute godsend, since it meant that I was free to develop my evening classes as they built up, to go out with Ewan, and to actively participate in some of the plays. We now had a car and this made life much easier as I could shop and drive to Stratford when necessary. Hamish would come with me or play with friends.

In 1954, a company meeting with Joan, Gerry, Ewan, and others spelt out the critical situation in no uncertain terms: we still needed to attract a larger audience in order to break even. The problem was no longer having to meet our touring expenses, but, like any conventional theatre, having to meet our necessary overheads. Meanwhile a healthy and growing 'Theatre Workshop Club' had been formed by a loyal fan of the company, Peggy Soundy. All too aware of our financial difficulties, she formed the club in an effort to support the theatre by holding various fund-raising events. With this in mind, I suggested that the company 'trinity' – i.e. the three of us: Joan, Ewan and I – should each take an evening class run by the local borough. Our friends in the club, many of whom were amateur actors, would benefit and it would also hopefully have the knock-on effect of attracting more local people to our productions. There was also the added advantage that we would also all get paid. The motion was passed without any great enthusiasm: rather like our highly successful summer schools, it was still a ploy of 'last resort' for us all. Another minor source of extra revenue was a series of Ballads and Blues concerts that Ewan later presented at the Theatre Royal, following the broadcast of the programmes themselves on the B.B.C. Ewan had worked hard on this series, along with Alan Lomax, Bert Lloyd, and Humphrey Lyttelton. The folk clubs were yet to be established, but interest was growing, and Ewan was asked to sing at a few folk-song concerts before bringing it back to the Theatre Royal – a good shop window for future folk enthusiasts.

Prevailing conditions at the Theatre Royal were a mixed blessing. For those actors who had recently joined the company, the concentrated rehearsals and regular performances were of paramount importance. Workshops had also become available for the technical staff, and they experimented with all sorts of design construction. Coming through the side door, one was met by a hive of industry – sawing, hammering, and painting – and a terrible smell: the foul and pervasive stink of size (needed to cover untreated canvas) mingling with the asphyxiating gases rising from the basement boiler.

Sachiko Takamura and Mark Britton at Pineapple Studios 1953

With autumn came the evening classes I had proposed. I was still doing my part-time stint at the theatre taking movement classes, but saw no problem in taking one evening out a week to teach others. I was going to teach movement, Joan acting, and Ewan 'voice', in a local evening institute in Stratford. My classes started well but it was not long before Joan reneged on her commitment: rehearsals, naturally, had priority. At first, I stepped in for her. But as the weeks went by, everything else seemed to take priority, and it was obvious that her acting classes would not survive. I felt some sympathy for the institute's pompous little principal as he strutted and tutted before me, incredulous that anyone should consider his evening class so unimportant as to delegate the work to me. Things might have been easier if Ewan had turned up regularly for his classes. Unfortunately, I was standing in for him, too. Joan's acting classes I could just about cope with; taking a voice class was quite another ball game, not least since I can't sing. To get the principal off my back, I twisted Ewan's arm one day, and he grudgingly arrived on time to take the class. Ignorant of the rituals currently in force, Ewan neglected to collect the register from the office – prompting 'Humpty-Dumpty' (as I called the rotund little principal) to rush out and confront him as he strode across the playground, determined to show his sovereignty. 'I don't know you,' he exclaimed. 'Who are you, and what are you doing here?'

Nonplussed, Ewan explained that his name was Ewan MacColl and that he was from Theatre Workshop.

'But do you have any proof of who you say you are?' he blustered. 'You haven't collected the register and . . . and . . . how do I know who you are . . . who you say you are?'

The object of his suspicions turned on his heel. 'Well, I'll go then,' he said, and headed gratefully for the gate and freedom, leaving an open-mouthed Humpty-Dumpty to put things together again.

Rather less anarchic than Joan, I still found such petty rules a source of profound irritation. My entry into the world of evening classes had been long ago in Bolton during the war, with the kindly, whiskered old lady who insisted on plying me with food. This was an altogether more stressful experience. It was a bureaucratic condition of these two-hour classes, for example, that the register be taken exactly two minutes after the official commencement of the lesson – and then again, exactly two minutes into the second hour: I was taken to task for filling in both sections at the outset. The caretaker, anxious to get home, would then noisily walk through my class ten minutes before the end, in a none-too-subtle warning that it was time to pack up. Clearly, this was no easy way to concentrate on our intensive work, and I said as much to my class. Although Joan and Ewan's classes fizzled out by Christmas, however, my own students arranged for me to move to a private hall, and paid the hire charges in exchange for the tutorial services I volunteered. This was like a burden being lifted off my shoulders. The atmosphere was excellent and our numbers increased. We now even had a small kitty.

These were the inauspicious beginnings of the London Dancers, the young and exciting dance company with whom I would travel to Europe for the next two biennial Youth Festivals. When I handed in the register to Humpty-Dumpty for the last time, I realised that, for all his rigid instructions, I had marked all the attendance ticks on my classes' roll-calls on entirely the wrong page. I had inadvertently turned Spring into Autumn. In terms of my career, the very opposite proved to be the case.

Jean Newlove - Yum Di Dee Dah

At Pineapple Studios

Chapter Twenty-Four

London and Warsaw

1954–1955

Ewan was now becoming increasingly committed to the folk scene, and to some extent so was I. My own interest stemmed from the gradual demise of the old Theatre Workshop working traditions and the poor showing of British folk dance in Bucharest. It was a way of continuing to work in my own field of movement. Both of us agreed that the existing folk culture must be encouraged to survive, and that young people should be encouraged to learn the old songs and dances and have the opportunity to create their own in a living tradition. In spite of that commitment, I was still continuing to help out at the theatre although no longer on a daily basis. Both Ewan and I were in the last performance of 'The Other Animals'. I also did some work on 'Richard II' and 'Arden of Faversham', and arranged the wedding dance for 'The Midwife' by Julius Hay. At Christmas I took a part in Alan Lomax's production of 'Big Rock Candy Mountain'.

By the New Year of 1955, my dance class at Stratford had grown, both in its size and in the dedication of its members. I was reading numerous books on the history of folk dance and one in particular, the Carmina Gadelica, interested me very much. This described ancient Scottish dance rituals, two of which I was later to use as the basic inspiration for new choreographies. My aim was to create a body of dancers that were able not only to dance well in the streets – I still remembered the lacklustre performance of English dancers in Bucharest – but also to be of a high enough standard to perform on stage, before a critical audience, at the forthcoming Youth Festival, to be held in Warsaw that summer.

'Richard II'
courtesy of Theatre Royal Stratford East Archive

'Richard II'
courtesy of Theatre Royal Stratford East Archive

We had already left the grim auspices of Humpty-Dumpty's institute in Stratford for more central premises in Greek Street, Soho. Before long, we had moved again to the nearby Italia Conti Stage School, which had a large studio with a sprung maple floor. As word spread of our work, and our membership increased, we were able to hire the facilities more often. We eventually increased our nightly sessions from once to three times a week. Politics played no part in the training of my dancers, though most, I'm sure, were left-wing. I know two were Communists, but two others were Catholics, and we had a fair share of 'don't knows'. The only commitment we all shared was to train as dancers and attend the next Festival as performers. Lisa Ullmann occasionally came down to visit us as a guest, and Laban and I remained in regular contact. My dancers realised we would have to be very good to compete on an international front.

A warm-up, followed by some barre-work, preceded the main study course, which I based on Laban's principles of movement. When the training (usually three hours a night), began to produce results, I introduced a deceptively simple dance arrangement to a lively Scottish air. The foot-work required precision, the jumps proper technique, and the whole dance had to exude confidence and joy. (I had been much impressed by the performances of visiting song and dance ensembles from Eastern Europe.) It was then that Ewan invited us to take part in a Ballads and Blues concert at the Festival Hall.

Costumes became my next headache. We selected a small group of six women dancers, myself included. What should we wear for this new dance using Scottish steps and traditional Scottish music? From my reading, I knew that in the old days women never wore the kilt. Walking down Charing Cross Road after a class one evening, I peered into a second-hand bookshop window and saw what I was looking for. Displayed there was a print of a young girl wearing Scottish dress of the mid-eighteenth century. I coveted the picture and went in to ask the price – fifteen pounds! It might as well have been fifty. What little we had in the budget was for material, and I was still working without payment. I explained the situation to the sympathetic shopkeeper, who allowed me to come back and sketch it the following evening. I spent the best part of an hour drawing the costume in every detail. I decided that our first costume must be a modified version of the print, and the effect turned out to be quite suitable for street dance. Apart from the first engagement, we would be doing a lot of street dancing, and the costumes would inevitably undergo much wear and tear and need regular washing. Later on, when we had earned it, both technically and financially, we would have the whole superb outfit. For now, though, our costume consisted of black ballet shoes, white cotton blouses decorated with red ribbons and tartan taffeta skirts gathered to a tight waist with a black velvet waistband. Underneath were very full, layered, waist petticoats which were heavily starched. The material for these would have been beyond our means so we asked for donations of white single-sized sheets! For our street performances we added a few tiny bells to the inside of the lower hem, which both attracted audiences in the noisy bustle, and provided some additional percussion as we danced.

Before a packed audience, we were announced from the stage of the newly opened Festival Hall as 'The London Dancers'. We were greeted by polite applause – and after our performance (of which I remember very little) the audience was literally roaring for more. Unfortunately, however, we were unable to oblige, since this was the only dance in our repertoire. We nevertheless received many compliments, both on the dancing and the costumes, and offers came in for us to perform at a gratifyingly large number of events. I felt pleased with our first performance and as we continued the quite rigorous training, I extended our repertoire by inviting two specialists to come along and teach us some authentic highland dances, such as the Highland Fling, Sword Dance, and Foursome Reel, as well as the Scotto-Irish jig and the English Hornpipe. All these required as much technique as any conventional ballet class. They were conceived as show pieces for an audience, and I felt they could stand up well against any European competition.

Of course, one of the defining characteristics of country dance, or community dancing, is its enjoyment by everyone, regardless of age or ability, but my own interests always lay in performance and, at that time, on improving the image of British folk dance at international festivals. I still vividly remembered the friendly crowds in Bucharest quickly losing interest in the British contributions.

Dance in Eastern Europe was then strictly divided into two camps: classical ballet was considered as a highly professional art form, while folk-dance was strictly amateur. This was an extraordinary anomaly because very many of their folk groups were state-subsidised and training went on full time. Would-be dancers auditioned for places in the company and in every respect worked as professionals. With the inclusion of folk singers and musicians, the best groups became the Folk-Song and Dance Ensembles who represented their countries abroad. At the other end of the spectrum, the small village groups may have been truly amateur but were still supported in numerous ways; their costumes were superb and their expenses paid. As for the London Dancers, in stark contrast, we had no backing from anyone. I started with two girls from the East End who used to visit Theatre Workshop. As the membership grew and we moved from the hassles of the evening-class environment, the class levied a small sum to cover the hire of the room. Later, we pooled any extra cash in a kitty. We had a professional attitude to work, and while I was willing to work without payment, we paid our two guest teachers the going rate. Getting full value for money, we worked with grim determination to master the different techniques.

Another problem, as I saw it, was the insularity of our folk dancers: English, Irish, and Scottish dancers never attempted to learn each other's dances. I could never understand, for example, why an Irish step dancer should not be at least sufficiently interested enough to have a go at a Highland Fling, and vice versa. And the English meanwhile seemed happy to settle for the less demanding techniques of country or square dancing. Few of them attempted the Sailor's Hornpipe or the Broom Dance, even among younger practitioners. I must confess, however, that I never myself succeeded in getting around to Irish step-dancing. One reason for this was that I did not like the 'arms by the sides' approach: I could not believe that this unnatural behaviour was truly traditional in its style. The teachers I spoke to considered it authentic, but their interest in research was limited and their definition of 'authenticity' rarely went back further than before the First World War. Surely, I thought, somewhere in the history of Irish dance, it had all been more joyous? Rightly or wrongly, the passive arms hanging limply by the dancers' sides, always spoke to me of oppression . . . or depression. I did wonder what it might be like to execute a brilliant step-dance with naturally lively, spontaneous arm movements. Temporarily, I settled for the lively, bouncy three-and-seven steps Irish country dance, as in the Fairy Reel. Another reason was that I have always heartily disliked the current 'traditional' female Irish costume. Mainly because it seems to have no true links with the past, and the Celtic designs are used rather indiscriminately. It has never seemed a happy union to me. Again, more research is needed to find something a little more authentic. The contemporary dancing of Michael Flatley and his troupe has recently settled for a simple black costume, which seems more appropriate. I am aware that much has been lost but I still think that at least the dress materials could be improved upon. For our Irish country dances, we wore the traditional red flannel skirt with two black bands around the hem, a rough shawl, and occasionally an apron with one corner tucked into the waist-band. Had there been enough money in the kitty, I would have added the traditional long, hooded cloaks with their Celtic designs; they were dramatic enough for any stage.

For the most part, we danced barefoot, though a set of clogs were specially made for us and sent down from Lancashire for our attempts at English clog dancing. We had a hilarious time practising with them and suffered a lot of minor injuries in consequence. As training progressed, we also bought tap shoes for the Hornpipe and the Scotto-Irish Jig. This latter, no longer performed in Ireland, travelled with the immigrants to Liverpool and Scotland where it became part of their own folk culture. Essentially a woman's dance, I was told the tossing of the skirts and shaking of the fist were originally directed against the English occupying forces in Ireland. Whether or not that was just a good Irish tale, I don't know, but later versions suggested it was a wife railing against her husband. Certainly the fiery tap steps and clicking of heels supported this behaviour. Either way, audiences loved it. By the time we came to perform in Moscow in 1957, we also wore hand-made kid ghillie shoes for the Highland numbers.

The 'London Dancers' were as highly dedicated a company as the Theatre Workshop had been. The fact that some of them already had young families to look after and the rest needed to work, did not stop us. For a few years, the group's activities took over all their spare time, encouraged by supportive families. Much later one girl laughed as she told me, 'Jean, if you only knew how many babies had been delayed because of our involvement with the dance group!' We were committed to becoming a unique group. With a Laban training, we would not only perform a variety of our own Irish, Scottish, and English country dances, we would also have the technical expertise to perform the 'show' dances of those countries.

But our aims did not stop there. We started to work at weekends on choreographies based on ethnic tales. As a result of my reading in the Scottish Carmina Gadelica, two of our male dancers were sent off to observe the behaviour of farmyard cockerels: the way they walked, moved their heads, used their eyes, preened themselves – and fought. By the time we staged 'The Cockfight', the men wore a complete tartan outfit in the muted colours of the original vegetable dyes – colours reminiscent of the plumage of the birds. We used Laban's efforts – the dimensions and emotions stemming from human effort he spent his life analysing – to clarify and inform the logical sequence of events we presented. After all these years, two moments still stand out vividly. The beginning, with the cocks circling warily round each other on stage, heads giving a jerky forward movement with each step, eyes wide, all-seeing, elbows jutting outwards. And the final sequence, in which one of the protagonists is dying, his wings moving convulsively as the other springs for the coup de grâce, digging his spurs into his opponent's body: a lone fiddler played a dying note as the lights dimmed.

This extraordinary piece had required extra rehearsals but, broke as we were, it was difficult to find studio space. I still remember the thrill of hearing that there was a large room available in my neighbourhood. As the house was due for demolition we were not charged rent. It was midwinter and the banked snow had just started to melt. The disused, dilapidated space was freezing-cold, and water dripped steadily from two large cracks in the ceiling. We put the one available bucket under the worst of these, and agreed to take turns to empty it. Glancing around as we all changed into our kit – shivering with cold, pinch-faced, red-nosed, our hands and feet numb and ungainly – it struck me that we must all surely be mad. But we cleaned the floor as best we could, and put the music on. Before long we were warming up and soon gently sweating. Hands and feet took longer to come back to life, so the lunch break was kept short by common consent. At five o'clock we finished our session: we had been going since nine-thirty that morning. All smiles, we dispersed to enjoy what little was left of the weekend.

Our dedication slowly began to pay off, and we were soon in a position to accept professional engagements – and therefore also charge a modest fee. These were usually on large concert platforms, for various charity events or garden fêtes, and any nominal fees or leftover expenses went straight into the kitty. I remember turning up to perform a single Highland Fling before a group of exiled and inebriated Scots in a London restaurant one Burns Night. There was scarcely room to swing a cat, but I dutifully performed my dance in solitary splendour before the haggis was piped in, I picked up my five-pound cheque, and had disappeared before the drone of the bagpipes had echoed into silence.

After the success of 'Arden of Faversham' and 'Volpone' at the Paris Festival, Joan had met with a setback at the Devon Festival in Barnstaple in July 1955. I heard from the company that Bertolt Brecht himself was threatening to bring an injunction unless Joan played the title role in the forthcoming production of his Mother Courage. It had never been her intention to play the character, so a battle of wills ensued. She continued to rehearse an actress from Theatre Workshop as Mother Courage, believing that Brecht would eventually accept this substitution. In the event, however, he sent an ultimatum demanding absolutely that Joan play the role or else not stage the play at all. Her last-minute return to the part came too late, and the result was not good.

Meanwhile, my London Dancers had met with greater success – albeit on a smaller scale. Hearing of the Bethnal Green Festival of Arts, I had entered the company in the heats of the International Dance section of the competition, where we were set to perform both the English Broom Dance and the Irish Mountain Road. I had several reasons for entering this competition. Not least, I wanted to see how we fared against the international 'opposition'. I also reckoned that no other English country dance groups would opt for the athletic and virtually unknown 'Broom Dance'. At least our performance might help keep it from dying out and, who knows, maybe encourage others to try it. It was also important to me that our dancers gained as much experience as possible in front of a live audience. Finally, and perhaps most important of all to me, was the challenge I felt at choreographing a dance in the Irish tradition. I had been helped with a lively tune composed by Michael Gorman, a brilliant Irish fiddler who often played with Willie Clancy (Uilleann pipes) and Martin Byrnes (fiddle and tin whistle) at folk concerts. (All three were regular guests on Ewan and Alan's B.B.C. programmes.) It was extremely fast, and the dancing required split-second timing. In a line, hands by their sides, the dancers performed the most intricate steps in complete unison. Close together, if one dancer had made a mistake, the outcome would have been disastrous. One keen member of the group burst into tears when she was learning it and threatened to leave. Fortunately she persevered and mastered it. Done well, it was quite spectacular and very ambitious for a group who had only been together such a short time. But how would it be received?

The Broom Dance had gone well. Other dance groups followed, beautifully dressed in their European costumes, performing delightful national dances – including more than one troupe of Irish step-dancers. I looked at my dancers, barefoot in our own traditional Irish costumes, and crossed my fingers. Now came the moment I had waited for. Arms at their sides but with smiling faces, the dancers in the Mountain Road performed their highly intricate steps with real expertise – and no mistakes. They deserved the spontaneous applause, the audience loved it.

While the judges were busy, our rival Irish dancers and their teachers milled around Michael while I made a tactical withdrawal. The questions were coming in thick and fast. They had never heard that tune before. It was great, but which part of Ireland was it from? And the dance? Did that come from the same place? Who could teach it? Where had we found it, and who had taught it to us? Michael smiled serenely and answered them all politely and sincerely, while actually telling them nothing factual at all. In the end we came second. More importantly, however, I now knew that we were on the right track: audiences were at last beginning to notice our work, and it was time to find new audiences abroad. Arguably Ireland's top touring folk band, The Chieftains, finally got a copy of Michael's beautiful Mountain Road and the Bulgarian men in their national Dance Ensemble learnt my dance. We both went into history!

The second World Youth Festival was held in Poland later that same summer of 1955. Ewan had written another of his ballad operas, 'See You in Warsaw, Johnny', a simple tale about a young boxer wanting to go to the Festival. It contained a number of songs especially written for the occasion. Without a trained cast, however, this new production could not be overly ambitious. The company was now beginning to feel the pinch, as old stalwarts like Harry Corbett, Joby Blanchard, and George Cooper had all left to take up other theatre work. Nevertheless, there were a few 'old timers' like Howard Goorney, Barry Clayton, and George Luscombe joined us, and Joan directed the piece. George, a Canadian actor, played the lead; I was Mary, his girlfriend; and Howard – cast against type – played George's trainer. I seem to remember that Barry played a kind of spiv. The London Dancers were also part of the cast and joined in the jollifications, with the Irish musicians playing their hearts out. Ewan had a singing and acting role.

The journey to Warsaw followed a similar pattern to our earlier trip to Bucharest. This time we all travelled together on the boat-train. After crossing the German frontier, crowds greeted us at the stations, bands played, choirs sang, badges were exchanged and photographs were hastily taken before clambering aboard to continue our journey. However, this time it was very different for me, since I was taking my own group of dancers. There were about twenty of them altogether, officially appearing in the ballad opera, as well as on specially erected stages in the city's parks, and at a couple of scheduled indoor concerts. Ewan was already known as a popular singer–performer from his performances in Bucharest and was in much demand. My London Dancers were also recognised as a truly British group, of international standard – it was the first time that a company had been trained to perform English, Scottish, and Irish dance to such a high level.

*A musical that TW took to Warsaw
courtesy of Theatre Royal Stratford East Archive*

Meanwhile rehearsals on Johnny were proving difficult. Joan's method of working was very individualistic. It was perfectly suited to professional actors, under circumstances where everyone could concentrate intensively on their parts. What she now overlooked, however, was the fact that this festival offered an enormous variety of experiences, and our cast were a mixed bag with other commitments. Crucially, she couldn't rehearse all the hours she was used to because the festival always intruded, expecting members of her cast to attend other functions considered by the organisers to be equally important. Fortunately, the dancers presented no problem: I was the only one with any lines to learn, so the festival ceremonial dance was not in jeopardy. I think she would have had a mutiny on her hands if she had required them to stay! As it was, she expected the Theatre Workshop actors to rehearse all through the day of the grand opening. Having been at Bucharest, I had already told them of the splendid international atmosphere in the stadium, which reminded me of the Olympics. Howard voiced the actors' strong resentment at this directive, but Joan retaliated with true Littlewood fury, rather bizarrely accusing him of being a misanthrope. While I felt some sympathy for her wanting to work for a better show, this was simply neither the time nor the place to do so. It was far more important for everyone to mix and take advantage of such a unique occasion. As things turned out, the Warsaw Festival was also unique in another respect: it was the last time that Ewan, Joan, and I – the 'trinity' of Theatre Workshop – ever worked together as a threesome.

My dancers started out mid-morning, joining the parade as it passed through the crowded streets of Warsaw. Apart from my work with the London Dancers and the ballad-opera, I had also been invited to join a panel of official adjudicators for the classical ballet competitions. This was a huge honour for me: to find myself sitting next to the Russian maestro Leonid Lavrovsky, the choreographer of the brilliant Bolshoi ballet, Romeo and Juliet, and the other judges were from as far afield as China, Bulgaria, Poland, Austria, and Brazil. Since I had had a classical ballet training from a very early age, and had passed all the usual exams, I felt quite at home with my fellow panellists – despite having long ago forsaken the discipline in favour of Laban. Indeed, I found the Laban training helped me immensely in my observation and analysis of the performances.

These classical competitions took place in the Palace of Culture, a vast skyscraper building 'presented' to the Poles after the war by the Soviet Union. The architectural style did not please everyone, and with their usual wit the Poles nicknamed it the 'Wedding Cake', claiming that the best available view of Warsaw was to be had from on top of it – because it was the only view of Warsaw from which you couldn't see it.

Like Bucharest, stages had been erected in the parks for the many folk dance performers. The audiences for these ran into the thousands, and a Tannoy system relayed the music from the stage way back into the far distance. Our group and our musicians were extremely popular with the crowds and the judges presented me with an award as choreographer, and a testimonial. I felt that I had made a start since visiting Bucharest two years earlier, and that I was on the right track, but still had a long way to go. In another two years we hoped to be going to Moscow.

When the time came to return home, Ewan and Bert Lloyd were invited to go off on a week's folk-song trip. I joined the others on the train. On the way back, after an uncomfortable night, we stopped in the early morning at the Polish town of Oswiecim– better known to the world as Auschwitz – for a pre-arranged visit. Although nine years had elapsed since the end of the war, it was all too easy to visualise the horrors perpetrated there by the Nazis. The guide told us that the prisoners had arrived at this very station, but in cattle trucks. They had also followed the road up to the camp but they marched while we took our time. I looked at the inhabitants of nearby houses who had come out to stare at us. They seemed curious and a few smiled slightly. I wondered if they had been there when it was all happening and what they thought about it all and how they could bear to smile at us or even, to live in such close proximity to a camp which had now become a shrine of suffering to the rest of the world.

We entered the massive gates with their villainous slogan, 'Arbeit Macht Frei', across the top. Rooms with large hermetically sealed glass fronts displayed false teeth, artificial limbs, glass eyes, spectacles, toys, pitiful clothing belonging not only to adults but also to children and babies. Anything of real value had already gone to the fatherland. In one corner there was parchment which turned out to be human skin. There was a yard where inmates were brought to be shot. Bullet holes pock-marked the brickwork and I could not help feeling that it must have been a merciful release. Better than dying in a tiny punishment bunker built for one person with not enough room to stand upright or sit down. At times, a second person would be forced into the bunker. Their manner of death must have been horrifying. I'm 'glad' I saw it all – the huts, latrines, crematoria, and the 'shower' rooms where thousands were gassed. We saw bones in the ovens and walked along paths shining white in the sun, crushed bones of the victims. One terrible photograph blown up to cover a whole wall showed a screaming mother being forcibly restrained by a German soldier whilst his colleagues laughed as one of their group reached high with his bayonet to collect a falling object, the mother's baby. I can never forget that picture and man's inhumanity. When I returned to England, and spoke about my visit to the camp, I was surprised, and rather shocked, at how very few people were willing to listen.

Returning to the train, I was offered one of two spare air tickets from Prague to London that had just become available. I was given first refusal with another girl – though she turned it down, being terrified of flying. In fact she was far more honest than me, since in those days I was just as nervous of flying myself. But no one took me up on the offer of my ticket, and I was unwilling to confess my own fears: so the guitarist Bryan Daly and I travelled together to Prague, and joined an ancient Dakota aeroplane for a rather bumpy ride over the Black Forest, the North Sea, and home.

Chapter Twenty-Five

The Soho Festival

1956 – 1957

My work at Stratford E.15 in the New Year of 1956 was limited to a little movement training on Marlowe's 'Edward II' and Brendan Behan's 'The Quare Fellow'. From now on, however, I came across more and more newcomers in 'our' Theatre Workshop productions who went straight into rehearsals without taking any Laban training sessions. It was disheartening to see all that I had worked so hard to build up disappear due to the exigencies of the theatre's new policies for survival. On the other hand, the London Dancers were now thriving. When the Bulgarian Folk Song and Dance Ensemble visited London in the year, for example, the London Dancers met up with them on stage after one of their performances. We were not total strangers as we had seen each other's performances at the Warsaw Festival. We showed them the Mountain Road, which particularly interested the men, who went through the steps while their pipers picked up the tune as we sang it. Such exciting moments compensated for my anxieties over Theatre Workshop, and I tried to look upon the situation as philosophically as I could. Hamish was now at primary school, and I used a lot of my new-found time to work out more programmes for my dancers, to arrange our engagements, and to read anything that would give me more information about the origins of worldwide folk dance.

With the next Youth Festival in mind – to be held in Moscow in 1957 – we continued to train hard. One of my ideas was to add a square dance to our repertoire. This demanded some expertise in the choreography to find a way of presenting it on stage. In the end, I came up with a simple and humorous story line requiring some dramatic interpretation, leaving the simpler versions for our street performances. We now had a number of men in the company, and were therefore able to attempt the Butterfly Whirl. This required four men to join hands and four women to hold hands round their necks. Then they start to spin and before long, the women take off with the centrifugal force, becoming horizontal in flight. With two or more groups it is visually stunning. The girls loved it, and the fellows were proud of their manly strength until we rehearsed it over and over again as a safety precaution – at which point, they suggested it was their turn to try flying and wanted the girls to spin them off their feet. This type of traditional couple-dance led quite naturally to the moves of the new 'rock and roll' and we experimented with a few of the more exciting ones involving lifts and spins. No dance was set, but everyone learnt some of the most lively sequences and it became a natural follow-on to the square dance and a good ending to our shows. It seemed to be such a popular part of our present day culture that it was important to include it.

Hearing word of the forthcoming Soho Festival, we decided this would be a good time to earn some much needed cash. Our group had expanded – we were now some thirty strong – so we needed to invest in more swords and some expensive kid ghillie shoes for the highland dancers, as well as new woollen tartans for the eighteenth-century costumes I had previously drawn, and velvet for the bodices. Only those who had reached the highest standard were chosen to perform these, but the whole company participated in the less demanding dances. No expense was spared on costumes. We would also need new materials for the square dancing – the skirts were complete circles of felt in bright colours, worn over the ubiquitous white petticoats. The Soho Festival organisers invited us to perform regularly at certain venues and at other times we performed from after lunch till nearly midnight every day to raise money.

We knew that the Festival would only last a week and, although we were the official dance group, there would be other performers hoping to earn money. Our dancers divided into two groups, changing daily and switching from Irish with the Irish musicians and Scottish with a piper. However the piper occasionally couldn't make it and the Irish musicians kindly acted as substitutes. These two teams were set up to compete against each other, The Irish costume would be worn when the Irish musicians were accompanying the team and the Scottish costume would be kept for our Scottish bagpiper. Night after night, the groups came straight from work and danced from six o'clock until the last trains. Competition was fierce. I started out with the Irish musicians playing like a dream. The difficulty was they got so thirsty that I found them constantly disappearing into the nearest pub. This was a hazard that I had overlooked. We saw our huge audiences getting impatient for the dancing to begin and one dancer rushed after them when she thought they had overstayed their time, calling after them, 'Do hurry up, we are losing our audience'. Our programme was quite short, about fifteen or twenty minutes, after which we moved to another location, carefully avoiding our rival dance group. We went down well with the crowds and it was gratifying to hear their complimentary remarks. We gained a few recruits too. Collecting on the first day was not highly organised and the crowds dispersed before we could get around them all. This was quickly put right by stationing friends strategically among the crowds, their tins at the ready, containing enough coins to make a nice sound. Only recently a great friend of mine said she always danced in Soho in our other group looking pointedly at her bare feet, hoping it would swell the takings! Most of us wore black ballet shoes but by the end of the Festival they were in ribbons and we were reduced to our bare feet too. One evening we were congratulating ourselves on having done exceptionally well when some 'ladies of the night' came up to us and said we were ruining their business! I think we reached an amicable compromise and switched locations.

I would rush for the last train home with Sylvia, our team's treasurer. Carrying our heavy tins, we would be met by her husband and go to her house to pour out our spoils onto her carpet. Then the real business began of counting. A few odd coins were disgustedly cast aside and great appreciation voiced when a note appeared or half crowns piled up. Everything was made ready for the bank in the morning. Then a call would come from Queenie, the treasurer of our rival team, we would find out which group had earned the most, and calculate the total night's takings. I usually stayed for supper prepared by Sylvia's husband. It helped us to unwind and he liked to hear of our adventures before running me home.

This temporary arrangement did not go down well with Ewan, who had started to complain about my coming back so late. I explained that I really felt too tired to prepare supper for myself and Arron, Sylvia's husband, had rustled something up. The following night I arrived back late again, having already eaten and was greeted by Ewan looking like a demented housewife. He said he had tried to keep my supper hot. I thought he had succeeded very well. Carrying the scorching plate gingerly on a couple of tea-cloths, I looked at the burnt offering and tried to keep a straight face. It must have been in the oven for over five hours. I thanked him very seriously and managed to eat some of it. I did, I think, imply that this was totally unexpected. Had I known I would have come back earlier.

Sylvia and I went to her bank together one morning. We lifted the spoils onto the counter and she pushed them across to the cashier who looked up smiling. 'I see you had a good night in Soho, Mrs R!' Since Mrs R. was the wife of a respected doctor, it's no wonder that the rest of the customers looked rather bewildered.

Ewan's work was meanwhile going well and he seemed to be immersed in the folk scene. Asked to record some Scottish ballads, he bought a Ferrograph machine and I was introduced to the complexities of recording on it. Unfortunately the only time we could be fairly sure of not getting any interruptions was after midnight. It was then that I would test for balance and the session would start in earnest. The ballads were long – I seem to recall that twenty verses were nothing unusual. If Ewan coughed or faltered we'd have to start all over again. I remember once when we were actually on the last verse and a plane went overhead. Although it was wearisome work at the time, and we usually only managed one ballad a night, there was great pleasure at accomplishing a satisfactory recording. When those early records came out, I was quite proud of my 'engineering' prowess even though I never got a credit.

We began to help each other in other ways, too. He coached my dancers in singing technique and soon we had a good repertoire of folk songs. This arrangement was rather different from the folk song and dance ensembles of Eastern Europe, who were divided between singers and dancers. I think we felt rather pleased with ourselves as we could now do both. The male dancers also supplied the choruses for Ewan's recording of sea shanties with Bert Lloyd. This happened at weekends and now seven-year-old Hamish took over the Ferrograph. I continued to discuss Laban's theory of efforts with Ewan, which helped him in his own performances. He was also later to use this knowledge when training his own folk-song group, The Critics.

I don't now remember my first meeting with Peggy Seeger. It could have been at the Aldwych Theatre, where Ewan was singing the theme song, 'Mack the Knife', in a production of 'The Threepenny Opera'. It was a popular show and there were always a great number of fans crowding into the dressing rooms back-stage. What I do remember is returning to the flat in Croydon one day, after a long rehearsal, and being surprised to find her there. She became a regular visitor over the next few weeks. At first, I was pleased that Ewan had found another accompanist especially since the folk concerts were really beginning to take off. The venues were usually large rooms above pubs all over the country designated for the folk-song scene. I continued to go along to these events on a regular basis, but before very long I began to feel that I was a supernumerary figure, surplus to requirements. It was quite a painful experience. Finally I asked Ewan just what was happening to us. He denied any romance and I put the best light on the situation I could. After all, I knew what it was like to be driven in one's work, to be excited by ideas, and know the thrill of achieving something worthwhile. I had no wish to deprive him of this experience – and indeed I don't think I could have done so had I wanted to. Ewan had the ideas, and Peggy the musical knowledge to assist him: it was a good partnership, and there was no denying it. He was later to admit that having a fan half his age falling in love with him was flattering.

I stopped going to the concerts. As someone said, 'Ewan was now in the public domain and had suddenly lost his family.' Initially, I do not believe that he, or his new colleagues, expected the folk evenings to become as popular as they did. From a handful of devotees, the rooms above the pubs gradually filled with followers and Ewan began to bask in his new-found success as a folk singer. I was always of the opinion that his talent, together with his years of theatre training, enabled him to put a song across better than any of his fellow singers. Certainly, few could manipulate the audience or hold them spell-bound so well. It was also a much easier task than playing night after night to a theatre audience because he was now able to concentrate his focus entirely on his own performance and his audience was enthralled. How different from the hours spent alone writing the next play followed by acting rehearsals and company policy meetings fast becoming even more difficult as we tried to cope with a rep. programme. In his own autobiography, Ewan recalled this time as 'a period of great change, of excitement and discovery in my work, of happiness, despair and uncertainty in my personal life'.

The public was well able to sympathise with his dilemma; the fans could smile readily, overlooking his foibles; and the Communist Party would remember only his allegiance to their cause. Written or sung, the brilliant flurry of his articulate words always showed a man of perception, charm, humour, and talent. This was the man I had fallen in love with some nine years earlier and continued to love during this difficult time – a man who had so often expressed his dependency on me in emotional crises. Now we were facing another one, perhaps the most serious yet. I still retained some optimism (shades of the transcendental idealist remained!), and I made up my mind to do whatever I could to help him. The fact that he was also the main bread-winner, earning far more than my part-time salary with Theatre Workshop, also added to my anxiety. But I reckoned that we would, with luck, weather this crisis too. Not having Ewan's gift for words, I can only say that I too was going through a period of 'despair and uncertainty in my private life'. Did he notice, I wonder? I think not. He was totally immersed in his own feelings at this stage, whereas I was trying to save our marriage, and was also desperately concerned for Hamish's well-being.

It seemed that Ewan was unable to deny himself anything if such a denial resulted in his emotional distress. He wanted to go ahead with the new work – and the new relationship – but was not prepared to sacrifice the family life that he was later to say had given him the stability he had longed for. Ideally, he wanted us all to work harmoniously for the new direction his life had taken – in plain language, he once agreed that this was called 'having your cake and eating it'. I began to deplore and resent his lack of common sense. As for me, my central concern remained our marriage. I supported Ewan where I could, singing rehearsals took place at our flat and I recorded them on the Ferrograph when Hamish was at school.

My own work with the theatre and the dancers was not so demanding at that time and I somehow managed to juggle everything satisfactorily, including taking Hamish to and from school and attending school functions. If ever a serious clash of timetables arose, Ewan's mother was still with us, ready to jump in and cook for him or make sure his shirts were laundered and waiting.

It was to be another four years until Ewan at last acknowledged the end of our marriage, and that was in part due to my own final decision. Romantic anguish is never too far removed from comedy, even farce. At the back of my mind, I was conscious of Ewan writing and directing a scenario for us in which the role I was studying was diminishing before my eyes. I didn't see it as funny at the time. I seemed to be adrift in uncharted waters, out of my depth and very much alone. The most painful part of infidelity, in my experience, is not that it happens, but rather the deceit that often accompanies it. It is hard not to make judgements, not to despise someone for their lack of courage in not owning up to their actions. And it's always nonsense to say that it is because they are afraid of hurting their partner: it only exacerbates the misery. And I was angry for Ewan too: he seemed diminished by this behaviour.

Peggy went back to the States while her visa was renewed. Ewan and I managed to resume some sense of normality, and once again started to appear at various functions together. Since our move to London in 1952, we had been inundated with all sorts of formal invitations to parties, dinners, even embassy functions, and we also threw one or two good parties of our own. Our guests would include artists, musicians, actors, and MPs – lively evenings, full of music, dancing, laughter, and song. But by the spring of 1957, they were a thing of the past.

It seemed no time at all before Peggy was back in England, and family life was once again disrupted. There is no doubt that Ewan had missed collaborating with her, but it would also be true to say that he had been coping well without her. Ewan's mother meanwhile continued to do much of the housework, no doubt done for his comfort, and certainly by her own choice. I was in no position to try to introduce changes during this difficult period. But I have no doubt that she was fully aware of what was going on. Never easy to live with, she now became excessively moody – though, paradoxically, her ill-humour was never directed at Ewan, the root cause of her unhappiness. But her relationship with Hamish was good; she had a proper grandmotherly pride in him. There were dangers, however. She was already beginning to do everything for his comfort, and I knew I must try to establish a healthier balance, for his own sake, before he was much older. She continued to largely prefer her own company, and even after all this time, I was sorry there was no real warmth in our relationship. It was an amicable enough arrangement, though; we shared the odd joke, and I learned to ignore the sporadic outbursts of her bad temper. But I never knew what to expect from one day to the next, and I could only try to keep in mind her indomitable strength during the hard times thirty and more years before.

As Ewan and I were walking down the Charing Cross Road one morning, I was suddenly hailed by another voice from the past. My old friend 'P', who had come to visit me in my A.T.S. days, all those years ago, in Blackdown Barracks, suddenly rushed up, full of his usual good-natured banter. I introduced him to Ewan, and after recalling happy memories we promised to keep in touch. He asked for our phone number and Ewan wrote it out for him. I was disappointed that he never rang back. Many years later, when I met 'P' again, and asked him about that meeting, he told me that he had been given the wrong number.

Chapter Twenty-Six

Moscow

1957

The London Dancers had by now grown into quite a large company, technically strong and becoming more experienced in performance. It hardly seemed possible that so much had been achieved since the Bucharest Festival less than four years before. I continued our training sessions in the evenings, busily preparing for the Moscow Youth Festival where we were scheduled to appear at several concerts as part of the official programme, as well as entering the International Dance Competition.

To accustom the dancers to performing, we meanwhile took on a number of engagements in the Greater London area. Money was still a problem. At no time did we ask for or receive financial support from anyone. Once again, we took it in turns to raise money by busking at weekends. We did well at Brighton, in spite of a biting wind. It rained all day in Crawley and we had to return on a better day. Soho was rewarding but there was now far more competition, resulting in greater restrictions and diminished income. Somehow we eventually raised the necessary funds to cover expenses and once again set off from Ostend to travel as far as the East German border on a Western train.

This time we were heading for the International Youth Festival in Moscow in company not only with Theatre Workshop, the London Dancers, but also folk and jazz musicians, choirs, professional ballroom dancers and representatives of the UK's national theatre. John Osborne had been invited as a result of his recent hit, 'Look Back in Anger', which became part of the 'kitchen sink' genre of the period. This international gathering celebrated a future of peace and prosperity for all young people throughout the world.

This artistic contingent changed on to a very basic, third-class-only train. From here onwards we chose to dance on every platform when the train stopped. People had heard propaganda about shortages of food in the West and we were given individual food parcels at very regular intervals. We felt rather guilty at accepting so much largesse from people who didn't look as though they had too much to spare themselves.

Things improved at Brest-Litovsk when our new transport hoved into sight continuously blowing its whistle in welcome as we boarded for our final destination. To show our appreciation we danced on the platform in front of the flower-bedecked engine. Inside the train further surprises awaited us. A larger gauge meant it was wider than normal trains and the mahogany and frosted glass belonged to an Edwardian era. At the end of each compartment sat a young woman with a samovar ready to hand out glasses of tea at any time. Some people ate in the dining car, others preferred to eat in their compartment. The blankets, starched white sheets, and pillow cases were very welcome and many of us got an excellent night's sleep.

For the first time in eleven years, Joan, Ewan, and I had all gone our separate ways and were presenting our own very different programmes before an international audience. Ewan was representing Britain as a folk singer, accompanied by Bruce Turner, Jim Bray and others. (There was also a small American folk contingent, including Bertice Reading – and Peggy Seeger.) Joan also attended the Festival, bringing Theatre Workshop's controversial modernization of 'Macbeth'. I was approached by a Festival organiser who asked if my London Dancers would lead the British contingent in the gala opening parade. We were thrilled at the honour and I arranged a processional dance where the leading male dancers performed a sword ritual and the leading women moved from side to side swinging their plaids. All were wearing individual authentic tartans and the girls' velvet bodices matched them. Behind our leading dancers the rest of the company carried wands with white doves and blue streamers. We later found ourselves on the front of Life magazine. Accompanied by the bagpipes, we followed the rest of the parade into a huge Olympic-like stadium with the Russian word 'Mir' (meaning both peace and world) lit up in lights. We processed round the stadium to the applause of the audience – an unforgettable moment. Later that day Joan, who had been in the crowd came up to me and said she thought the London Dancers had looked magnificent.

Looking back over fifty years or more, I remember Moscow in a series of flash-backs. I can recall the modern building where Ewan and I shared a room. An extra room was set aside for the voluminous dance dresses belonging to the ballroom dancers. Their stiffened skirts caused a great deal of wonderment and humour. I remember the friendly Russian students working so hard in the restaurant, waiting patiently as the British deliberated over the vast choice of food set before them. The quantities were enormous. Steak and eggs was a regular breakfast for those stalwarts who could face it. I also discovered that Russian ice cream was the best in the world.

The McPeakes, a traditional Irish group, were very popular, as were the London University Jazz band, led by John Picton. Richard Harris, now part of the Theatre Workshop cast, found a drinking companion from one of these jazz groups, and both enlivened the scene with their own raucous celebrations. Bruce Turner, clarinettist with Humphrey Lyttelton, was asked what Moscow was like on his return and replied, 'Full of red squares, Dad' ('Dad' being his hepcat nickname for almost everyone). John Osborne was also sceptical, though less endearingly. He was not popular with his colleagues, and eventually returned home early, publishing a scathing attack on being 'duped' by the Soviet propaganda.

Among many outside venues, the London Dancers gave a performance in the Kremlin grounds, and I later heard that Guy Burgess had been spotted nearby – a year before his famous meeting with the actress Coral Browne, an encounter subsequently immortalised in Alan Bennett's 'An Englishman Abroad'.

The East Europeans didn't know what to make of the ballroom dancers with their heavy make-up and enormously 'over the top' dresses, though I suspect that some of the Russian women would have liked a little of this colourful flamboyance for themselves. On the other hand, their reaction was surely tinged with awe at so much blatant 'decadence'. Perhaps it was made all right by the strict timing and the deadpan delivery, with neither a hair nor a foot out of place.

It was not always easy to keep track of my flock. My friend Denise, the bare-footed dancer of Soho, was travelling to an engagement at the Yugoslavian Embassy with the London Dancers in her best Scottish costume when she spotted an open lorry transporting two white horses. She shouted, 'Stop!' (it being the same word in Russian). The driver pulled up, the horse-mad Denise left the coach and in no time was disappearing in the direction of the Moscow Hippodrome seated happily next to the lorry driver. I am told that she was the first (and probably the last) rider to appear there wearing an authentic tartan costume.

Attending an indoor concert on our busy schedule, I noticed that the wings of the stage were blocked with male folk-dancers. Some, unable to get a clear view of the stage, had crept out of the dark auditorium and sat squashed like sardines, in front of the first row of seats. Mouths agape, they were staring goggle-eyed at the soloist. I was intrigued by what terpsichorean masterpiece can have enthralled so many professionals. Then I understood. A plumply curvaceous, almost nude, Egyptian dancer was performing a belly dance. I suppose it could, at least in theory, be called a folk dance ... Well aware of her charms and the impression she was making on the males in the audience, she shimmied and wiggled symmetrically and – as far as I could see – asymmetrically, too. Tassles responded accordingly and the girls in the audience, in their beautifully embroidered folk costumes, suddenly looked far too prim and over-dressed. It was patently obvious that this was the first time East Europeans had been exposed to the delights of Egyptian culture.

At another performance, this time indoors, we were fascinated by the forbidding sight of four Stalin-moustached dancers from

Georgia, all from different villages, we heard, who had been chosen as the very best dancers of the region. Taking their place in the wings, they each loosely held an elaborate dagger, gently feeling the sharp edge with their thumbs. Our cockney colleague Grace was not impressed. 'They aren't really sharp,' she murmured, 'I s'pect they're as blunt as anything.' Then suddenly, like coiled springs going off, the stage was filled with their whirling, stamping, jumping on toes, triumphant shouts, and flashing knives. The furiosity increased as the daggers were thrown into the floor of the stage, digging deep into it, hafts quivering from the dynamic force as the dancers continued to jump over and around them, twirling non-stop. I realised that their black tight-fitting boots were made of the finest kid – with little protection against the knife-blades if a foot landed in the wrong place – and that they could jump onto their toes and actually dance en pointe. I looked across at Grace who was ashen. By the time the dance was over, and the men were leaving the stage in a lather of sweat, she had fully recovered. She smiled kindly at them. 'That was orl right,' she said.

Ewan and I were invited to a Formal Ball at the Kremlin. I imagined it was the equivalent of being invited to Buckingham Palace, and wore my favourite French dress from Galeries Lafayette. Tight-bodiced with a full layered skirt in two tiers, the colourful print had a black back ground. I looked forward to this evening very much – ballroom dances had not featured prominently in our penurious Theatre Workshop lives. The ballroom was huge and around the sides of the room were coffee tables and chairs for those wishing to sit out. Very soon, Ewan was chattering away to a group of friends and I was on the dance floor being whirled around in a Viennese waltz by a gentleman – could it have been Sinbad? – in baggy, colourful trousers and embroidered slippers with turned-up toes. Ewan was a little put out that I was in such demand, which in the light of recent events seemed rather illogical. I suggested he danced with me, which he did, but soon gave it up for the greater pleasure of a political discussion. I returned to the dance floor and the action. Rumour had it that Bulganin, the Soviet premier himself, was among the dancers, but I didn't recognise anybody. It was enough to be surrounded by so many good dancing partners of all nationalities.

We attended three other events together. A visit to the Writers' Union was followed by a day trip to a writer's dacha in the country. The dacha, a primitive wooden chalet, was beautifully situated amidst a forest of birch trees and provided a welcome respite from our busy schedule. Our third event was a formal dinner in Ewan's honour, again arranged, I imagine, by the Writers' Union. Never much of a drinker, Ewan was concerned when he saw the sheer amount of vodka lined up on the table. The only other liquid refreshment seemed to be water. Each place setting had two glasses, a large tumbler for water and a smaller one for the vodka. I told him not to worry and to drink only from his own vodka glass. The speeches began. So did the toasts. We all stood up and the men drained their vodka glasses at a gulp. So did Ewan, with a mild look of surprise on his face. I sat down quickly and added a little more water to my large glass, surreptitiously spilling it into Ewan's smaller glass as I set the carafe down. Toast followed toast, my sleight of hand passed unnoticed, and Ewan was able to knock his glass back with the best of them. The atmosphere was becoming increasingly jolly as the vodka flowed, and when Ewan rose to reply, upright and clear-headed, he thanked his hosts, raised his glass, and knocked back its entire contents in one gulp. Those still able to stand roared their approval: here was a man after their own hearts. I think their admiration was due as much to his ability to drink most of them under the table as to his work as a writer.

The International Dance Competition was held in a theatre over several days. There were hundreds of entries from China, the Soviet Republics, Brazil, Europe, and Canada, to mention only a few. I knew we had little chance of winning, but I wanted to see how we stood up against such strong competition. It was essential for us to see other dance artists at work and go back refreshed and inspired to carry on. I was also extremely keen that our own training and choreography be seen by as many people as possible, since it was entirely based on Laban's movement theories of efforts and spatial harmony. These were to be beautifully demonstrated in our opening piece, 'The Cockfight'.

My two male dancers took up their positions at the back of the large stage in complete darkness. We left a few moments of utter silence, and then, upstage right, a lone piper began playing a tune representing the breaking of day. As the stage lighting slowly increased, Dickie in a red tartan, and Colin in a green tartan, stepped out of the shadows on either side of the stage, and confronted each other. In an instant they were eyeing each other as cockerels prepared to fight to the death. They were both excellent dancers, and had researched the movements of cocks and their mannerisms in their spare time, adapting and finessing the movements they observed for the stage. They circled each other with sharp head movements and sudden elbow movements, most of the time on demi-pointe with bent knees, as if prepared to engage if they saw the opportunity. Their analysis of movement stemmed purely from their Laban training. The Red Cock's movements became suddenly harsher, and his head started to thrust as he jumped into the attack. At first, the Green Cock displayed strong defensive efforts, but it was clear that he had been wounded. Driving home his apparent victory, the red cock increased his speed and without preamble jumped on his opponent, cruelly using his spurs to force him to the ground. The wounded cock was unable to rise and it was clear that he had lost the fight. The victor strutted around the dying bird in a show of strength – sharp movements of the head, bent knees, and again on demi-pointe, circling closer on his opponent, before delivering the coup de grâce with his spurs. The piper ended his lament at that very moment with a long drawn out cry, as though from the dying bird. There was a moment of complete silence, then a slight murmur went through the huge audience, and isolated clapping started to break out into applause, ending in a roar of approval and a chorus of bravos.

The lighting dimmed for a moment to allow the two dancers to get off stage, and most of the company came forward slightly as full lighting rose on them. The girls, accompanied by our violinists, now mimed the gathering of sheep's wool, individually criss-crossing the stage, before ending up in their own space to enact the process of carding and spinning. I had read a great deal about the lives of the women on the crofts in South Uist and other islands, and their work was often described in great detail. My ambition was to choreograph my own version of these traditional island practices. Although we wore thoroughly accurate folk costumes, it was not folk-dance in the narrow meaning of the word. Nevertheless, we were illustrating the life of the crofters through dance, just as the Mongolian fishermen had illustrated their daily lifestyle through dance on a stage in Bucharest. The dancers were now able to sing as they mimed soaking the tweed, beating it twice on the table, and pulling it along to their neighbour, stretching it as it went. This very rhythmic song – known as 'mouth music' (or puirt à beul in the Gaelic) – was accompanied by the authentic working actions I had researched. Our Laban training was invaluable: I had carefully analysed the 'efforts' of the working actions, and honed them, if not to perfection, at least to a pretty high standard.

Next, the whole company danced to a selection of Strathspeys, jigs and reels. We started slowly, emphasizing the grace of the Strathspey, passing through each other's lines like the court dances of old. Suddenly the musicians changed the tempo to a jig which was then followed by a reel. As the country dancers faded into the background, eight new performers now positioned themselves onstage. Each couple carefully placed their swords on the stage with the two blades crossing and took up a position facing one other. After a brief introductory skirl from the piper, the sword dancers started their neatly measured steps, from side to side over the swords and turning at each corner. In highland dance the dancers' arms represent the antlers of the stag, and as a result are held very differently from classical ballet. The footwork is extremely light with high springs, with turning and strong beats of one leg on the calf of the other leg. If the dancer can do more than one beat on the leg at a time then he has quite a good technique. All our dancers were in unison as they danced clapping the piper to up the tempo. Now they were dancing across the swords themselves and turning over them as they each arrived in a new position. The sword dance traditionally increases in speed, but we went still further, our dancers' feet flying over the swords as the springs and turns went by in a dazzling blur. The dance ended sharply with the performers all facing the audience in unison, arms on hips, stepping to the side and bowing. I breathed a sigh of relief that no one had sent any swords scattering, or even touched one. The audience burst into another round of lively applause (allowing the sword dancers to quickly get offstage), only subsiding because the rest of the company now filled the stage in preparation for the finale.

A dozen or more couples faced each other across the stage, as the music began to a slow tempo that gradually increased in speed as the dance progressed. I had modelled this closing dance on the Reel of Tulloch, but our dancers did not follow the traditional dance, instead moving into different directions adding variety and liveliness to the whole. My inspiration for this was based on Laban's ideas on diagonals. This enhanced the effect of mobility: it was pure – and very ambitious – showmanship, but on this occasion it worked flawlessly. As the tempo's crescendo reached its wild climax, everyone spun on the spot, the girls undoing their plaids and throwing them high into the air as the stage was blacked out. For a moment the audience was left with the memory of flying plaids: then the lights came up on the entire company as they bowed to an audience who clapped and cheered their thunderous approval. The total reliance I had invested in the dedication of my dancers had paid off.

Relaxing in a backstage studio afterwards, the door was suddenly flung open, and a line of male Bulgarian dancers came in, hands on shoulders, beautifully performing my very own Mountain Road dance, and accompanied by Bulgarian pipers! I don't know whether it had gone into their repertoire or not, but I was delighted by their homage. We greeted them like old friends – I always knew it was a good dance! When their company had last been in London my dancers had been invited to go backstage after the performance. The girls had shown them the Mountain Road and the Bulgarian men had liked it so much they had taken the trouble to learn it.

The results of the competition came through a few days later. Because of the sheer numbers of competing groups, there were ties for the top places. Not surprisingly, the Chinese Classical Opera Company took first place with (as far as I remember) a Russian group. To my proud astonishment, however, we were the only group from the West among the top four places. I personally was presented with a medal for choreography by the judges. My framed citation, in beautiful Cyrillic calligraphy, still hangs on the wall beside my desk.

Our final concert was in Gorky Park, before an audience of twenty thousand people, whom we wowed with our interpretation of Bill Haley's 'Rock Around The Clock'. After our dancers had finished with the rock-and-roll number, the blues-and-jazz singer Bertice Reading followed onto the stage, looking stunning in a white evening dress and with sequinned eyelids. We must have provided a baptism of fire for the audience, thus exposed for the first time to a live performance of a supposedly decadent Western culture! Even so, I was asked if my London Dancers might be willing to appear in a film being made in a television studio on the city's outskirts. They were particularly interested in our rock-and-roll sequence. We immediately agreed – though I did wonder whether we had been selected in order to portray the decadent culture of Western youth.

After a long, long day, we finally set off for the television studios. Starting work at ten-thirty at night, we did not emerge until nine hours later. We went through most of our Scottish traditional dances, and the ever-popular Scotto-Irish Jig. We also regularly shattered the studio floor, which was made of large squares of strengthened glass resting on a wooden base. At about four in the morning we had got as far as the Sword Dance. As our tired feet clipped the swords, the glass splintered and we had to wait while the cleaners appeared with brooms. They swept up and replaced the glass in silence. The regular noise of breaking glass was becoming extremely embarrassing. It also meant we had to start all over again to complete a proper take. The studio technicians were perfectionists but also patient and sympathetic. By half-past seven the next morning, everything was 'in the can' and we were nearly on our knees with weariness. As we prepared to stagger out to our coach, we were bade farewell and each handed a wad of what turned out to be rouble-notes. It slowly dawned on us that we were actually being paid for our time – a thoroughly novel experience. Exhaustion disappeared in a trice, especially as the more business-minded among us spread word that the money had to be spent that very day. We couldn't take it out of the country, and had only a few hours before leaving for home. There was really only one place where foreigners were encouraged to shop, and that was the famous and enormous GUM department store off Red Square, in those days a complex arcade of shops, with first-floor walkways and bridges. I only had an hour or so to spend my unaccustomed wealth, and came away with four silver glass-holders and an embroidered Chinese tablecloth with napkins.

Our journey home was marred by a terrible tragedy, when an Aeroflot plane crashed off the coast of Denmark when trying to land. This episode still haunts me because Ewan and I had originally been offered the tickets. Although I had overcome my aversion to flying, I still felt I wanted to travel back home by train with my London Dancers, and persuaded Ewan to do the same. The awful thing was that the tickets instead went to a young couple in the British contingent who had recently become engaged. We heard the news of the plane-crash while boarding the cross-channel ferry at Ostend. There were no survivors.

The 1957 Moscow Youth Festival proved a decisive turning-point both in my life and in the history of Theatre Workshop. Joan's production of 'Macbeth' had met with a very mixed reception. The origins of this venture were vexed. Joan had originally suggested to Ewan that Theatre Workshop take his new play, 'So Long at the Fair', to the Festival, but Ewan had claimed there was insufficient time for him to complete it and for the company to rehearse it. Joan then proposed 'Macbeth', with Ewan playing the lead – but he thought the choice of play inappropriate and in this the Moscow critics certainly agreed. As Howard Goorney put it, 'They felt the modernization of the play undermined the belief of the audience in the truth of what was happening on the stage.' 'If Shakespeare has any significance today,' Joan is quoted as saying in Howard's book, 'a production of his work must not be regarded as a historical reconstruction, but as an instrument still sharp enough to provoke thought.'

Ewan's disagreement with Joan over the 1957 Festival probably represented his final severance from Theatre Workshop. The trip had also exposed a complicated development in my marriage to Ewan. (The small American contingent, including Peggy, had been invited to travel further east and into China, at the end of the Festival – and this was later to present difficulties for those wanting to return to the States.) From a purely professional point of view, however, it had been a triumph for the team effort of my London Dancers, and it was immensely satisfying to see all our hard work being recognised on the international stage. I was personally delighted that the dream I had held since my visit to Bucharest nearly four years before had come true. Starting with only two volunteers, the company had now grown to thirty practitioners, trained to professional – indeed, now award-winning – standards.

It was also a great pleasure to recognise that the Laban techniques I had used for our training had proved so successful, both in using the 'efforts' in dance actions and in deploying the notion of 'spatial harmony' in the overall conception of my choreography. We had all worked extremely hard, and our success was all the sweeter for the daily slog it had taken to raise the funds, in various squalid surroundings, to travel to the Festival in the first place. Many of our East European counterparts were due to depart on state-funded family holidays after the Festival. In the after-glow of our success, the fact that we were all immediately going back to work did not, at least for the moment, matter in the least.

Chapter Twenty-Seven

London – and Paul Robeson

1957–1958

I had of course kept in touch with Laban and Lisa throughout these years, taking Hamish down to see them at their new studio near Weybridge. Invited to give a performance for Lisa's students some time after our return from Moscow, the London Dancers were excited at finally meeting the man who had influenced so much of our work. They were given a warm welcome, and I had a bear hug from Laban, which took me back to the evening when I had arrived unexpectedly from Blackdown and met him on the stairs.

I chose a selection of our work to present, which naturally included 'The Cockfight', and now they had had Ewan's coaching, the group were also able to sing. Lisa's students watched with great interest and it was a pity that we didn't have more time to talk about our trip but Laban and Lisa wanted a private chat and our bus waited. They were very interested in our methods of work and choice of material. Some of the group were able to use the large icosahedron in the room to show their understanding of his spatial harmony. This delighted them both, and when I explained how we had used the Laban 'efforts' in our performance work, he understood completely. As for the singing, we were able to show him how Ewan too had used the efforts in teaching us to sing.

Laban was immensely proud of my Moscow medal for choreography, particularly when I explained that the Russians still only recognised classical ballet and folk dance: ballroom dancing and 'modern dance' of any kind seemed totally disregarded. I explained the link we had made between Scottish traditional mouth music and the work of the women crofters who made the tweed by hand, and the Mongolian fishermen who described their work in movement. The two strands, 'dynamics' and 'spatial harmony', enabled me to describe these activities in dance movement. For me, the most satisfying results were those when dance and working movements blended into each other and it was difficult to distinguish one from the other. We later privately discussed the possibility of working together again, but very sadly; this was to be our last meeting because Laban died on 1 July 1958.

*

After a brief break with Hamish, I became involved with rehearsals for Shelagh Delaney's play 'A Taste of Honey' and, later, for Brendan Behan's 'The Hostage'. During this summer Ewan and I were invited to the Polish Ambassador's residence. We were among a mixed bag of artists and politicians gathered to celebrate the return of Paul Robeson's passport by the American Government to him. It was a glittering occasion with everyone dressed in their finery and I was glad of the opportunity of wearing my Moscow dress again. We were formally welcomed by the Ambassador and his wife then led through to a large room with a table resplendent with a variety of delicious foods and waiters serving drinks. Going through to the next, even larger room, a small gramophone was playing and a number of fellow guests were standing and chatting awkwardly, sipping their drinks.

Some of the guests looked as though they would like to dance but were unwilling to be the first on the floor – the Ambassador's wife obviously noticed this too. Getting down on her knees, she organised a team of helpers to roll back the carpet to reveal a beautifully smooth parquet floor. There was a slight moment of uncertainty as the honoured guests, Paul Robeson and his wife, entered the room. On this special occasion he was not there to sing, so the gramophone started up again, and people were soon happily fox-trotting. The Ambassador's wife obviously enjoyed dancing very much, and as one dance followed another, a tango started. Much to my surprise and delight, Paul Robeson came up to me and asked me for the honour of a dance. He was, not surprisingly, an excellent dancer and we soon started to improvise. We separated slightly, eyeing each other as we circled, I in a slightly coquettish manner, and we soon became aware that everyone else had stopped dancing and that we were the centre of attention. So we played out our roles to the end of the music, amidst great applause. 'I could watch your wife dance all night,' Robeson told Ewan, after escorting me back. We were invited to stay the night, but I wanted to get back to Hamish. More flattery came my way when the well-known Polish artist Felix Topolski lifted up one of my shoes lying discarded under my chair. Courteously remarking on its small size, and gallantly holding it aloft, he said he would like to drink champagne from it – a rather impractical suggestion as it was toeless.

Over the next few days, Ewan and I started talking again. It seemed that in spite of everything else, we still loved each other. Life was certainly never black and white to Ewan! My resolve to lead an independent life was suddenly being scuppered by the very person who had engineered the whole scenario. After receiving a long letter from Ewan in which he said he still loved me, I rang him, and before very long we were reconciled. I was contemplating the run-up to Christmas with something like quiet optimism. Unfortunately, that mood did not last for very long. By the end of the year he was obviously having problems. Peggy was domiciled in France owing to visa difficulties. As I have described in greater detail in 'Sun on the Water', my book about my daughter Kirsty, Peggy managed to return to England around Christmas and in the New Year of 1959 Ewan and I separated. I heard that Peggy was pregnant and she gave birth to a baby in March; I had meanwhile discovered that I was myself pregnant, and expecting a baby – Kirsty – in October.

Now – and finally – on my own, there came a sense of relief. It had been hard to shoulder Ewan's feelings of guilt, and there is no doubt that he had not found it easy to separate from our family. But I was now determined to enjoy my next few months, sharing my time between Hamish, my work, and planning for my baby. We had shows running in the West End and Joan asked me to go round to each of them and give notes in her place. London was looking at its best, I remember, in that glorious summer of 1959. 'A Taste of Honey' had transferred from Stratford East to Wyndham's Theatre in February; it was to move to the Criterion in June. Meanwhile we were now working on Frank Norman's 'Fings Ain't What They Used T'Be' with, among others, Barbara Windsor, Toni Palmer, Miriam Karlin, Yootha Joyce, Glynn Edwards, and James Booth. I can only speak for myself regarding this production, but to my mind the old Theatre Workshop had by now effectively ceased to exist. While improvisation had always been a part of our policy, it had never before taken the place of training. Newcomers did not share our 'aspirations'. How could they? Joan appeared to be on a treadmill, a victim of a success not of her own choosing. And whereas we had all once seemed to share a common artistic goal, this was no longer the case. The newcomers, I believe, had no interest in this aspect of the company: they simply wanted to work in London, preferably the West End, with a successful producer. Suddenly there was no time any more. The wonderful spirit of unity we had maintained throughout our poverty, despite the rows at company meetings, was over. Old members of the company who had benefited so much from the training were in great demand and were offered good salaries. For the first time they had the opportunity to provide adequately for their families: who could blame them for spreading their wings? And meanwhile actors and actresses, both well-known and unknown, flocked to the theatre doors to audition for parts so they could say they were from Theatre Workshop. From time to time, old members of the company returned and, for a brief period, it almost seemed like the old days. Everyone now had a reasonable wage – success and the West End saw to that. Gerry Raffles could pay the bills without worrying. But for my part, I felt something precious had been lost when commercialization dictated policy.

April 1959 saw us all flying over to Paris, delighted to be returning to the Théâtre des Nations (previously the Théâtre Sarah Bernhardt) to represent Great Britain with Brendan Behan's play 'The Hostage'. The British Council had finally decided to support us and both Shelagh Delaney and Frank Norman came along for the ride. To celebrate the occasion, I wore a silky grey linen suit and perched a shiny pink bowler on my head. Howard sent a jokey word down the plane that the pilot would like me to remove my hat since it dazzled his eyes. On arrival, those of us not directly engaged in the production took time off to find our hotels and snatch a quick meal. Peter Walker was our costume designer – though he was more used to creating gorgeous costumes for Glyndebourne than the current production. He and I decided to go and find a restaurant. Harvey Webb, who played the fiddle in the show, reckoned he had the time to join us. As we shared a bottle of wine, I told them the news of my pregnancy. They decided to lash out on another one to celebrate.

Arriving back at the theatre, we were amazed at the transformation that had taken place. Flowers were everywhere and a red carpet covered the foyer. I walked along it sinking into the deep pile and, proudly wearing my bowler, entered the auditorium. Chandeliers sparkled and glowed. This was indeed a far cry from Boggart Hole Clough, the Manchester Park where we had once performed with a dog joining us on stage. There was just time to wish everybody luck. Peter and I rushed outside to see the V.I.P.s arriving in their Rolls-Royces and Mercedes. There was even a guard of honour, who now lined up in full dress uniform.

The play was a tremendous hit. Brendan managed to remain sober enough to stand up and acknowledge the cries of 'Auteur!', and I later walked through the streets with him and Joan. She and I wondered whether this would be a real breakthrough, at long last. Whatever the future held, tonight was a success, the audience had brought the cast back time and again. This went far beyond our expectations.

I left them at the door of my hotel. Gerry had made all the bookings and while none of us expected five-star treatment, this place was definitely seedy. I was sharing with Ann Beach (playing Miss Gilchrist in the show), who would be some time yet. I discovered our room was reached by a spiral iron staircase on which a number of odd couples loitered. 'Excusez-moi,' I smiled, and passed them. While not actually hostile, they seemed extremely reticent. Years later, Yootha Joyce, who was also in the cast, wrote an article for the Radio Times which at last explained

London – and Paul Robeson

the oddity: it seems that Gerry had inadvertently booked us into a brothel! In the middle of the night Ann and I were awakened by a terrific banging on the door. There stood Roy Kinnear, holding all his clothes and bedding, saying that his room had been commandeered, and could he sleep on our sofa?

The company returned to their London productions while Joan and Gerry left for a summer holiday in Cassis, in the South of France. Before leaving, she asked me to do the rounds of the theatres and give notes to the two companies. (Both 'A Taste of Honey' and 'The Hostage' were playing in the West End.) I would sit through the shows and make what notes I thought were necessary. Afterwards I'd join the cast in their dressing rooms for a chat. Avis Bunnage and Murray Melvin were old mates from the earlier Theatre Workshop days. I would also occasionally drop in to see Wendy Toye's production of 'Die Fledermaus', visiting friends backstage later.

The London Dancers 1959

The London Dancers 1959

The summer of 1959 was a beautiful one, and I kept extremely well. I hoped that the baby would enjoy being surrounded by music. All this activity helped ease what could otherwise have been a very lonely period. Instead, there were times when I experienced great happiness. It was a year in which I learnt a lot about myself, and found that, given time, I was strong enough to take charge of my own life. I was determined to look back on this pregnancy with sheer joy – and I do. It was a golden period. Glowing with health, I kept busy, and if ever I felt down, I never allowed the mood to last. After all, I had so much good fortune: a beautiful son; a new baby on the way to look forward to; and my theatre work and dance group. I realised I was a survivor.

A letter arrived, brief and to the point. 'Madame Littlewood requests the pleasure of the company of Mlle Newlovna and Master Hamish MacColl . . .' : we were invited to Cassis for a fortnight. As usual with Joan's plans, I was to leave immediately and send a wire confirming the day of arrival. Saturday saw me booking our journey through to Marseilles, reserving seats and also overnight accommodation at a hotel in Paris, directly opposite the station. There was only one slight flaw: the clerk at the booking office could not accept a cheque as it would have to be cleared, and that would take three days. As I was booked to leave the following day, I paid cash, and phoned Ewan, who promised to send a money order out to me in France. We left England with about ten pounds.

The hotel in Paris was extremely pleasant. Breakfast was ordered for seven o'clock, which gave us ample time to take up our reserved seats on the nine o'clock train for the south . . . I woke up at eight-thirty – no call and no breakfast. Rushing down, we left amid profuse apologies from the management, and Hamish was handed a bag with our breakfast in it. But it was all to no avail. We saw the end of our train disappearing round a bend in the track. A kindly porter told me that if I was quick, there was another train leaving in two minutes from the opposite platform. Seven months pregnant, carrying a huge suitcase, I laboriously 'ran' with Hamish and we launched ourselves into the open door of the last carriage. It was immediately slammed behind us and we were off. Everywhere I looked, there were people sitting, standing, and lying across luggage. I had no idea how we were going to survive until six-thirty that evening.

First things first. We sat on the case and enjoyed our belated breakfast. After about half an hour, an angel of mercy, in the shape of a ticket collector, arrived, took one look at me and my case, and expressed his horror in typical Gallic fashion. He picked up my case and told us to follow him. I never knew that a train could be so long. Using our case as a buffer, he made his way for us, through carriage after carriage. It seemed we had been walking for at least twenty minutes when he finally arrived at the door to another compartment, which he now unlocked. There was another surprise in store: opening a second door, he showed us into an empty compartment. Our saviour wouldn't take a tip – for which I was extremely grateful: having paid the hotel bill, I was now down to about five pounds and a handful of small change. We shook hands and he kindly indicated that I should put my feet up. Next door to us was a tiny bar with drinks and sandwiches. Utter bliss. For the rest of the journey, we travelled in state. Only one other person joined us at Dijon.

Six-thirty and we were on the platform at Marseilles. 'There she is!' Joan extricated herself from the crowds, her face wreathed in smiles. 'Gerry said that no one would be crazy enough to come out of the blue, just like that, but I knew you would!' It was meant as a compliment. I also knew that she would be there to meet us, come hell or high water.

It began as an idyllic holiday. Joining the other 'enceinte' ladies at the resort, I would regularly launch myself off the steeply shelving sands into the cool green waters, where I would float like a contented whale, soaking up the sun. Getting out was more difficult. We all had to help each other amidst a great deal of shrieking and laughter. Sometimes Gerry would take the four of us further up the coast in his boat, and I would drop off and follow at a stately pace to cool off.

I awoke one morning to the sound of one of Joan and Gerry's arguments. She was expected to fly to Sicily or somewhere to collect a theatre award; there would be other 'stars' of stage and screen at the ceremony. She made all sorts of excuses, but in the end Gerry won her over. With extreme reluctance and in a belligerent frame of mind, wearing shorts and a cotton top, she left, refusing point-blank to 'dress up' in any way.

That evening, Mish and I sat on the terrace eating our dinner. The fairy lights, strung across a line of plane trees, were reflected in the dark waters of the harbour. We dawdled over the meal and went to bed in a very contented frame of mind. Tomorrow, he was going to try out his new fishing rod. Fate had other plans, however. During the night he became delirious and developed a high fever and a swollen arm. As soon as I could, I asked the hotel to send for a doctor. A young man arrived, who lost no time in checking Mish over, and only after that squeezed his arm. Matter shot high into the air: it seems that an insect bite had caused a severe infection. The young medic left some antibiotics, and I promised to pay him that afternoon when my money was due to arrive from England. It seems churlish to mention it, but I clearly remember being very surprised that he departed without washing his hands. I left Mish, now sorted out and clearly on the mend, surrounded by comics and cool drinks: it was time to sally forth with my passport and find the post office, where my money order would be waiting for me.

I queued up in the heat as the line inched towards the counter clerk. Yes, there was some money for Mrs MacColl. Could she see my passport? Yes, of course she could – but as I handed it over I suddenly realised that it was in my maiden name of Newlove. Her eyes grew steely and suspicious as she looked me over. No, my son's passport, emblazoned the name MacColl, would certainly not do: the money order was addressed to a Mrs MacColl, whoever that may be, and that was the only person she would give it to. She didn't care who I was or wasn't: my passport said Newlove and that was that.

Determined not to be defeated by this little autocrat, I turned on my heels and headed for the Tourist Office – the Syndicat d'Initiative. After all, initiative was what was needed. There I was met by a charming Fernandel character, dressed completely in white, who stood up to greet me with old world courtesy. He offered me a seat, and listened to my tale of woe with little sympathetic clicks of his tongue. His manners were exquisite, his gestures showing his genuine concern. My situation and all-too apparent condition obviously appealed to his Gallic chivalry. He picked up his cane, reached for a white Panama hat, and escorted me out of the office. Locking the door, he pocketed the key, and held out his arm. I took it, and we walked slowly, but purposefully, through the increasing heat to the post office, which with lunchtime approaching was soon to close.

We made quite a scene as we processed along the street, and I would not have been surprised to hear a film director shout, 'Cut!' The locals were curious, following at a discreet distance – first the children, some wheeling bicycles, then the adults. By the time we arrived at our destination, it seemed that half of Cassis were waiting to enter the post office, the simply curious joining the queue of its genuine customers. Bicycles were now thrown against the wall as the 'extras' jockeyed for position; one or two of the more daring climbed onto the window sills for a better view.

Strangely enough, the queue in front of us melted away at the sight of my white knight. The lady behind the counter prepared herself for what can only be called a counter-attack. My white knight tried reason, then gentle persuasion, appealing to her to think of my sick child and my present condition. This was an unfortunate tactic, since I'm sure she suspected me of being an unmarried mother. He grew angry. She raised her voice. They began to hurl insults at each other. The crowd ranged itself, for the most part, on our side. The rest remained neutral. The state of play was relayed to the unfortunates left outside. Finally, she waved and taunted us with the money order before slamming it into a drawer, and we left defeated. The crowd were sympathetic. I thanked my champion for his support, really feeling sorrier for him than for myself. He was glorious in defeat, but a defeat it nonetheless was. I watched his stiffly erect figure disappear down the long street, this time alone, and wondered whether he would ever again tilt at windmills.

To cut a long story short, I did finally receive the money order, but only after it – and I – had been returned to England. I duly changed the name on my passport to accommodate the authorities. Joan returned from her trip with amusing tales of the ceremony and gave the invalid Hamish the statuette she had been awarded – though he was thoroughly unimpressed by the gift, saying it made him feel worse. Despite that, however, he was now eating heartily, and in a few days we resumed our golden life of the 'idle rich'.

For the return journey, I had only booked one couchette for the two of us, forgetting that my condition required extra space. As our compartment was empty, we took over the two top bunks. Whenever I heard the ticket collector, I jumped the divide in case I was occupying someone else's reservation. I became quite adept at these aerial flights although so far, they had all been false alarms. Then someone stopped at the door. Another false alarm? This time I left my rocket launch a fraction too late. The door opened, and a figure draped in black gasped and crossed itself as I flew with practised ease over his head to the other side of the carriage. Look, no wires, and no safety net! The priest was horrified and looked on the verge of fainting. To quieten his fears, I accepted the offer of his lower bunk and he went atop. Once back in Paris we were able to travel back by ferry the same day, arriving late evening.

The summer continued hot and sunny on our return. I felt very well, and although there were moments of emotional pain and depression, they didn't last. I spent a lot of time with Hamish, preparing for the much wanted baby; went to see all my mates in the theatre; and helped with auditions for Wolf Mankovitz's musical, 'Make Me an Offer'. I seemed to be surviving.

In an excess of zeal, I decided to join an antenatal class. This was a mistake. I was late, and after missing the bus had to run all the way there. To my further consternation, the classroom was up three flights of stairs. After throwing myself with gusto into the leg-raising exercises, I briefly succumbed to the effect of my recent exertions, and nearly fainted. The teacher was very sympathetic, fussing over me as she worried that I had left the exercises too late 'for a beginner'. Of course, as the 'movement lady' at one Britain's most dynamic theatre companies, and with nearly twenty years of theory, training, and practice behind me, I was mortified at this humiliating lapse, and never went back.

Just before the baby was born, Hamish wanted to go out and buy it a present. We went to a local toy shop and after much careful consideration he decided on a green Dinky car. Within a couple of days I was in labour and my friend Dr Arron Rapoport drove me to hospital. The next day I was the very proud mother of a beautiful russet-haired little girl. I called her Kirsty.

With Hamish

With Kirsty in Regent's Park

Jean Newlove - Yum Di Dee Dah

Epilogue

2013

Pip's 90th birthday

Now, almost 71 years since I met Laban at Dartington my enthusiasm for his work remains undiminished. I am grateful, despite walking difficulties, that I am still in demand for classes.

Laban believed that it is essential to physically experience spatial harmony and dynamics. He believed that bringing this experience to all would enable the human race to achieve a more peaceful and rewarding existence.

It would seem in the present climate we have a long way to go before we achieve such 'harmony'. In recent years two problems have been brought to my notice by confused students wishing to study Laban's theory in depth:

A magnificent building has been erected at Creekside in London bearing the name 'LABAN'.

The prime movers in establishing this centre were Marion North and Valerie Preston Dunlop. Both were students of Lisa Ullmann's Art of Movement Studio. Many of us who were students in those far off Manchester days were delighted. Now Laban would have a real home and all his work would be covered. Students would study Laban's work on industry (which I pioneered during the war) and has now been taken over by Warren Lamb. Kinetography Laban, or Labanotation, would reach a high level (ICKL or International Congress Kinetography Laban) to enable whole ballets to be written down. My own area of actor training and choreography covers both spatial harmony and dynamics in depth.

Unfortunately this dream was not to be. The lottery money was allocated to create a contemporary dance school. Neither Marion nor Valerie had experience in the commercial professional theatre. Marion looked to America for dance tutors and was greatly influenced by contemporary ex-dancer Bonnie Bird in the school's planning. I find nothing wrong in that providing students wishing to study Laban's work in depth are adequately catered for.

Laban modules have appeared in some courses but it seems from the many frustrated students coming to me that they are returning to Latin America, USA, Germany and England without knowing the basics. They were sometimes advised by their contemporary dance tutors to find me for help. In the few days available I recorded answers to their queries and they moved through the scales on my lawn. Luckily it was the end of term and the beginning of the summer holidays.

Valerie, I am told, has been influenced by the American choreographer William Forsythe and the 'A' Scale has changed from what Laban taught us. Even so, they enjoyed her classes in choreology 'spatial harmony'. Walli Meier, greatly influenced by Laban, has done sterling work for children with disabilities. And I

Epilogue

have several good contemporary dancers coming to me for a belated Laban training!

The second problem brought to my attention was the work of the celebrated Swedish dancer Yat Malmgren. When he met Laban at Dartington he was given some notes which would help in the training of actors. These were later published in Laban's book 'The Mastery of Movement'. There appears to be no doubt that he found the notes useful as indeed, he continued to use much of the vocabulary. It was only when I took a master class at Arts Educational School that I realised their Yat training had changed the third dimension, making a nonsense of an actors' Laban training. The students seemed to think my explanation was much more logical.

Acting and Dance students working together at the Havana National Dance School in Cuba in 2003.

Jean Newlove - Yum Di Dee Dah

Acting and Dance students working together at the Havana National Dance School in Cuba in 2003.

I don't think any of us in the early days of Theatre Workshop thought beyond the immediate future. Joan, Ewan and I realised we were breaking new ground and through our joint work the young post-war company was inspired and totally committed. But surviving on a daily basis also exercised our wits and ingenuity. For the most part we were ignored by organisations who could have made life a little easier for us, our contribution to theatre was recognised abroad and the company was feted wherever we played. Joan, Ewan and I were interviewed after each performance and I found myself taking classes with professional actors in Sweden after Birgit Cullberg's review.

When the company settled in London we became, in Camel's words, a repertory company. Our actors were in great demand by other directors. One notable exception was Maggie Bury, Camel's wife at the time. Maggie was considered by most of us as a very hard worker at whatever she was asked to do; props, costumes or stage management. In rehearsal she listened intently to Joan and made copious notes. She certainly worked hard in movement

Epilogue

classes. She was not given major roles in the plays because, as Joan commented, all her hard work didn't come together in her stage characters.

For quite a long time she and I were out of touch. I was assisting Joan in several productions, all of which moved to the West End. During this time Maggie was not involved with our Theatre Workshop productions. Later I was preparing my dance group for Moscow and then busy with 'Make Me an Offer'. I gave birth to Kirsty in October1959. I met up in Angel Lane with Maggie, who was concerned about her future, asked me what she 'should do now?' I rather flippantly replied, 'What about starting a drama school?'. Later she asked me to join her and initially we were the only tutors. She found the premises, students and called it the East 15 Acting School although I believe it was never actually based in Stratford. My role was simply to train the students and choreograph certain plays.

'Oh What a Lovely War' (above)
with permission of Ramano Cagnoni and Theatre Royal Stratford East Archive

Jean Newlove - Yum Di Dee Dah

*'A Taste of Honey' March 1958
Murray Melvin, Frances Cuka
courtesy of Theatre Royal Stratford East Archive*

Epilogue

'The Hostage' October 1958
Murray Melvin (The Hostage – Centre), The Company
courtesy of Theatre Royal Stratford East Archive

'Make me an Offer' October 1959
Tom Fletcher, Martin Lawrence, Bernard Martin, Bernard
Goldman, Daniel Massey, Milton Sills, Roy Kinnear
courtesy of Theatre Royal Stratford East Archive

Epilogue

'Fing's ain't wot they used ti be' February 1959 (above)
Glyn Edwards, Eileen Kennally, James Booth, Brian Murphy,
Edward Caddick
courtesy of Theatre Royal Stratford East Archive

With a baby and young son, I had no time to sit in on any of Maggie's sessions. Situated in Plaistow and later at Rectory Lane, it was quite a long car journey from my home in Selsdon in Surrey. I continued teaching there for a few years and remember at some point, Sarah Aucott, an acting student, taking my Laban diploma course when her studies were finished and returning as Head of Movement. When she left, the Laban work went into decline. This was certainly not Maggie's fault. 'Laban' teachers came and went and, I am told by my ex-students, their work bore no resemblance to mine. When some of them became directors and returned to the school, they were frustrated by the students ignorance of basic Laban theory.

With the passage of time, many of these early students have told me how much they owed Maggie. I respect their opinions. My problem, until very recently, was equating Maggie who was not an actress according to Theatre Workshop yet highly praised by her drama students. I think I have the answer. In 1939, at the beginning of the war, Maggie was almost 19 years (I was 16) of age. There was little choice at that time for school leavers. It was the services, factories or teacher training colleges and Maggie chose the latter. By the time she joined Theatre Workshop she was a qualified teacher with five years experience. She was now able to pass on all Joan's notes which she had carefully written down. The students were actually inspired by Joan's direction first hand thanks to Maggie's diligence.

As far as I am concerned, it matters not one jot that she was never considered an actress. Her role as a teacher passing on Joan's work as a director first hand has proved invaluable. Whatever occurred in later years does not in any way diminish her valuable role in furthering the artistic development of Theatre Workshop. I am reminded that Camel said Maggie's metier was teaching, not acting, and on one occasion when we all needed to earn, she took on home tuition. I am glad that she had the opportunity to pass on Joan's work so brilliantly.

*

Epilogue

In the last twenty years I have been asked to take master classes at a number of well-known Drama Schools including East 15. Many of them purport to 'have Laban' as part of their curriculum. Their classes often bear little resemblance to what I learnt from Laban. Classes should be dynamic and engage one's understanding of movement. Rather like peeling an onion, there is always something new to discover.

The East 15 School has now become Essex University and the movement department I hear is about 500 strong with five or six tutors. I would like to think, in time, they will increase the Laban training. They have just celebrated their 50th anniversary.

I remember the very first group of students to complete their studies, such as Ann Mitchell, Marji Campi and Kate Williams. They all seem to want to talk of two things. After fifty years they say they remember the rigour and excitement of my Laban movement-into-acting classes, sometimes three-hours long, in the freezing cold gymnasium in a boys' club which we could not afford to heat during the day. Then they want to talk about how Laban is built inextricably into their acting and of the joy of those rare occasions when they work with a director who knows of Laban's work.

For Kate Williams who also now directs, often in drama schools, Laban is an essential part of building a character or capturing the tempo of a speech or a scene in a way that, because of its physicality, is meaningful to any actor.

When another ex-student of mine, Philip Hedley, turned from acting to directing, he assembled a company largely drawn from East 15 Acting School to work at Lincoln Theatre Royal for nearly three years. It included Jane Briers, Yvonne Edgell, Ron Hackett, John Halstead, Howard Lloyd Lewis, Diana Rayworth, Annabel Scase, Trevor T. Smith, Alison Steadman and Brian Tree. Laban was at the basis of their work whether it was a classic text, commedia dell'arte or a drawing room tragedy. Stanislavski and Laban provided the basic tools of the rehearsals, just as much, if not more so, when rehearsal time was desperately short.

A guest director at Lincoln was Mike Alfreds who was influenced by seeing Philip Hedley's rehearsals at the London drama school LAMDA. Soon after his Lincoln experience he established one of the most innovative and physically expressive theatre companies in British theatre in the seventies and eighties, the aptly named Shared Experience.

In his book 'Different Every Night', Mike Alfreds discusses at length his use of Laban efforts in rehearsal. He says, "I've used them for a good forty years and each time I've done so I learn some new application for them." The name of his company, the title of his book and even its sub-title, 'Freeing The Actor', all contain elements in theatrical activity of which Joan and I would strongly approve. It is very gratifying to hear of good, lively work being done by people one may never have met and yet you know you are a link in a chain that has passed certain qualities on.through my own work based on Laban's theories.

Many are now senior citizens and still working as actors, directors or teach on drama courses. We keep in touch.

*

I think it is important to explain my role as a choreographer with Theatre Workshop.

Working with a ballet company or with dancers, the choreographer's work is obvious, his or her, creation is on view to an audience. The choreographer's role within an acting company where the spoken word is an important means of communication, is very different.

My company was sufficiently trained to perform a Chess Ballet and an Atom Ballet within the plays in our repertoire. Far less recognisable to the general audience was the close working relationship between my own role and that of the director. I can only describe it to being the opposite of a musical where the characters go from acting to singing to dancing and it's all very clear.

Epilogue

I have always been concerned with the movement of the actor and helping him/her to explore his role. The actor should be able, for instance, to move across a stage as himself, as an expressive character turning the quality of movement, if necessary, imperceptably into dance-like movement but not dance unless we choose to dance. One example of this was in 'The Other Animals' when the ghosts of past comrades haunt Hanau's fevered imagination and rise from the dead together, silently raising an accusing arm with a finger pointing in his direction. Moving silently and together to Mahler's 2nd Symphony, it surpassed all words.

Through the years this has been my major passion and I have used my understanding of Laban's theories to develop and explore this method. Joan Littlewood found it a great help and we often attended each other's rehearsals in the early days. With Ewan's plays and Camel's sets lending themselves so brilliantly to the work of the choreographer and director, we achieved a 'unified whole' appreciated by audiences. It was only experts such as Michael Redgrave, Sam Wanamaker (actors), Sigurd Leeder (Jooss Ballet director) and Birgit Cullberg (Swedish Royal Ballet choreographer) and A. V. Coton (journalist and biographer of the history of the Ballets Jooss) who singled out the actors' movement for special praise.

*

Kirsty's boys are now grown up and it seemed right for me to spend time with Hamish. So I sold my London flat and moved to France last December after enjoying nine farewell parties! Kate Williams, ex East 15 organised a party on stage at the Theatre Royal. It was lovely to see so many early students mixing with some of the current East 15 trainees. Ann Beech of Theatre Workshop, a great friend, sang a song from 'Johnny Noble'. My last evening was spent with good friends Harry Greene and Barbara Young. It had been Harry that checked the theatre over with Gerry before we moved down from Glasgow and Barbara suffered Belmont Street with the rest of us. So many laughs and stories.

At the moment I am staying with Hamish but have bought a plot of land nearby and, all being well, a kit bungalow will be erected very soon. My team will come and work with me as the lounge is spacious enough to accommodate dancers. However, many newcomers are showing interest in another course so we may have to hire a studio locally. Previous students from my European courses have been in touch with me. I look forward to meeting them all.

*

Anyone wanting to study Laban in depth should apply to my team of practitioners: Darrell Aldridge, Sarah (Aucott) Henderson, Lindsay Royan and Jenny Frankel. Look at the courses run by Jenny Frankel in Swiss Cottage. Please refer to my website at **www.jeannewlove.com** for further information.

The team and I have studied for many years the various aspects of Laban's work. They have travelled with me to teach in Holland, Germany, Austria and Cuba. The last time was as guests, exactly a year ago when a theatre in Havana was renovated and opened in Kirsty's name. Her fans had raised the money to rebuild it.

Post Script

I wonder what Ewan, Joan and Gerry would say to this welcome, if belated, recognition? Gerry has his name on an East London square, the Gerry Raffles square, next to the Theatre Royal E15.

This year, Joan will have a statue erected on her birthday, October 6th, and a musical about her life is planned for 2014 at 'The Other Place' in Stratford-on-Avon! Ewan is a celebrity in his hometown of Salford and has a plaque in the town centre and another plaque in Russell Square, London.

Kirsty was believed by musical colleagues to be reaching the height of her creativity when she was killed. In Los Angeles there is talk of making a film about her. In London there is a bench dedicated to Kirsty in Soho Square, organised by her fans. Every year at noon on the Sunday closest to her October 10th birthday, fans, friends and family meet there and sing a few songs before heading to the nearby Phoenix Artist Club for a happy musical evening. The gathering seems to attract more people each year and there are the regulars who have come every year since 2001. On Sunday October 13th 2013, I shall be there with Kirsty's sons as usual.

*

Other books by Jean Newlove

Sun on the Water

writing as Jean MacColl
2008, John Blake. ISBN 978-1-84454-549-0

Kirsty MacColl led a dazzling life - tender, creative, heroic and full of love. This book charts with moving insight Kirsty's early years, celebrates her brilliant career at the front rank of the music business in the 1980s and '90s, and mourns her tragic and untimely death - killed by a speedboat in Mexican waters in December 2000. It also tells, with heartfelt truth, the shocking story of the elaborate cover-up and gross miscarriage of justice that followed, and appeals for justice to be done in her name. This remarkable book is in equal parts a celebration and an appeal for truth.

Laban for Actors and Dancers

1993, Nick Hern Books. ISBN 1-85459-160-6

This book, written from a lifetime of experience, is a handbook for teachers and students wanting a simple, practical introduction to the Laban system of movement. We are guided step-by-step through the concepts of Space, Time and Weight and the Eight Basic Actions. Each chapter is complete with easy-to-follow graded exercises. The book ends with practical examples of how the movement training can be used in the development of characters in specific plays.

Post Script

Laban for All

with John Dalby
2004, Nick Hern Books. ISBN 978-1-85459-725-0

This book offers a simplified version of Laban's system which can be used by relative beginners upwards. We are introduced to the kinesphere - which simply means the personal space surrounding each one of us extending as far as we can reach. Then to the Dimensional Cross - which is simply a way of describing movement in three dimensions: high/ low, forwards/ backwards and side to side. Then we learn about Pathways and Trace Forms, Levels and Zones ... Each new term is accompanied by very specific exercises - clearly illustrated with line drawings and diagrams - designed to strengteh and deepen our understanding. When we have grasped - and practised - the basic vocabulary, we move on to its expressive possibilities in drama and dance. The result is a thorough - and thoroughly practical - grounding in the most significant system of modern times.

Index of Photographs

1. Bathing belle 1925 — 5
2. William G Newlove, Paris 1912/13 — 6
3. Norrie L Newlove, Holidays 1937 — 7
4. Pip and Jean, 1928/29 — 13
5. 1934 — 14
6. 'London Bridge' — 19
7. My family on holiday 1938 — 19
8. A break from working on the land, 1940 — 23
9. Pip in Tobruk — 26
10. Rudolf Laban 1944/5 — 39
11. Physical Training Course, ATS 1944/45 — 87
12. The Art of Movement Studio in Denmark 1948 — 137
13. At Elsinore Castle, Denmark 1948 — 138
14. 'The Flying Doctor' * — 148
15. 'Johnny Noble' * — 149
16. 'Operation Olive Branch' * — 155
17. 'Johnny Noble' * — 175
18. Lisa and Laban at Moreton Hall — 179
19. 'The Other Animals' * — 187
20. 'The Other Animals' * — 188
21. 'Don Perlimplin' * — 214
22. 'Don Perlimplin' * — 214
23. My son Hamish — 245
24. Hamish — 270
25. 'Lysistrata' 1947 * — 273
26. 'Lysistrata' 1947 * — 274
27. 'Paradise Street' 1953 * — 275
28. 'Paradise Street' 1953 * — 275
29. 'Uncle Vanya' 1953* — 281
30. 'The Devil's Disciple' * — 282
31. 'The Government Inspector * — 283
32. Sachiko Takamura and Mark Britton 1953 — 285
33. At Pineapple Studios — 288

Index of Photographs

34. Richard II *	290
35. Richard II *	290
36. A musical that TW took to Warsaw *	299
37. The London Dancers 1959	329
38. The London Dancers 1959	330
39. With Hamish	336
40. With Kirsty in Regent's Park	337
41. Pip's 90th Birthday	339
42. Havana National Dance School 2003	341
43. Havana National Dance School 2003	342
44. 'Oh What a Lovely War' **	343
45. 'A Taste of Honey' March 1958 *	344
46. 'The Hostage' October 1958 *	345
47. 'Make Me an Offer' October 1959 *	346
48. 'Fing's ain't wot they used ti be' February 1959 *	347

* courtesy of Theatre Royal Stratford East Archive.

** with permission of Ramano Cagnoni and Theatre Royal Stratford East Archive.

Made in the USA
Middletown, DE
24 May 2015